Romantic Cities Series

ROMANTIC

DAYS AND NIGHTS IN

New York City

INTIMATE ESCAPES IN AND AROUND MANHATTEN

by Pamela Thomas

Happy birthday
Mike..
love
Mum + Dad

The Globe Pequot Press

OLD SAYBROOK, CONNECTICUT

Cover and text design by Mullen & Katz
Illustrations on pages 1, 23, 33, 55, 63, 77, 89, 109, 117, 127, 131, 145, 159, 177, 189, 205, 217, and 233 by Maryann Dubé. All others by Mullen & Katz.

Library of Congress Cataloging-in-Publication Data

Thomas, Pamela, 1946–
     Romantic days and nights in New York City / Pamela Thomas. — 1st ed.
         p.   cm. — (Romantic cities series)
    Includes index.
    ISBN 1-56440-970-8
    1. New York (N.Y.)—Guidebooks. I. Title. II. Series.
   F128.18.T43   1996
   917.4'10443—dc21
                                    96-36878
                                    CIP

Manufactured in the United States of America
First Edition/First Printing

To the memory of my friend
Ken Sansone,
who knew so much about the romance of New York

ACKNOWLEDGMENTS

While it was always a pleasure to research and write this book, I leaned on the romantic expertise of several of my friends in order to really get at the essences. Now I'd like to thank them.

Most particularly, I want to thank my friend Susan Cook, who spent many hours tramping through the streets of Manhattan with me, exploring everything from the fabulous penthouse at the Ritz-Carlton to the boardwalk of Coney Island. Susan's sophisticated sensibilities, her fine eye, and her terrific sense of humor were a great help to me. I also want to thank Susan's husband, Richard Bennett, for sharing his knowledge of the New York culinary world, for cluing me in to the makings of a perfect martini, and, mostly, for his genuine interest in this project.

I also want to give special thanks to my good friend and gifted travel writer, Eleanor Berman. Eleanor generously shared with me her expertise, her contacts, and her knowledge of New York with sensitivity, generosity, and grace.

Several other friends also shared their knowledge of New York and its romance with me, and remained patient with me as I raced to complete the manuscript. Specifically, I want to thank Mary Lou Brady, Grace Young, George Lang, Jenifer Harvey Lang, Susan Seibel, Nancy Shuker, Dirk Kaufman, Kari Sigerson, Maggie Anson, Venable Herndon, Carol Scatorchio, John Hadamuscin, and Mel Lavine.

Finally, a few people at the Globe Pequot Press were extremely helpful to me. Laura Strom was a kind, patient, creative, and meticulous editor. Doe Boyle did a fine job of copyediting. My old pal Dana Baylor, recommended me for this job, and over the years her level-headedness and support have served me very well. For all of this, I am grateful.

Contents

NEW YORK CITY

NEW YORK ENVIRONS

BRONX

HARLEM

Yankee Stadium

145TH ST
135TH ST
125TH ST
116TH ST
110TH ST
W 96TH ST
W 79TH ST
W 72ND ST
W 57TH ST

Central Park
The Reservoir
The Lake

Upper West Side
Upper East Side

CENTRAL PARK WEST
COLUMBUS AVE
AMSTERDAM AVE
WEST END AVE
RIVERSIDE DR.
Riverside Park
HENRY HUDSON PKWY.
WEST SIDE HWY

Lincoln Center
BROADWAY
CENTRAL PARK SOUTH

Museum of Modern Art

E 96TH ST
E 79TH ST
E 72ND ST
E 60TH ST
E 57TH ST

Guggenheim Museum
Metropolitan Museum

FIFTH AVE
MADISON AVE
PARK AVE
LEXINGTON AVE
THIRD AVE
SECOND AVE
FIRST AVE
YORK AVE

MADISON AVE
LEXINGTON AVE
THIRD AVE
SECOND AVE
FIRST AVE
YORK AVE

FRANKLIN D. ROOSEVELT DRIVE
Roosevelt Island
Queensboro Bridge

Rhinebeck
Hyde Park
Poughkeepsie
Litchfield Hills
New Preston
CONNECTICUT
Shelter Island
Sag Harbor
East Hampton
South Hampton
Long Island Sound
LONG ISLAND
Atlantic Ocean

Hudson River
NEW YORK STATE
NEW JERSEY
MANHATTAN
Staten Island
Coney Island
Taconic State Pkwy.

202
84
7
684

14
25
5
29
10
26
7
8
13
1
6
30
9
4
18

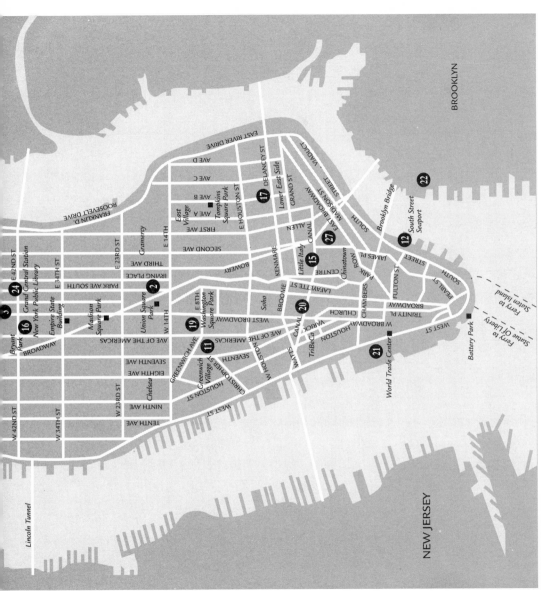

Numbers on map correspond to itinerary numbers (see Table of Contents).

I have lived in New York City for twenty-eight years, and I love it. From my earliest days here I was utterly enthralled with the life of the city. As with any great love, I was captivated by its charms, all of which can be defined in superlatives: the biggest buildings, the best cuisine, the most fabulous art, the most remarkable theater, the most interesting people, the most excitement, and, yes, the most romance.

This is a book about the romance of New York. Like any deep love, the romance of New York has many sides. The most obvious, of course, is its *electricity*. All you have to do is walk down Fifth Avenue during the Christmas season, go dancing at the Rainbow Room, or walk through the theater district just before curtain time to sense the excitement.

The romance of New York also has much to do with *nostalgia*. New York City has a rich history, from the incredible contributions of its old families like the Stuyvesants and the Roosevelts to the remarkable rise of its immigrants, particularly the Jewish, Italian, and Asian peoples. In a single day, you can witness vestiges of New York's 400-year history in virtually every neighborhood in the city—a remnant of a cobblestoned street, a well-preserved Federal house, roses climbing the walls of a beautiful nineteenth-century cathedral—or be dazzled by the twentieth-century glass towers of modern New York.

Best of all, New York has *sex appeal*. This remarkable sexiness somehow involves New York's excesses—the grit, the noise, the occasional quirkiness, the constant stimulation and yes, the expense. But, again, like any profound love, you somehow learn to accept certain aspects that may at times seem annoying. In fact, these are the very characteristics that make New York City so vital.

Whenever I return to the city after a vacation from its excesses, I am struck by its powerful ability to turn me on. As my plane circles Manhattan Island, and I see the Statue of Liberty standing majestically in the harbor, the Empire State and Chrysler Buildings jutting up against the sky, and the twinkling lights of ships lumbering down the East River, my heart begins to pound. The only other time I've felt such palpitations have been on the few times in my life when I have fallen head-over-heels in love.

New York is a place to love, and a place to be in love, a place to explore together. It is a marvelous place to come for a romantic weekend. You'll be stimulated, entertained, and cared for in incredible style. And you'll create memories to last you a lifetime.

ABOUT THIS BOOK

The Audience

First, this is a guide for couples, specifically couples who are in love. It's for young couples who have just met, honeymooners just beginning their lives together, middle-aged couples who want a weekend away from their kids, and older couples celebrating an important anniversary. It's for rich couples, reasonably comfortable couples, and couples who are traveling on a budget. By definition, this is a "travel guide," a book designed for visitors. Yet, it is also a book for New York City residents who want to explore aspects of New York City from a fresh point of view. Part of the romance of New York City is that you can always find a shop, a hotel, a restaurant, a block, a neighborhood—or an entire borough—that you have never explored before.

The Itineraries

   This book includes thirty romantic itineraries. In my experience, exploring a new city (or a new romance) is always made easier when the adventure is tied into a theme. Therefore, I have hinged each of these itineraries to a particular interest, neighborhood, or holiday. Some of these weekends focus on activities for which New York City is famous: art, opera, baseball, literature, art, and jazz, for example. Others celebrate New York's colorful multiethnic history, with itineraries designed around Italian, Irish, Jewish, Asian, African-American, and French aspects of the city. Still others focus on the unique qualities of some of the city's special enclaves, such as Central Park, Brooklyn Heights, and South Street Seaport. Since New York is at its best over holidays, I've also centered itineraries around Easter, Thanksgiving, Christmas, New Year's Eve, and, of course, Valentine's Day.

   The itineraries vary in length from one afternoon and evening (which make for ideal "first dates") to as long as four days and nights. Moreover, the book is designed so that various itineraries can be interlocked ("A Honeymoon in June" can precede—or follow—a weekend in "The Hamptons à Deux"; a day spent exploring Central Park ("The Garden of Eden") can easily be added onto a weekend exploring New York's art museums ("Art for Lovers").

   Finally, three itineraries lead you toward weekend getaways located within about 100 miles (or a two-hour drive) from Manhattan. These include the famous "Hamptons," an incredibly romantic trip up the Hudson River, and a winter weekend in Connecticut. By linking these getaways together with one or two weekends in New York, you could easily plan a week (or more!) in and around New York City and get a romantic taste of America's Northeast.

Hotels

Very often my decisions with regard to hotels have been utterly personal. New York City is full of wonderful hotels, and my primary goal was to suggest those that are most romantic. In order to create cohesive itineraries, however, I've sometimes had to make choices based on expense, location, and appropriateness to the itinerary. As a result, you may be surprised—and I hope delighted—by some of the choices. (For a complete listing of recommended hotels, see "Romantic Hotels, Inns, and B&Bs on page 287).

Restaurants

New York City is jam-packed with restaurants. Literally hundreds of places to dine line every street of Manhattan and its boroughs. As I researched this book, I realized something quite fascinating. Often the restaurants most noted for their chefs and cuisine were not particularly romantic in ambience. The food might be sublime, but the public rooms lacked intimate little tables in the corner, candlelight, crackling fireplaces, and other conventional romantic trappings. Conversely, sometimes the restaurants that were most romantic in ambience offered rather conventional fare on their menus. To make matters even more complicated, three of my favorite restaurants—all of which offered both romantic ambience and top-notch menus—are at this writing closed. These are Le Cirque, Bouley, and the Russian Tea Room.

Still, although I've had to make concessions either to taste or ambience, I certainly have been able to suggest many restaurants that are both incredibly romantic and gastronomically delightful. For a complete listing of recommended restaurants, see "Romantic Restaurants" on page 282.

Entertainment

I have suggested a wide variety of entertainments, from theater and ballet, to walking tours, to night clubs. For details of events during your stay, check local newspapers or magazines, such as *The New York Times, The New Yorker, New York* magazine, or the *Village Voice*. All these journals are available at newsstands and bookshops. See "Nightlife," on page 287.

GETTING TO, FROM, AND AROUND MANHATTAN

Air Service

Getting to New York by airplane is relatively easy. Every major domestic and international airline in the world serves the New York area at one or more of its three airports. These include **John F. Kennedy International Airport (JFK),** located about 15 miles from Manhattan but about an hour's travel time from any given midtown hotel; **La Guardia Airport,** located about 8 miles from Midtown and the easiest airport to access; and **Newark International Airport,** located 16 miles from Manhattan.

The most convenient way to get from any New York airport to midtown Manhattan is by **taxi.** Taxis are available at designated taxi stands at the three New York airports. Fares are metered, costing anywhere from $25 (from LaGuardia) to $50 (from JFK). You will also be required to pay bridge or tunnel tolls, tips (15%), a $.50 surcharge between 8:00 P.M. and 6:00 A.M., and in the case of a ride from Newark Airport, a $10 out-of-state surcharge.

Car services are becoming an increasingly easy way to travel from the airports to

Manhattan. These are safe and legitimate and are licensed by the New York Taxi and Limousine Commission. Call them in advance, and a driver will be waiting at the baggage claim area holding a sign with your name on it. Car services charge a flat fee for trips to Manhattan, which can result in a cheaper ride than in a taxi, especially if you are arriving during rush hour when you might get caught in traffic. These services also usually take credit cards. When you are ready to leave, you can also call one of these services in advance and have them pick you up at your hotel and drive you to the airport. Good choices include Carmel (212–666–6666), Allstate (212–741–7440), Sabra (212–777–7171), and Tel-Aviv (212–777–7777 or 800–222–9888).

Bus service is also offered between the airports and midtown. You can take **Carey Transportation** (718–632–0509) to and from JFK and La Guardia airports to midtown Manhattan, where the buses stop near Grand Central Station (125 Park Avenue at 42nd Street) or at the Port Authority Bus Terminal (Eighth Avenue between 40th and 42nd Streets). The charge is $11 per person each way to JFK; $8.50 per person each way to La Guardia. Buses run about every thirty minutes.

From Newark Airport, you can take **Olympia Trails** (212–964–6233) to Grand Central Terminal (Park Avenue at 42nd Street), Pennsylvania Station (Seventh Avenue between 31st and 33rd Streets) or One World Trade Center (Vista Hotel on West Street); or **New Jersey Transit** (212–564–8484) to the Port Authority Bus Terminal. The charge is $7 per person each way. Buses leave the airport every twenty minutes.

The **Gray Line Air Shuttle** also offers bus service to and from the airports. Call 800–AIR–RIDE for locations, times, and charges.

By Train

Amtrak (800–USA–RAIL), America's primary intercity train service, runs frequent service from Pennsylvania Station (Seventh Avenue between 31st and 33rd Streets), to many cities, especially those along the northeast corridor, including Boston, Philadelphia, Baltimore, and Washington, D.C. Commuter rail services run to all suburban New York locations; call the appropriate line for departure points, arrival points, and charges to locations you wish to visit. For Westchester and upstate New York, call **Metro-North** (212–532–4900 or 800–638–7646); for Long Island, call **Long Island Railroad** (718–217–5477); for New Jersey, call **New Jersey Transit** (201–762–5100 or 800–722–2222); and for Connecticut, call **Amtrak** (800–872–7245).

By Car

I do not recommend coming to New York City by car. If you must drive to New York, park your car in one of the many parking lots and parking garages around the city and leave it there for the duration of your stay. (Most hotels offer parking services.) Although parking a car in a lot or garage in Manhattan is expensive, the cost far outweighs the hassle of parking on city streets and the possibility of having your automobile broken into or stolen. During your stay, use taxi service, car service, or public transportation.

By Taxi

Taxis are the easiest way to travel around the city, and the drivers are reliable. The initial charge is $1.50 with charges added every one-tenth mile or every minute while waiting in traffic. A fifty-cent surcharge is added to your fare from 8:00 P.M. to 6:00 A.M. Tipping is expected and 15 percent is the norm.

By Subway and Bus

In the twenty-eight years of my life in New York City, hardly a day has gone by that I have not used the **subway system.** For $1.50 (you must buy a token), you can travel from the north Bronx to Coney Island, and to any point in between—relatively quickly. The subway is clean, air-conditioned, and, despite its reputation, safe. Still, after 9:00 P.M. it is safest to avoid the subway and take a taxi.

Many New Yorkers prefer the **Metro bus service**, which is excellent. It is also sometimes slow and often crowded, with standing room only for some riders. The charge is $1.50; exact change or a subway token are required. Generally, it is safe to ride the bus at any time of day.

Maps to the subway and bus services are available at Grand Central Terminal, Pennsylvania Station, Port Authority Bus Terminal, many newsstands, and most hotels. All services run 24 hours a day.

FOR FURTHER INFORMATION

Your first stop for planning your exploration of Manhattan should be the **New York Visitors Center** (2 Columbus Circle, New York, NY 10019; 800-NYC-VISIT or 212-397-8222). Even before you come, you can telephone for free literature and recommendations. (The Visitors Center may move from its present Columbus Circle location in the near future; telephone ahead of time to confirm its location or ask at your hotel.)

Ten Most Romantic Activities in New York

1. *Riding the Carousel in Central Park*
2. *A midnight ride on the Staten Island Ferry*
3. *Dancing at the Rainbow Room atop Rockefeller Center*
4. *A late evening tram ride to Roosevelt Island*
5. *Lingering on the Promenade in Brooklyn Heights*
6. *Walking across the Brooklyn Bridge at sunset*
7. *A hansom cab ride in Central Park*
8. *A stroll around Old St. Patrick's Cathedral*
9. *Cocktails at Windows on the World*
10. *Tea at the Plaza, especially at Christmastime*

The prices and rates listed in this guidebook were confirmed at press time. We recommend, however, that you call establishments before traveling to obtain current information.

SPRING

ITINERARY 1
Two days and one night

QUINTESSENTIALLY MANHATTAN

*S*everal years ago writers Owen Edwards and Betty Cornfeld put together a marvelous book entitled *Quintessence*. In that work, they talked about the persons, places, and things that possessed quintessence—"a rare and mysterious capacity to be just exactly what they ought to be." To expound upon that thought, they spoke about how things quintessential exhibited the "pure, highly concentrated essence of something. In other words, something quite like a soul."

To me, these thoughts describe New York City. For starters, New York City is jam-packed with "things quintessential." For example, when you think of skyscrapers, you conjure the Empire State Building; when you yearn for bohemia, you go to Greenwich Village; when you talk of theater, you speak of Broadway; when you ponder bridges, you imagine the famous one from Manhattan to Brooklyn.

What's more, New York's quintessential soul is much more than a sum of its quintessential parts. Its "soul" is made unique by its colorful history, its collection of ethnic denizens, its sophistication, its sensuality, its inexorable sense of surprise—in other words, its romance.

This itinerary guides you to much that is quintessential—and therefore romantic—in

New York. I have borrowed many of these ideas from my friend Susan, who presented this weekend to her longtime boyfriend, Joe, for his birthday last year. Joe was thrilled, and you will be, too.

Practical notes: This weekend, like the name of the hotel, is appropriate any time of year. It's expensive, designed to celebrate a special occasion such as a birthday or anniversary.

One of the features of this itinerary is attending a carefully chosen (that is, to suit the two of you) Broadway play. As always, it's best to book ahead of time either through the theater or through one of several ticket bureaus, some of which will deliver the tickets to your hotel. (See "Theater", page 288, for more information.) If you want to try your luck at **TKTS,** where you might find tickets to your favorite play for up to 50 percent off, head for Broadway at 47th Street or Two World Trade Center. You can only buy what is available on the day of the performance, and you'll probably have to stand in line.

Romance at a Glance

♥ *Spend a night in sleek luxury at the Four Seasons Hotel (212–758–5700).*

♥ *Dine at Orso's and Periyali, two of New York's trendiest and most romantic restaurants.*

♥ *See a Broadway show, then have drinks at Joe Allen's.*

♥ *Listen to jazz after dinner over a martini and a cigar.*

DAY ONE: MORNING

The stunning **Four Seasons Hotel** (57 East 57th Street; 212–758–5700; expensive: double rooms: $430 to $530; suites: $695 to $6,000 per night) was designed by I. M. Pei, one of America's premier architects. To use his words, his multi-terraced lobby is a "stage for urban theater." When you enter, you'll be awed by the 33-foot-high backlit onyx ceiling and the floor-to-ceiling limestone-covered pillars. The lobby is ideal for both people-watching (while researching this book, I ran into supermodel Claudia Schiffer) as well as for intimate conversation.

But you'll want to see your room as quickly as possible.

Depending upon your budget, you can book rooms from $450 to $6,000 a night. Regardless of what you spend, the rooms are pale, sleek, and modern. Even the smallest is spacious and airy. Despite the ultra-modern decor, the rooms, with their soft-colored pastel walls and linens, buttery leather chairs, and king-size beds, are serene, almost silent. Also, each has a gigantic bathroom with a glass-enclosed shower and a huge bathtub (that fills in sixty seconds). Of course, each bath is outfitted with fluffy bathrobes and massive towels.

After seeing your room, you'll no doubt be tempted to lock your door and stay all weekend in this blissful dreamland, but you'll have plenty of time to luxuriate here after you venture outside. So, make your way to lunch and the matinee.

Turn right as you leave the hotel and walk west to Fifth Avenue. (If it's raining, ask the doorman to hail a cab for you.) Turn left and stroll down "the Avenue"—one of the most famous boulevards in the world—and take in Trump Tower, the chic shops, and Rockefeller Center at 50th and Fifth. Cut across Rockefeller Center by the skating rink, and head west to Broadway.

When you get to 50th Street and Broadway, you'll find yourself on a little rise. Look down (south) along the Great White Way. This glittering thoroughfare is theater personified. (It's even better at night!) It's a little tacky, but so what? That's part of its romance!

Lunch

Make your way down to 46th Street and turn west. You'll be lunching at **Orso's** (322 West 46th Street; 212–489–7212; moderate to expensive), perhaps the most popular spot on "Restaurant Row." (Book your table well in advance of your visit.) Orso's is at once cozy, with a somewhat rustic Tuscan atmosphere, and sophisticated. Lots of celebrities hang out here, not because it's a place to be seen, but because it's so comfortable. The pastas are the best dishes on the menu, but if you don't feel like eating anything quite that heavy, order one of the delicious salads.

DAY ONE: AFTERNOON

Orso's understands about getting you through lunch in time for your show. For this itinerary, I would recommend a comedy. (To me, the best part of romance is laughter.) For Joe's birthday, Susan chose *Defending the Caveman*, a long-running Broadway one-man show that was universally considered hilarious. But these days, Broadway is replete with marvelous shows. In any case, choose something light and entertaining.

After the theater, head for a cocktail at the unpretentious **Joe Allen's** (346 West 46th Street between Eighth and Ninth Avenues; 212–581–6464; moderate). Another theater district favorite, this restaurant and bar is as popular with actors and other theater professionals as it is with theater buffs. Joe Allen's is always packed, yet it is romantic in its easygoing way. (By the way, if you can't get into Orso's for lunch, you might try Joe Allen's. The burgers are the best, or you might want to go for one of their terrific salads. If time is running short, you can usually be served quickly at the very friendly bar.)

DAY ONE: EVENING

After your late-afternoon cocktail, make your way downtown to dinner. If the weather is balmy, you may want to walk down Broadway. I particularly love the stretch of old Broadway between 34th Street and 23rd Street. This was Theater Row in the late nineteenth and early twentieth century, and the Tin Pan Alley often referred to in song and story was actually 28th Street between Fifth and Sixth Avenues. Look up as you walk along Broadway and take note of the remarkable architecture. When you reach 23rd Street, head south on Fifth Avenue; turn right at 20th Street and continue west until you come to Periyali.

Dinner

Periyali (35 West 20th Street between Fifth and Sixth Avenues; 212–463–7890;

expensive), considered the best Greek restaurant in New York, is much more than just an ethnic favorite. It is a marvelous restaurant by any standard.

In contrast to the sleek modernity of the Four Seasons Hotel, Periyali has a cozy "country" feel to it, with a white tented ceiling, colorful Greek tiles on the floor, and stucco walls. (Ask to be seated in the back room, which is a bit more intimate than the main dining room.) Periyali's coziness is as sophisticated as its menu. Try any of the appetizers, particularly the *pikantikes salates,* a tasty vegetable plate. The fish dishes are incredibly fresh, grilled to perfection, and lightly seasoned, and the lamb dishes are equally divine. The salmon baked in phyllo with spinach and feta cheese is ambrosia.

Linger over dinner. You might be tempted to imagine that you're on Mikonos with the sea lapping in the background, but take the time to reflect on each other and the fact that you are dining in one of Manhattan's most sophisticated restaurants.

After dinner, catch a taxi back to the Four Seasons. (If you're lucky, you'll flag down one of the few remaining Checker cabs, one of the items deemed "quintessential" by Edwards and Cornfeld.)

You can't spend a night at the Four Seasons without having a martini (again, another quintessential item, according to Edwards and Cornfeld) at the **Fifty Seven Fifty Seven**

Bar. The bar itself is as sleek as the rest of the hotel with hardwood floors, high ceilings, and exquisitely designed furniture by Dakota Jackson and Don Ghia. The walls are adorned by drawings by French artist Kimon Nicolaides.

The bar's martini selection features fifteen types of four-ounce martinis served on a lacquer tray with a shaker on the side. Among the martini styles are the Gotham (Absolut vodka, blackberry brandy, and black Sambuca), the Passion Fruit Martini (Tanqueray gin, Sterling vodka, Grand Passion liqueur, a hint of Remy Martin, and cranberry juice) or, to arouse the testosterone, there's the James Bond Original ("shaken, not stirred").

Best of all, jazz is performed nightly (on weekends until 1:00 A.M.) by pianist John Campbell and saxophonist Jerry Dodgion, who performed with Benny Goodman and Dizzy Gillespie.

Then, to bed.

DAY TWO: MORNING

Breakfast

Breakfast in bed is a must. Chef Susan Weaver, the general chef at the Four Seasons, has been well reviewed by New York's gourmet press, and her Lemon Ricotta Pancakes were declared the "best pancakes in New York" by *New York* magazine. (At the Four Seasons, room service fare is identical to food ordered in the restaurants, and you can enjoy breakfast in the privacy of your room.)

෴

If possible, allow enough time for both of you to enjoy a massage served up in the Four Seasons Fitness Center. The hotel has created a "massage menu" featuring eight distinctive massages (like "Gentle Voyage," "Sports Performance," and "Pre-Nuptial Massage"), each coupled with an appropriate beverage, from a steaming cup of chamomile tea to a glass of

bubbling dry champagne. You can have the massage in your room or at the Fitness Center.

If you are Manhattan natives, stroll home through the areas you undoubtedly know well. If you are visitors—and have more time to tour the Big Apple—move on to your next venue. But whatever your plans, you can be assured that you've just enjoyed a quintessential Manhattan weekend.

FOR MORE ROMANCE

After dinner on DAY ONE, you may want to catch the late show at **The Blue Note** (131 West 3rd Street; 212–475–8592), one of Manhattan's quintessential jazz clubs. The Blue Note always features the greatest of the jazz greats, and with the club's location in the heart of Greenwich Village, it offers one of New York's most memorable experiences.

ITINERARY 2
Two days and one night

THE AGE OF INNOCENCE

*N*ovelist Edith Wharton, a member of New York's upper class, wrote several heart–wrenching novels about New York life in the late nineteenth and early twentieth centuries. *The Age of Innocence* is perhaps her most poignant work. It concerns the longing of Newland Archer for a life of freedom with Countess Ellen Olenska, the woman he loves passionately. In true romantic tradition, Archer relinquishes his love to retain his honor.

This itinerary pays tribute to *The Age of Innocence,* as well as to the romantic notion of ineffable longing, the emotion central to literary Romanticism and to the novel. You'll view many of the landmarks that Wharton draws so beautifully in her novels, including Fifth Avenue, Grace Church, West 11th Street, and lower Broadway as it was in the Knickerbocker Old New York, days. New York has changed completely since the time Wharton described, yet occasionally you'll view a remarkable remnant of those long-gone times—and it may move you to tears. In many ways, this is the most truly romantic weekend in this book.

Practical notes: This itinerary is romantic any time of year. In the novel, New York City is described in every season: spring, after Easter, when many weddings were planned; summer, when most New Yorkers left the city for Newport; autumn, when New York is at its

Romance at a Glance

♥ *Stay at the Inn at Irving Place (212–533–4600).*

♥ *Dine at The Gramercy Tavern, Verbena, or The Knickerbocker.*

♥ *Shop along The Ladies' Mile.*

♥ *Tour Edith Wharton's New York, including the Morgan Library and the Frick Museum.*

♥ *Take a hansom carriage ride (wear gloves).*

♥ *View the Bougueraus, Cabanels, and Corbets at the Met.*

most beautiful; and winter, when New York is at its social height.

You'll be staying at the Inn at Irving Place—the perfect address for an *Age of Innocence* weekend. When you make your reservations, try to reserve the Madam Olenska room, which features a charming window seat where you can gaze longingly out the window. If the Madam Olenska room is booked, however, don't be disappointed. All the rooms at the Inn have unique charms.

DAY ONE: Morning

Drop off your bags at the **Inn at Irving Place** (56 Irving Place; 212–533–4600; $250 to $325 per night). You may be bemused when you arrive on the street outside the inn. The Inn gives absolutely no indication that it is a small hotel. Instead, it looks like a typical private home of the late nineteenth century. Just look for number 56, which is above the stoop to the left of the Verbena restaurant.

When you enter, you'll be enchanted by the fabulous Victorian furniture and decoration. You'll also be charmed by the graciousness of the Inn's staff. The Inn offers breakfast every morning and tea every afternoon in Lady Mendl's Tea Salon, in front of the parlor's fireplace. Keep in mind that most of the guest rooms have fireplaces, so you may well decide just to enjoy the privacy of your room. All of the rooms are romantic beyond belief. All have huge, comfortable beds, including some four-posters, and all have luxurious private baths.

You may be tempted to just close the door of your lovely room and stay there all weekend long. I don't blame you. But if you want to tour a bit before snuggling up, leave your bags and head out to explore the streets of Edith Wharton's New York.

Turn right at the bottom of the steps of the Inn and walk to the end of Irving Place. You'll find yourself at **Gramercy Park.** When New York City was first being planned, the city fathers wished to imitate London and create intimate squares or small parks every few blocks to ensure beauty. Unfortunately, the city grew so fast that only a few of these squares were built. In addition to Washington Square and Union Square, two central squares of the early and mid-nineteenth century, only Gramercy Park, Stuyvesant Square, Madison Square, and Tompkins Square Park survive.

Created by real estate developer Samuel B. Ruggles, Gramercy Park is considered by many to be the most beautiful of these city landmarks. It is protected by a beautiful wrought-iron fence, designed to be locked so that parents who owned houses around the park could be assured that their children would have only the most suitable playmates. The park is locked to this day, and only those who own apartments in the buildings surrounding the park are permitted to have keys.

Many fine houses from the late 1800s line the park. Pay particular attention to **The Players Club** (16 Gramercy Park South), which was founded in 1888 by actor Edwin Booth, brother of Lincoln's assassin, John Wilkes Booth. A statue of Edwin Booth as Hamlet stands in the center of the Park. Writers Herman Melville, O. Henry, William Dean Howells, Nathaniel West, S. J. Perelman, and others have lived in the Gramercy Park neighborhood. Although Edith Wharton herself never lived in Gramercy Park, she mentions it in many of her books and sets some of her stories in houses along the square. Her parents once lived in a house on nearby East 21st Street, but by the time Edith was born in 1862, the family had moved to West 23rd Street.

For a taste of mid-nineteenth-century life lived to its fullest, head over to the **Theodore**

Roosevelt Birthplace (28 East 20th Street; 212–260–1616). A National Historic Site, the museum is fascinating not only because it was Theodore Roosevelt's childhood home, but because it allows visitors to step back into the mid-nineteenth century. The house and its fine furnishings give an accurate picture of the life of a wealthy and influential New York City family.

DAY ONE: AFTERNOON

Lunch

Just down the block from the Roosevelt House is one of the hottest restaurants in New York, **The Gramercy Tavern** (42 East 20th Street; 212–477–0777). Despite its current celebrity, it has a warm, traditional quality to it. The restaurant is expensive, but the tavern room offers delicious sandwiches, grilled vegetables, salads, and cheese plates that are not outrageously costly. It's the perfect place to stop for a light lunch.

೧೯೬

After lunch, walk east to Park Avenue South and turn left and walk down to **Union Square.** On Monday, Wednesday, Friday, and Saturday, Union Square (and several other locations around the metropolitan area) plays host to a remarkable farmers market known as the **Greenmarket**. Farmers from upstate New York, New Jersey, Long Island, and even Pennsylvania come to sell their produce.

Union Square also has a colorful history that long precedes the Greenmarket. In the early nineteenth century it was a central square where the most fashionable families owned beautiful houses that lined the beautiful oval. It was officially named Union Square during the Civil War when Union troops congregated there.

Later, in the early twentieth century, it became a center for New York's radical movements, serving as a forum for soapbox speakers, much like Speaker's Corner in London.

The neighborhood was thought remote, and the house was built in a ghastly greenish-yellow stone that the younger architects were beginning to employ as a protest against the brownstone of which the uniform hue coated New York like a cold chocolate sauce.

—Edith Wharton, from *The Age of Innocence*,
describing a house on 39th Street

In the 1980s, the park, which had become seedy and dangerous, was renovated. New buildings were built nearby, and the subway station was revamped. Today, it is once again a popular meeting place for New Yorkers and visitors alike.

Stroll through the Greenmarket, and when you come to the northeast corner of the Square, walk up Broadway. The stretch of Broadway between 17th Street and 23rd Street is a famous part of the **Ladies' Mile**, a shopping district that was prominent in the late nineteenth century. The Ladies' Mile extended up Broadway, west along 23rd Street, down Sixth Avenue, and east along 14th Street. Many famous department stores lined these avenues, including the original Macy's, W. & J. Sloane, and Lord & Taylor. In the past decade, many of the beautiful Victorian buildings in the neighborhood have been renovated. **ABC Carpets & Home** (Broadway at 19th Street) has become one of the choicest stores in the city, and its eclectic displays of carpets, furniture, and home decorations of all sorts are reminiscent of those nineteenth-century department stores. Be sure to stop in and ogle ABC's marvelous—and very romantic—wares.

When you get to 23rd Street, stop long enough to take a close look at the famous

Flatiron Building, New York's first skyscraper—that is, a building constructed with steel girders. The Flatiron Building was given its name because of its unique shape, rather like a homemaker's iron.

The point created by this architecture at the intersections of Broadway, Fifth Avenue, and 23rd Street can be very windy. In the nineteenth century, young men used to stand on the point waiting for young women to walk by. The wind would often capture the ladies' skirts, allowing the boys to catch a glimpse of an ankle. The police would then come by and tell the boys to "skidoo," hence the expression "23 skidoo."

Across the street from the Flatiron Building is one of the early parks that survived the rapid growth of New York City: **Madison Square**. In the Gilded Age, Madison Square was a center of New York life, the equivalent of Rockefeller Center today. The famous Fifth Avenue Hotel faced the west side of the park, and the original Madison Square Garden sat just across the park on 26th Street.

West 23rd Street is not very interesting these days, but make your way along 23rd Street to Sixth Avenue, then head south. Stop at several of the stores that have recently opened on Sixth Avenue, including **Bed, Bath and Beyond** (620 Sixth Avenue) and a spectacular **Barnes & Noble** superstore (675 Sixth Avenue at 22nd Street), both of which inhabit luxurious buildings that were once fancy department stores. (Alternatively, you could stroll down Fifth Avenue between 23rd Street and 14th Street, a stretch that in recent years has become one of New York's chicest shopping areas.)

Make your way south to **West 11th Street**, and take a turn on the block between Fifth and Sixth Avenues. This is one of the most beautiful blocks in Greenwich Village, and the street on which Wharton's Newland Archer and May Welland lived throughout their married life. Continue walking east, crossing Fifth Avenue and University Place. You'll eventually come to Broadway again and the magnificent **Grace Church**, at 11th Street. This elegant Episcopal church was designed by James Renwick when he was in his early twenties; late in

In addition to The Age of Innocence, *novels by Edith Wharton that concern New York include* The Custom of the Country, The House of Mirth, Old New York *and many short stories. You'll want to read Edith Wharton's novels now that you can identify many of the sights she described so well. Also, be sure to see Martin Scorcese's lush film version of the novel, available on videotape.*

life, he designed Saint Patrick's Cathedral. Being the church where all wealthy New York Episcopalians were baptized, married, and eulogized for many generations throughout the Victorian and Gilded Ages, it was, of course, the setting for the fictional wedding of Newland and May.

Turn north on Broadway, east on 14th Street, and make your way back to Irving Place, and turn north to 17th Street and the Inn. You may want to take a nap, change for dinner, and just enjoy your elegant room—and each other.

DAY ONE: EVENING

Dinner

Have dinner at **Verbena** (54 Irving Place, between 17th and 18th Streets; 212–260–5454; expensive), the lovely restaurant located just beneath the Inn. If the weather permits, ask to sit in the garden terrace, which may well be located just below your room. Chef/owner Diane Forley has cooked at some of Manhattan's best restaurants including the Gotham Bar & Grill and Petrossian. The atmosphere is intimate, and the food is marvelous, featuring American cuisine infused with Forley's French training. Particularly, try the warm salad of shrimp on an artichoke griddlecake or wild mushrooms on toasted pasta.

⌘

Depending upon your mood, you can linger over dinner or venture uptown to the theater, a concert, or the opera. New Yorkers from Newland Archer's time congregated at the opera when the Academy of Music stood just down the block at Irving Place and 14th Street. The Academy of Music is long gone, but you can either go to the Metropolitan Opera or the New York City Opera at Lincoln Center.

It is **Carnegie Hall** (57th Street and Seventh Avenue; 212–247–7800), however, that most closely resembles the ambience of a Gilded Age theater. Carnegie Hall offers everything from grand classical concerts to performances by popular artists like Betty Buckley or Liza Minnelli. Its main hall hosts visiting orchestras from around the world and its smaller concert halls offer a marvelous array of musical artists.

You can't possibly have an *Age of Innocence* weekend without taking a **hansom carriage ride** around Central Park. It will cost $34 for the first twenty minutes: and $10 for each additional 15 minutes. Cabs line up on Central Park South (59th Street) by the entrance to Central Park, and you should have no trouble finding them. In Martin Scorsese's film of *The Age of Innocence,* he staged one of the most erotic love scenes ever filmed. While riding in a hansom cab, Newland unbuttons Ellen's glove and kisses the inside of her wrist. This is rather a tame gesture by late twentieth-century standards, but it is incredibly steamy in the film. Take your cues from The *Age of Innocence*, and end your evening by invoking the passion that existed between Newland and Ellen.

DAY TWO: MORNING

After your romantic night's sleep, enjoy breakfast in bed. Croissants, coffee, and tea are served on elegant porcelain, making you feel, once again, as though you had stepped back in time.

If the weather is good, spend the morning strolling the streets of New York. In *The Age of Innocence,* May Welland's aunt lived in a mansion at 809 Fifth Avenue near what would now be about 65th Street. Today, 65th Street is almost midtown, but in the late nineteenth century, 65th Street was considered to be unfashionably far uptown. At one point in the novel, Ellen Olenska walks from Madison Square to her aunt's home, a distance of about 2 miles. You might want to make the same walk, and try to imagine how dramatically life—and New York City—has changed.

Retrace your steps through Gramercy Park and walk north on Park Avenue South to 23rd Street. Turn left and walk west one block to the southeast corner of Madison Square, which is formed by the junction of Madison Avenue and 23rd Street. Walk north 13 blocks until you come to the **J. Pierpont Morgan Library** (29–33 East 36th Street at the corner of Madison Avenue; 212–685–0008 or 212–685–0610; open daily 11:00 A.M. to 6:00 P.M. Sunday 1:00 to 5:00 P.M.; $3 contribution requested).

The Morgan Library is actually a collection of several buildings and additions. The older building (which you can enter from Madison Avenue) was originally the home of financier J. Pierpont Morgan, perhaps the most influential banker and businessman of the nineteenth century, eclipsing even the glittering lights of his contemporaries John D. Rockefeller and Andrew Carnegie. Pierpont Morgan was as astute a collector of art, books, and ephemera as he was a businessman. He gave most of his great works of art to the Metropolitan Museum of Art, which he helped to found, but he built a library to display his collection of books, manuscripts, and incunabula.

The library (which you enter from 29 East 36th Street) was designed by Charles McKim of McKim, Mead and White, who based his design on the attic story of the Nymphaeum of 1555 built in Rome for Pope Julius III. The exterior of the building is of a refined design

with a marvelous Palladian arch, but the inside is luxurious almost beyond belief. An addition to the library was built after Morgan's death in 1928 and a glass pavilion was added to the rear of the library in 1991.

Take time to explore both the library and the Morgan house. Be sure to look at one of the original Gutenberg Bibles and original letters from such romantic writers as Balzac, Byron, and Keats. Also, as you take in this magnificent place, bear in mind that this was how upper-class people lived in New York in Wharton's day. Not all were as wealthy as Morgan, but Madison Avenue and Fifth Avenue were lined with spectacular mansions much like this one.

DAY TWO: AFTERNOON

Lunch

Either have a light lunch at the Morgan Library in their delightful glassed-in atrium, or else, venture north to **The Villard Houses** (actually, a part of the New York Palace Hotel; 455 Madison Avenue at 50th Street; 212–888–7000; expensive). Like the Morgan Library, the Villard Houses were built for another tycoon, Henry Villard, in 1883–84. The architectural firm McKim, Mead and White also designed this structure, incorporating six brownstones into a U-shaped design modeled on the fifteenth-century Italian Palazzo del Cancellaria.

Enter the hotel from the courtyard and note the magnificent Villard fireplace on the second floor. Have lunch in the **Hunt Room**, or if it's after 2:00 P.M., have tea in the **Gold Room,** which was once the original music room.

After lunch, take a taxi or walk to **The Frick Museum** (1 East 70th Street at Fifth Avenue; 212–288–0700). The Frick is considered one of the most beautiful small museums in the world. The building itself is a palatial mansion built in 1914 by industrialist Henry Clay Frick, precisely the type of nouveau-riche New Yorker that Edith Wharton described so well. (Although the house is of a later period than those described in *The Age of Innocence,* it exudes the same level of opulence.) Frick was a remarkable collector of fine art, and the house is filled with paintings by such masters as Rembrandt, Turner, Vermeer, El Greco, and Fragonard as well as eighteenth-century French furniture, Chinese vases, and Limoges enamels. The house and its artwork are dazzling. Moreover, the center Garden Court is a romantic urban oasis, where concerts are often heard. The Frick is open from 10:00 A.M. to 6:00 P.M. Tuesday through Saturday and 1:00 to 6:00 P.M. on Sunday. Admission costs $5.00. Put a romantic close to your *Age of Innocence* weekend with an intimate tête-à-tête in this beautiful place.

FOR MORE ROMANCE

Take a scenic day trip by boat up the Hudson River to **Kykuit,** the house built by John D. Rockefeller, creator of one of America's greatest family fortunes. Stroll through the immaculately kept garden terraces and antiques-filled interior. Marvel at the sweeping vistas of the Hudson Valley. Getting there is almost as pleasurable as seeing the mansion. Call **NY Waterway Sightseeing Cruises** at (800) 533–3379 for reservations and details. Boats depart from Pier 78 at West 38th Street and Twelfth Avenue.

If you have more time, spend a weekend in Rhinebeck (see "Paradise on the Hudson," page 45, for details). Such a weekend was popular during the Gilded Age, and the Hudson River mansions are precisely the sort of country homes that Wharton's characters visited.

ITINERARY 3
Two days and one night

KISS ME, I'M IRISH

After Plymouth Rock lost its allure, a bigger rock in the sea, called Manhattan, emerged as the landing point of choice for Europe's tired, poor, and huddled masses. Ireland's emigrants, particularly the million who came to America during the Potato Famine of 1845–51, became a template for future newcomers. Work hard, play by the rules, face down the ridicule and stereotypes, and find a mix between being who you were and who you will become.

The Irish contributed much to Manhattan's colorful history. James Duane, son of an Irish-born merchant, became the first Irish-American mayor in 1784. De Witt Clinton, who became Mayor of New York City and then Governor of New York State, was a visionary, responsible for creating the New York Historical Society, the Free School Society, and the Erie Canal. Margaret Sanger was the founder of Planned Parenthood, and Eugene O'Neill was one of America's most extraordinary playwrights. All were Irish New Yorkers.

Every year on St. Patrick's Day, New York pays homage to the Irish and all that they have given to New York City. Typically, it is a day and night of boisterous partying, so come and join in the fun. If you're Irish—or even if you are not—this itinerary will give you a little taste of the joy and romance of Irish New York. And that's no blarney!

Practical notes: Obviously, this getaway is planned for St. Patrick's Day, but you can use it any day of the year. It won't be quite as festive, but it will certainly be less hectic. If you do it on or around March 17, come prepared for all kinds of weather.

It won't surprise you to know that all New York's Irish restaurants and pubs are booked solid weeks—and sometimes months—in advance on St. Patrick's Day. Make your reservations as far in advance as possible.

Romance at a Glance

♥ *Stay at Fitzpatrick Manhattan Hotel (800–367–7701).*

♥ *Dine at O'Flaherty's Ale House, Moran's, and the Landmark Tavern.*

♥ *Watch the St. Patrick's Day Parade.*

♥ *Explore points of Gaelic Gotham.*

Unlike Little Italy or Chinatown, no single New York neighborhood remains relatively intact to commemorate Irish heritage. Irish immigrants lived, at different times, in various sections of the city: the Lower East Side; Greenwich Village, Hell's Kitchen, Yorkville. In order to catch a glimpse of Irish New York, you'll be jumping around a bit in this itinerary.

In terms of romance, this getaway—being a celebration of the fun-loving Irish—is not of the quiet-little-table-in-the-corner variety. You'll be spending a fair amount of time joking with the "boyos," so try to steal a few moments here and there just to be with each other.

DAY ONE: MORNING

There's only one place to stay in Manhattan when you're here to celebrate Irish heritage: **Fitzpatrick Manhattan Hotel** (687 Lexington Avenue, between 56th and 57th Street; 800–357–7701; $180–$250 per night). It is the only Irish-owned hotel in Manhattan and is managed by the Paddy Fitzpatrick Enterprise, a family corporation that operates several hotels in Dublin, Shannon, and County Cork. With its

European ambience and Irish friendliness, it has proven to be a home away from home for both Irish-Americans and transplanted Dubliners.

The moderately priced rooms and suites are comfortable, and the service is the friendliest in New York. Waterford crystal chandeliers and hand-woven Kelly green carpeting make the lobby charmingly Irish. The most comfortable accommodations are the seven Presidential Suites, each named for an Irish President, including DeValera, Robinson, and Hyde. Make St. Patrick's Day reservations early—some guests book as much as a year in advance.

Plan to arrive in mid- to late morning. Settle yourself in your room, then fortify yourself for the grand day with brunch in **Fitzers,** the hotel's charming Irish pub-type bar and restaurant (moderate).

Brunch/Lunch

Don't miss Fitzers "Irish Breakfast." It's such a classic and well-loved meal that Fitzpatrick's serves it from early morning until 10:30 at night in order to accommodate travelers arriving from any time zone. Naturally, the breakfast is a hearty one, featuring Irish scones, Irish brown bread, Irish soda bread; Irish oatmeal; eggs with a rasher of Irish bacon and bangers (that's sausages); grilled tomatoes; Irish black & white pudding (a savory dish akin to Scottish blood pudding); and Irish Morning Breakfast tea.

If breakfast fare is not your cup of tea, Fitzers offers other Irish dishes, including lamb stew, steak and kidney pie, oak-smoked salmon, and a special dish called Chicken Hibernia in Irish Whiskey Sauce.

You can also enjoy afternoon tea in the Irish Coffee corner, which offers tea Irish-style with scones and other Irish sweets. And if you're really Irish, you'll warm up with a neat whiskey or a jar of Guinness.

Pick up a copy of the Irish Voice *at any newsstand. This newspaper reflects the news and opinions of young Irish Americans. It also carries a comprehensive listing of cultural events and community happenings with addresses and telephone numbers.*

DAY ONE: AFTERNOON

Now you're ready to brave the streets. If you've never been to New York City on St. Patrick's Day, be warned. The Irish, the Irish-Americans, and all Irish-American wannabes (that includes most New Yorkers) are out in force. The St. Patrick's Day Parade begins at noon and weaves its way along Fifth Avenue from 42nd Street to 86th Street. It runs for several hours, so unless you're a glutton for punishment (or Irish nostalgia), an hour-long viewing of the parade will be sufficient.

Fitzpatrick's is on Lexington Avenue, three long blocks from Fifth, but as soon as you walk out the door of the hotel, you'll undoubtedly observe that the streets are teeming with happy people, most of whom are wearing green hats, green shirts, a shamrock or two, buttons demanding "Kiss Me, I'm Irish," and a warm blush surely the result of a few nips of whiskey.

Wend (or elbow) your way west to Fifth Avenue. (You'll probably be able to hear the bagpipes and the brass bands.) Religious observance is probably the furthest thing from your mind, but you cannot celebrate New York and Irish heritage without taking a turn around the magnificent **Saint Patrick's Cathedral** at Fifth Avenue between 50th and 51st Streets. Head south on Fifth to reach the cathedral—the heart of today's Irish New York and the focal point of the St. Patrick's Day celebrations. You'll spot famous politicians (certainly any that are Irish) and officials of the Catholic church, like Cardinal O'Connor, all of whom either participate in the parade or view it from the stand set up in front of the Cathedral.

Although it is almost dwarfed by the surrounding skyscrapers, Saint Patrick's is, in fact, the eleventh largest church in the world. When St. Patrick's was built in 1879 (designed by James Renwick, architect of the very Wasp Grace Church in the Village), it was considered too far out of town. It is finely detailed (many of the stained-glass windows were made in Chartres and Nantes) and well proportioned (the spires rise 330 feet in the air). Rest for a moment in the nave, observe the magnificent high altar (also designed by Renwick), and if the sun is shining when you leave, pause to see the reflection of the spires against the glass of the neighboring Olympic Tower. This sight is one of New York City's secret treasures.

If you've had enough of the parade and you have prayed for sustenance, head downtown to explore the birthplace of Irish New York. Make your way to the Lexington IRT subway stop at 51st Street. (Forget about taking a bus on St. Patrick's Day; you'll be caught in traffic for a week. If you want to take a taxi, go to Park Avenue—and lotsa luck.) As a matter of fact, the subway will also be "a trip," as they say—and you know what I mean—but you'll survive. Just hang on to your wallet. Take the downtown local train to the Astor Place stop.

When you come out of the subway, head south one block and then east to **McSorley's Old Ale House** (15 East 7th Street; 473-9148; expensive). McSorley's is famous in two ways. First, since 1854, it's been a hangout for Irish workers, some of whom were partially responsible for giving the neighboring Bowery a bad name; second, it was one of the first targets of the Women's Liberation Movement in the early 1970s, which was intent on forcing this formerly all-male bastion to admit women. The saloon admits women now, of course. It will be packed on St. Patrick's Day, but you'll want to stop by for a brew and a rest. Most likely you'll get the beer; you probably won't get any rest.

When you leave McSorley's, turn right, and when you get to the Bowery, turn left. You're about to walk back in time for an hour (and a mile) or so.

Walk down the Bowery until you reach East Houston Street. Turn right and walk two blocks to Mott Street, then turn left. Halfway down the block you'll come to **Old St. Patrick's Cathedral** at 264 Mulberry Street. This was one of New York's first Gothic Revival buildings, as well as the city's first Irish Catholic parish. (When the "new" St. Patrick's Cathedral was consecrated in 1879, this church became a parish church serving predominantly the Irish in the neighborhood; the Italian immigrants founded their own church several blocks east of here.)

Built in 1815 and restored in 1868 after a fire, the church is no longer as fine looking as it once was, since the fire damaged the facade badly. Nevertheless, the brick wall that surrounds the church and churchyard remains one of New York's most beautiful and romantic sights. The Irish (and the neighboring Italians) were the objects of tremendous discrimination, particularly during the Nativist period of the mid-nineteenth century. The pocks on the wall, the results of rocks and bullets directed at the Irish parishioners, can still be seen.

Turn right on Prince Street, then turn left at Mulberry Street. You'll no doubt observe that you've arrived at the heart of Little Italy. Historically, although the Irish preceded the Italians to Manhattan and, in this area, live close together, it is the Italian influence on the neighborhood that has survived. Continue to walk south through Little Italy all the way to Worth Street. Although this area now is built up with government buildings, it was once known as **Five Points**, a hideous ghetto where many Irish immigrants began their difficult New York life in the 1840s. (For more about this neighborhood, "La Dolce Vita" see page 131.) However, it's worth noting that today the park at the heart of the Civic Center is known as **Foley Square**, a testament to the Irish who ended up governing the city for more than a century.

Turn east and wend your way east along Worth. Cross the intersection of Park Row and the Bowery and make your way to Oliver Street. This three- or four-block area is the last vestige of the once largely Irish neighborhood.

At **25 Oliver Street** stands the childhood home of Alfred E. Smith, the onetime governor of New York State and the Democratic presidential candidate in 1928. Al Smith grew up in abject poverty, but his house and others in the row of buildings on either side date back to the 1820s when prosperous merchants lived in this neighborhood. By the time Smith's family moved in (in the late 1870s), the merchants were long gone and these single-family dwellings had become home to as many as seven families.

At the end of Oliver Street, make a right onto Madison Street. The buildings across the street make up the Alfred E. Smith Houses, a public housing project. Continue a few yards down Madison, then make a right onto James Street and walk until you come to the **Church of St. James** (at 32 St. James Place, on the right), established by Irish immigrants in 1837.

A plaque on the left side of the church commemorates the founding of the Irish benevolent society, the Ancient Order of Hibernians, in 1836. The AOH provided charitable services to Irish immigrants. It also rallied the Irish on many occasions to protect their churches and homes from nativist mobs. Across the street from St. James Church is **St. James Parochial School** where Al Smith received his entire formal education. Like many Irish boys of his time, he remained in school only through the eighth grade.

You're probably ready to relax for a few minutes. Unfortunately, this neighborhood does not offer much in the way of a romantic respite. The most convenient option is to retrace your steps back to Mulberry Street and have a cappuccino at one of the many Italian coffee-houses along the street. Then, if you care to, walk north to Spring then west about five blocks to **The Irish Secret** at 155 Spring Street. This delightful shop features men's and women's Irish imported clothes.

DAY ONE: EVENING

Dinner

At dinnertime, hail a taxi and ask the driver to take you to **Moran's** (146 10th Avenue at

19th Street; 212–627–3030; moderate). This family-owned pub, with its crackling fireplace and handsome bar, seems as Irish as a country pub in Galway. Although it is a neighborhood restaurant, it will be hopping on St. Patrick's Day. The waiters (many of whom are Irish) and the clientele couldn't be friendlier. If it's still early, linger over a lager or whiskey at the bar, then enjoy dinner. The fish dishes are especially good

၏

Now it's St. Patrick's Day evening. I can pretty much guarantee that most people who are still out on the streets and in the taverns are quite tipsy. As I said earlier, this is not a holiday that promises quiet conversation and intimacy. Rowdiness better describes the atmosphere. So, if you're still into the spirit of the day, catch a taxi and go to **Tommy Makem's Irish Pavilion** (130 East 57th Street; 212–759–9040). This is a pretty touristy Irish pub, but it's fun. The folk music is delightful, and, on St. Patrick's Day, Tommy (an Irish virtuoso) himself may be present. Best of all, it's located right around the corner from Fitzpatrick's, so when you've had enough reveling, walk (if you can) to your hotel.

At last, you can be alone.

DAY TWO: MORNING

Sleep in. (You did remember to bring aspirin, didn't you?)

Brunch

When you're ready to venture out, catch a taxi (or walk—it's about a mile from your hotel) to **O'Flaherty's Ale House** (334 West 46th Street; 212–581–9366; inexpensive). This is a real New York neighborhood public house that serves American staples like hamburgers and bacon and eggs but also features some Irish specialties like shepherd's pie. For a little hair of the dog, try a spicy Bloody Mary. When you're finished fortifying yourself, join in a game of billiards or darts.

After lunch you'll be ready to explore the surrounding streets. One interesting aspect of this neighborhood is that it is the heart of the theater district, so you may run into a familiar face. You can count on the fact that some of your fellow dart players or passersby will be actors, regardless of whether or not they are currently working. (Some may even be playwrights or novelists.)

This neighborhood is also the heart of Hell's Kitchen, once a rather dangerous Irish neighborhood. Later in the afternoon, stroll west and try to imagine growing up here—the way Senator Daniel Patrick Moynihan did. Stop in at the **Landmark Tavern** (626 11th Street at 46th Street; 212–757–8595; moderate). This 1868 authentic Irish pub will give you a parting taste of old Gaelic Gotham.

FOR MORE ROMANCE

The other great Irish celebration in New York is called "The Great Irish Fair" and is held at Coney Island in Brooklyn during the second weekend in September. An Irishman, Patrick Boynton, opened the Coney Island Amusement Park more than 100 years ago, and this celebration of Irish clans is organized by the Ancient Order of Hibernians, the same group that organizes the St. Patrick's Day Parade. It is a joyous fair with Irish folk singers performing on the boardwalk, Irish athletes competing in sports like Irish hurling, Irish boats racing to Sheepshead Bay, and a Colleen Queen reigning over the entire affair. If you can't make it to New York for St. Patrick's Day, try to schedule your romantic weekend around this affair.

ITINERARY 4
Four days and three nights

EASTER WEEKEND IN NEW YORK

*T*he poet T.S. Eliot once described April as the "cruelest month," and, in some ways, his observation is true. When the sky is gray, the temperature is chilly, and a still–wintry rain falls, early April can seem heartless indeed, especially in a city of brown stone and granite skyscrapers—like, uh, New York. However, when the sun breaks through on an April morning, New York is at its most spectacular. Churches ring with beautiful music, Central Park bursts into bloom, and Big Apple natives become welcoming and happy.

Easter Week is an ideal time to plan a getaway to New York. Easter normally falls in early April, and the week preceding Easter Sunday is a holiday for many people. This itinerary, therefore, allows for a long, three-day weekend, from Thursday night through Sunday. It also suggests some of the most lavish accommodations, food, and entertainment that New York has to offer. How better to celebrate the coming of spring!

Practical notes: For this itinerary, I've suggested several activities that surround the Easter holidays and, thus, the Christian faith. If you are not Christian or if you do not wish to participate in the religious observances suggested here, consider attending the theater, ballet, opera, or a concert. All of New York's performing arts have a season in the early spring.

If you wish a room at the Essex House overlooking the park, make sure you reserve well in advance. Be sure to make your dinner reservations at Les Celebrités and the other recommended restaurants at the time you reserve your hotel. All the restaurants suggested here are popular and will be booked solid during the holiday weekend.

This is a very expensive weekend. If you want to retain the basic itinerary but conserve your funds, consider staying at the Wyndham Hotel, which is located just a few blocks from the Essex House. (See "Puttin' on the Ritz" for a description of the Wyndham or see Hotels, page 287). All of the restaurants suggested here are pricey as well.

Romance at a Glance

♥ *Stay at The Essex House (212–247–0300).*

♥ *Dine at four of New York's most glamorous restaurants: Les Celebrités, The Terrace, Aureole, and Tavern on the Green.*

♥ *Explore several of New York's most exciting museums.*

♥ *Listen to music at New York's great churches and concert halls.*

DAY ONE: Evening

Plan to arrive in the city in the mid-afternoon. As you drive up to the **Essex House** (160 Central Park South; 212–247–0300; rooms $250–$350 per night, suites $400–$2,000), the excitement of spring in New York will greet you immediately. Located directly across the street from Central Park, the hotel affords you a view of the trees that will probably be about to bud.

The Essex House opened its doors in 1931 during an era of style and elegance when international travel began and ended at the West Side piers and fashionable ladies and gentlemen partied at the Stork Club. Today, the Stork Club and the piers are memories, but after a two-year renovation, the Essex House has been restored to its original opulence. The lobby pays tribute to the grand style of the 1930s with exquisitely restored etched-brass elevator doors and new dramatic black columns; at the same time, the hotel offers all the conveniences and luxuries of the 1990s.

If you've reserved a room overlooking Central Park, you'll be treated to a grand view of one of New York's greatest treasures: 843 acres of trees, lakes, and gardens—ideal for strolling, biking, roller blading, or just sitting. Take a moment to luxuriate in your lush room and then head out for your first holiday romantic evening.

It is Easter Week, and one of the most moving services of the season is the Maundy Thursday ceremony at **St. Thomas Episcopal Church Fifth Avenue** (Fifth Avenue at 53rd Street; 212–757–7013, parish office). St. Thomas is noted for its Boys Choir, which is ranked among the best boys' choirs in the world. As a result, the parish's liturgical music is sublime, and the ceremony commemorating Jesus' Last Supper and His betrayal is breathtaking. The service begins at 5:30 P.M., and you need not be a member of the church (or even an Episcopalian) to attend; it is open to the public.

St. Thomas Church is a fifteen-minute walk from the Essex House, and if the weather permits, I recommend walking. If you must take a taxi, allow thirty minutes to get from the hotel to the church. You may have trouble securing a cab, and rush-hour traffic is always congested. If you are walking, head east on 59th Street. Even if you've never been to New York City before, many sights will look incredibly familiar: the horse-drawn hansom cabs waiting at Central Park, the Plaza Hotel, and Fifth Avenue at its most glamorous. Turn right at the corner of Fifth Avenue and 59th Street and head south for six blocks to St. Thomas Church, which is located on the northwest corner of 53rd and Fifth.

Dinner

After the service, walk back to the Essex House and prepare for a marvelous dinner at **Les Celebrités** (153 West 58th Street; 212–484–5113; very expensive), one of New York's finest restaurants, which is located next to the 58th Street entrance to the hotel. (Remember to book ahead; make your reservation for 8:00 P.M. since the Maundy Thursday service will last until about 7:30 P.M.)

Les Celebrités has been described by restaurant critics as a "tiny jewelbox." The dramatic decor includes huge black columns and ruby-colored draperies. The walls are lined with paintings—luxuriously framed and lighted—by several celebrities (including Phyllis Diller, of all people), a feature that accounts for the restaurant's name. The table settings are exquisite, with red and gold Bernardaud china and elaborate Christofle silver. Yet, despite the drama, the restaurant has only fourteen tables, and a luxe intimacy is achieved with the help of impeccable service, an outstanding wine list, and a luscious (and expensive) menu.

Chef Christian Delouvrier, a French-trained artist from Toulouse in southwest France, has created a menu with intensely flavored French dishes with an Oriental element. He specializes in game birds, shellfish, foie gras, and truffles. The earthy roast squab with cabbage and the truffled mashed potatoes are not to be missed. Finish your dinner with a glass or two of light champagne. And off to bed.

DAY TWO: FRIDAY MORNING

Breakfast

Since this is the first morning of your Easter weekend holiday, you may want to sleep a bit late, then order coffee or tea from room service and enjoy the romantic tranquility of your beautiful room.

Don't tarry too long, though; there's a special day ahead of you. Put on comfortable walking shoes because you'll be doing a bit of hiking. (Don't worry; it's not too vigorous.) But first: Brunch. One of the great breakfast rooms in New York City is the **Edwardian Room** at the **Plaza Hotel** (768 Fifth Avenue; 212–759–3000; expensive), just two easy blocks away.

The Edwardian Room is known for its "power breakfasts," so if you did not spot any celebrities last night, you may run into a few actors or tycoons this morning. The magnificent beamed ceiling and oversized windows allowing spectacular views of Central Park and Fifth Avenue create a majestic, open feeling, and yet the large, widely spaced tables allow for privacy. You can order a French continental breakfast, a full American breakfast, or even an authentic Japanese breakfast. Enjoy the magnificent old-world charm as you soak up a real taste of New York.

DAY TWO: LATE MORNING/AFTERNOON

Now head for **The Cloisters** (Fort Tryon Park, 192nd Street between Riverside Drive and Fort Washington Avenue), one of New York City's greatest treasures and a part of the collections of the Metropolitan Museum of Art. See "Art for Lovers" (page 74) for directions and details.

Now that you've bravely ventured into the nether-reaches of Manhattan, spend the rest of the afternoon exploring a few other famous upper Manhattan landmarks such as Riverside Church, Columbia University, and the Cathedral of St. John the Divine. Begin by retracing your steps to the subway or bus you came on and heading to 120th Street.

Riverside Church, whose well-known pastor William Sloane Coffin made his name crusading against the Vietnam War and for other liberal causes, is located on 120th Street. The observation deck at the church (open Monday through Saturday, 9:00 A.M. to 5:00 P.M.; Sunday services at 10:45 A.M.) offers another incredible view of the Hudson River and Riverside Park. Your climb to the deck will take you to a seventy-four-bell carillon donated by the Rockefeller family. Spend a few romantic moments viewing Manhattan—and each other—from this unique vantage point. (Remember, this is Good Friday, and Good Friday services may be in progress. Feel welcome to participate or just sit quietly.)

After leaving Riverside Church, head south on Riverside Drive. At 116th Street, turn left and walk up just two short blocks to the entrance to **Columbia University** (116th Street and Broadway.) New York City's contribution to the Ivy League and one of the oldest universities in the United States, originally chartered in 1754. If either of you are an alumnus, then you'll have many memories to relive. If you've never seen the campus before, you are in for a treat. Walk through the gates and enter the main quad. (The university as a whole runs from 114th Street to 120th Street between Morningside Drive and Broadway). The focal point is **Low Library**, named after former Columbia president and former New York politico Seth Low. The statue of **Alma Mater**, designed by Daniel Chester French and situated in front of Low Library, may evoke fond radical memories since Columbia University—and the statue—were focal points of campus riots in 1968. Today the statue is decorated with photos of famous radicals of the sixties. You'll undoubtedly see many students on campus but these kids aren't quite as revolutionary as their parents were.

Another neighborhood sight not to be missed is the **Cathedral of St. John the Divine** (located between 110th and 113th Streets and Amsterdam Avenue). The Cathedral is just a short walk from Columbia's main quad. Exit the quad through the Amsterdam Avenue entrance at its east end, turn right, and walk three blocks.

Construction began on the Cathedral in 1892, is still going on, and is not expected to be completed for at least another 100 years. You may even see work going on in the stoneyard or on the Cathedral itself. The Cathedral evokes the great churches built in medieval times, but it is also very much a "living" church and an American church. Its stained-glass windows include a portrait of George Washington, a poet's corner is dedicated to American literature, and secular and social functions are on its active schedule. Despite its grandeur, it is a remarkably friendly place. Stroll through the nave, or relax quietly in one of the pews. Good Friday services may be in progress, but you will be welcome. You may well fall in love with St. John's and want to return on Sunday morning.

DAY TWO: EVENING

Dinner

I don't mean to sound sacrilegious, but by now you'll probably be ready for a cocktail and a fine dinner. Again, this neighborhood has its special place: **The Terrace** (400 West 119th Street at Morningside Drive; 212–666–9490; expensive). The Terrace is especially remarkable in the spring, and it is one of the most romantic restaurants in New York City. Although located on only the 17th floor of a Columbia University building, its unobstructed views—from the George Washington Bridge to Manhattan's midtown skyscrapers—make it almost as thrilling as the top of the Empire State Building. Step out on the Terrace before you sit down to dinner to get the full show.

You'll be lulled by the soft harp music and the scent of the lovely roses on every table. The menu is French and varied. Warm lobster salad and beluga caviar are among your choices. The service is discreet. All in all, it is a perfect place for a romantic dinner—and the end to a romantic day.

⌀

You'll have no trouble finding a taxi back to the Essex House. If you are not too exhausted from your meandering, take a hansom cab ride through Central Park before you retire.

DAY THREE: MORNING

Again, sleep late—and enjoy your holiday and your luxurious room. Savor your time alone: order breakfast from room service.

A weekend in New York is never complete without a few hours of shopping, and early spring is an ideal time to look for an Easter bonnet or a pair of new shoes. Of course, the shops on Fifth Avenue and Madison Avenue are particularly spectacular, so turn east as you leave your hotel and head over toward Fifth. You'll definitely want to window shop, but pay particular attention to the grand emporiums on Fifth Avenue between 50th and 60th Streets: **Trump Tower, Henri Bendel, Saks Fifth Avenue**, and **Bergdorf Goodman**. If you are in a playful mood, check out **F.A.O. Schwarz** at 58th and Fifth, the best place to find a perfect stuffed bunny. (Also, the "Barbie Boutique" is spectacular.) It's Easter, so you might want to indulge in a little chocolate at **Godiva Chocolatier** in Rockefeller Center or at 701 Fifth. If you prefer diamond "eggs" to chocolate ones, stop at **Tiffany** (Fifth and 57th), **Cartier** (Fifth and 52nd), or **Harry Winston** (Fifth and 56th).

Head over to Madison Avenue and stroll north. Madison Avenue between 57th Street and 96th Street is shoppers' heaven. Hundreds of fabulous shops selling everything from ladies' and mens' clothing, jewelry, and every sort of accessory to books and elegant provisions line both sides of the avenue. Many high-fashion clothing designers have shops on (or just off) Madison, including **Chanel** (3 East 57th Street), **Maud Frizon** (49 East 57th Street); **Givenchy** (954 Madison at 75th Street), and **Valentino** (823 Madison). Watch for my personal favorites: **Tenzing and Pema** (956 Madison at 75th Street), which specializes in objects for the "mind," and **Books & Co** (939 Madison), which also obviously sells works that appeal to the intellect.

Lunch

If you've been a super-shopper, you may well have made your way up Madison Avenue as far as 80th Street. Stop for soup, a salad, or a sandwich at **E.A.T.** (1064 Madison Avenue between 80th and 81st Streets; 212–772–0022), a sort of high-class delicatessen. It is owned by Eli Zabar, a member of the family that owns the famous Zabar's deli on the West Side.

DAY THREE: Afternoon

Not only are you in one of New York's best shopping districts, you are also close to many

Easter Church Services

The churches listed below are among the most famous in New York City—many, in fact, are well known throughout the world. Despite their grandeur, they all graciously welcome visitors, especially during the Easter holidays. All these churches offer services throughout Holy Week, including at least two services on Easter Sunday. Call the parish office to find out the schedule of services.

Cathedral Church of St. John the Divine
Episcopal; multi-denominational
Amsterdam Avenue at 112th Street
(212) 316–7540

Fifth Avenue Presbyterian
Fifth Avenue at 55th Street
(212) 247–0490

The Riverside Church
United Church of Christ
Riverside Drive at 122nd Street
(212) 222–5900

St. Patrick's Cathedral
Roman Catholic
Fifth Avenue at 50th Street
(212) 753–2261

St. Thomas Church
Episcopal
Fifth Avenue at 53rd Street
(212) 757–7013

Trinity Church
Episcopal
Broadway at Wall Street
(212) 602–0800

of New York's greatest museums, not the least of which, of course, is the **Metropolitan Museum of Art** (82nd and Fifth Avenue). Since you had a taste of the Met's incredible art collection at the Cloisters yesterday, you may want to stop and see more of the museum treasures. (Also, if your shopping passions have not been abated, check out the Met's gift shop, which is one of the best gift shops in New York.) On the other hand, since you brushed up on your knowledge of medieval art at the Cloisters, you may want a more contemporary change of pace. I would suggest spending an hour or so at the **Whitney Museum of American Art** (945 Madison Avenue; 212–570–3600). It is open from 11:00 A.M. to 6:00 P.M. Wednesday and Friday through Sunday and 11:00 A.M. to 8:00 P.M. Thursday. Admission is charged.

This is Holy Saturday, and many churches have late afternoon services. If you wish to attend one, check the list (page 41) for a church you would like to attend and call for the hours of the services.

DAY THREE: EVENING

Dinner

Easter is my favorite holiday of the year, but we need not get too heavy about it. I don't think God will strike you dead if you spend this evening having a delicious dinner and attending a play. However, just to ensure that you are blessed, have dinner at **Aureole** (34 East 61st Street; 212-319-1660; very expensive).

Aureole is not only one of the most romantic restaurants in New York but also one that consistently receives high praise for both its decor and its menu. The restaurant is located in a beautifully restored brownstone on one of Manhattan's prettiest streets, and the lush floral displays make the rooms breathtaking. The menu changes regularly, but since it is spring, lamb will probably be on the menu. In honor of spring, why not give it a try?

తోపొత

After dinner, see something fun at the theater, such as *Cats* or *The King and I*. If you didn't order tickets before you arrived, ask your concierge at the hotel to check around for last-minute seats.

DAY FOUR: EASTER SUNDAY MORNING

It's Easter—one of the most joyous days of the year for Christians. Again, enjoy breakfast in your room and savor the spectacular view of Central Park, which should be just about to burst into bloom. Then head out to church.

Church services for Easter are usually scheduled for 8:00 and 11:00 A.M. (Again, call the church you wish to attend and check the times. Plan to arrive at least forty-five minutes before the service begins, since all churches in Manhattan are extremely crowded on Easter Sunday.)

By late morning the famous New York Easter Parade will be in progress, regardless of the weather. After church, Fifth Avenue will be teeming with little girls in white gloves and Easter bonnets, drag queens decked out to the nines, and, of course, the Easter Bunny—or maybe several Easter Bunnies. Stroll up Fifth Avenue, have your picture taken with The Rabbit, and delight in this incredible array of humanity in celebration.

Brunch

Have a wonderful Easter brunch at the **Crystal Room at Tavern on the Green** (in Central Park at West 67th Street; 212–873–3200; expensive; reservations recommended). Some consider the Tavern to be garish with its Tiffany glass chandeliers, its gift shop, and its sheer size, but for most people it is a bit of glamour smack in the middle of Central Park. The views of the green and the twinkling lights (even in the daytime) make the Tavern festive and fun. Warner LeRoy treats his restaurant like a theatrical production—and he should know how since his father was Mervyn LeRoy, director of *The Wizard of Oz,* among other films, and Warner grew up in Hollywood. The chef, Patrick Clark, won the 1994 James Beard Award for Best Chef in the Mid-Atlantic Region, and his dishes are varied, subtly seasoned, and delicious—particularly anything made with salmon. Folks at the Tavern make a fuss over holidays, and you'll never know what will be cooking or going on. Maybe an Easter Bonnet contest.

DAY FOUR: AFTERNOON

After brunch, take a stroll through Central Park. Daffodils may be peeking through the earth. (You'll marvel not only at the flowers, but at the fact that no one picks them!) Buds will probably be bursting on the trees. Enjoy the pleasures of spring.

FOR MORE ROMANCE

Flowers are an important part of celebrating Easter and the coming of spring. Order a beautiful bouquet to decorate your room. Ask the concierge at the hotel for the number of a good florist near your hotel.

ITINERARY 5
Two days and one night

PARADISE ON THE HUDSON

$\mathscr{T}$he serene Hudson River can surely be considered among the great rivers of the world. Like the Thames, the Seine, and the Rhine, it has inspired artists to capture its beauty. Painters of the Hudson River School of the nineteenth century recreated scenes from the shores of the Hudson because they considered the area to be Paradise. Once the Hudson River School artists had designated the river's edge this side of heaven, millionaires and aristocrats such as the Livingstons and Roosevelts and, later, those "upstarts" the Vanderbilts and Rockefellers, decided that they agreed. Many of these families built fabulous mansions along the river. Today, many of the estates are open to the public. This getaway provides opportunities for romantic interludes by the river, quiet exploration of the lovely grounds and homes of several estates, and the time to take simple pleasure in each other.

Practical notes: For this itinerary, you will need a car. From Manhattan, take the Henry Hudson Parkway to the Saw Mill River Parkway and ultimately to the Taconic Parkway. (All of these highways connect; you'll have no trouble finding them.) Exit the Taconic at Route 55, go west into the town of Poughkeepsie and pick up Route 9; then drive north until you come to Hyde Park. After you have visited the mansions in Hyde Park, continue north along

Route 9 to Rhinebeck. Rhinebeck is about 100 miles from Manhattan.

If you don't have access to a car, you can take the train or bus directly to Rhinebeck and make your way around the town on foot. (You'll have to forgo Hyde Park, however, if you take the train.) For rail information, call Amtrak (800–USA–RAIL); the train takes you to Rhinecliff where drivers from the Beekman Arms will meet you. For bus service, check the Short Line from Manhattan to Rhinebeck; call (212) 736–4700.

For further information about this area, call the **Dutchess Country Tourism Promotion Agency** (3 Neptune Road, Poughkeepsie, New York 12601) at (914) 463–3131. Ask for pamphlets outlining historic county driving tours. You can also call the **Rhinebeck Chamber of Commerce** (Box 42, 19 Mill Street, Rhinebeck, New York 12572) at (914) 876–4778.

DAY ONE: MORNING

Start out early to begin your trip up the Hudson. Early Saturday morning traffic should be light, and after the cacophonous streets of Manhattan, you may be surprised by the beauty and quiet of the Saw Mill River and the Taconic Parkways.

When you arrive in Hyde Park, you will find two of the most famous of all the Hudson River estates: Springwood, the home and library of President Franklin Delano Roosevelt, and the Vanderbilt Mansion, one of the many mansions owned by the incredibly wealthy

Vanderbilt family. Together, these homes are formally managed as the Roosevelt–Vanderbilt National Historic Site. They are open every day from May through October, 9:00 A.M. to 5:00 P.M., and from Thursday through Monday at the same hours from November to April. Admission to the Vanderbilt Mansion is $2; to the Roosevelt Home, $5.

The first house you'll visit is the **Vanderbilt Mansion** (914–229–9115). The house is an opulent fifty-four-room palace owned by Frederick Vanderbilt, grandson of the famed Commodore Vanderbilt. Designed in the late 1890s by McKim, Mead and White (architects of many of the fabulous houses in the New York area), this enormous Beaux Arts structure was large enough to entertain literally hundreds—and the Vanderbilts often did.

If you like to walk and the weather permits, you can take a trail from the Vanderbilt Mansion to the Roosevelt Home and Val-Kill cottage (signs will direct you to the path, or ask at the mansion). The river path, separated from the riverbank by railroad tracks, allows intermittent glimpses of the river, and provides a quiet place for you to enjoy the day. If you don't want to walk, drive the short distance along Route 9 to the Roosevelt homes.

Springwood (914–229–2501), the main Roosevelt house, is not so much a showplace as a warm testament to an exceptional family who left the home stamped with their own personalities. Franklin Roosevelt was born and grew up here, and he, his wife, and their children returned here each summer to visit his mother, Sara. Both Franklin and Eleanor are buried in the rose garden beside the big house. The house itself is decorated as it was the last time President Roosevelt visited it in March 1945. The family photos, the leash and blanket of his dog, Fala, and the books and magazines that were here on that day remain. It is as though he could return at any moment.

In the library is more memorabilia, from FDR's boyhood pony cart to papers that shaped world history. The collection is arranged chronologically, with the primary focus on the years of FDR's presidency from 1932 to 1945. Records of Mrs. Roosevelt's humanitarian activities until her death in 1962 are also here.

Hudson River School

The Hudson River School was a style of landscape painting that flourished between 1825 and 1870. Many of the artists, including Thomas Cole, Asher B. Durand, and Frederick E. Church, lived and worked in Europe but chose the beautiful Hudson River Valley as a subject for their works. Their work centered on the belief that a faithful depiction of nature revealed the presence of God, a notion in keeping with the Romantic philosophy of the times. Although The Hudson River School was never accepted as an innovative artistic trend, it is viewed as historically important in that it was the first school of landscape painting begun in the United States.

Don't miss **Val-Kill**, Eleanor's modest house located just 2 miles from the big house. It was her private retreat while her husband was alive and the place where she chose to spend her last years.

DAY ONE: AFTERNOON

Lunch

Have lunch at the **Culinary Institute of America** (Route 9, Hyde Park; 914–471–6608; moderate). The Culinary Institute requires reservations for the restaurant you wish by the Tuesday prior to your visit; it is virtually impossible to get a table if you arrive without one. Jackets are required for men.

An American classic, the Institute is the nation's top school for chefs and is a pleasure to visit. The glass walls along the corridors let you look in on the classrooms of the students, who also cook and serve in all the dining rooms on campus. I strongly recommend the

American Bounty Room, which features classic American cookery. If you prefer something more formal, however, try the Escoffier room.

⸎⸎⸎

After lunch, drive north along Route 9 to Rhinebeck. Check into your hotel as soon as you arrive in town.

The Beekman Arms (4 Mill Street, Rhinebeck, New York 12572; 914–876–7077; $80 to $120 per night). Located at the intersection of Route 9 and Route 308, the Beekman Arms was a stagecoach stop dating to 1700 and has fascinated modern visitors with its venerable guest books. Yes, George Washington did sleep here, as did Aaron Burr, Horace Greeley, and William Jennings Bryan. President Franklin Delano Roosevelt wound up every campaign with an informal talk on the inn's front porch.

The Beekman Arms offers the best of both historic atmosphere and the latest amenities. All the ambience of an eighteenth-century inn remain—the wide-planked floors, the low ceilings, and the dark wood. In 1995, however, all thirteen guest rooms were redecorated and all the private baths were renovated.

If the Beekman is fully booked, you can stay at the **Delamater House Inn** (914–876–7080), which is operated jointly with the Beekman and is located just a block away. The Delamater encompasses seven buildings, only four of which are historic. The Delamater House itself is an 1844 American Gothic beauty, but its most convenient guest rooms are in its modern additions. Attractively decorated in period style with four-poster beds and working fireplaces, they have great bathrooms, TVs, and, in some cases, kitchens. Still, if you prefer the "real thing," ask to stay in one of the guest rooms in the Delamater house proper.

Whether you're staying at the Beekman or Delamater House, consider taking a long riverside walk after you're settled in your room. In the summer of 1996, Scenic Hudson, a nonprofit preservation group that has acquired many sites along the river, opened **Poets'**

Walk, a 120-acre park in Red Hook, New York, just north of the Kingston-Rhinecliff bridge. Scenic Hudson calls the walk a "romantic landscape park," and that it is. Ask at the hotel for directions to the Poets' Walk, and head there with, perhaps, a bottle of wine, some fruit, and cheese for a late afternoon picnic snack.

The walk offers a seductive blend of meadow, glade, and woodland, with many trails that wind down to the riverbanks. Small, roughhewn bridges cross streamlets, and a gazebo-like viewing pavilion offers a commanding view of the river at the end of the woodland trail. You can follow the mowed path across a meadow scattered with bachelor's button, Queen Anne's lace, black-eyed Susans, and daisies. After a rest in the pavilion follow the path through a cool forest downward to the summerhouse that overlooks a small pond and the river. Then pick up the trail and follow it back toward the meadow and back uphill to the starting point.

As you sit in the pavilion or the summerhouse watching the tranquil river, you may envy the folk who are lolling away the late afternoon in a sailboat. Hudson River area inhabitants are very proud of their river, and several enterprising boat owners offer visitors the opportunity to experience the Hudson's majesty. The **Great Hudson Sailing Center**, for instance, operates 43-foot sailing vessels out of Kingston at the Roundout Waterfront, not far from the Kingston-Rhinecliff Bridge. One of the most romantic ways to enjoy the Hudson is to take a sunset cruise. Great Hudson Sailing Center offers a two-hour tour that leaves Kingston at 6:00 P.M. The fare is $35 per person. Call (800) 237–1557 or (914) 429–1557 for information and specific directions to the dock.

DAY ONE: EVENING

Dinner

When you return from your river trip, dinner at the **Beekman 1776 Tavern** (located in the Beekman Arms, Route 9, Rhinebeck; 914–876–7077; moderate to expensive; reserva-

Rhinebeck is the site of several excellent fairs. In May, it hosts the Rhinebeck Antiques Fair, an outdoor fair featuring fine antiques from all over the Northeast. In late June, Rhinebeck is the center for Crafts at Rhinebeck, one of the best crafts fairs in the United States, featuring more than 350 of the finest artists and craftsmen in the U.S. In October, Rhinebeck offers a combined crafts and antiques fair. In addition, Rhinebeck hosts the Dutchess County Fair in August, an old-fashioned American county fair, with pie baking contests, displays of breeds of farm animals, tractor pulls, and other events that have been part of American country life for centuries. All the fairs take place at the Dutchess County Fairgrounds in Rhinebeck.

tions recommended) is a must. The kitchen is operated by Larry Forgione, one of America's leading chefs and owner also of An American Place in Manhattan. This quiet dining room offers wonderful, intimate, historic ambience with its elegant colonial decor, beautiful antiques, roaring fireplace, and candlelit tables. Mr. Forgione's menu features authentic American regional fare, with a special leaning toward fresh seafood. Try the traditional cedar-planked Atlantic salmon with roasted corn pudding—the perfect dish for this setting.

After dinner, enjoy a glass of port next to the fireplace, and then off to bed.

DAY TWO: MORNING

Breakfast

Have a hearty American breakfast or brunch in the Greenhouse at the Beekman Arms, or, if you prefer something lighter, head just a few doors down the street to the cozy **Calico**

Restaurant and Patisserie (9 Mill Street, Rhinebeck, New York 12572; 914–876–2749) for coffee and delectable homemade pastries.

ↄ◉ↄ

Near Rhinebeck are several of the most spectacular of the Hudson River estates. Perhaps the finest of these is **Montgomery Place** (River Road, Route 103 Annandale-on-Hudson, New York 12504; 914–758–5461). Located off Route 9G, Montgomery Place is an opulent twenty-three-room home built in 1805 by Janet Livingston Montgomery, widow of Revolutionary War hero General Richard Montgomery. It was remodeled in 1860 by Alexander Jackson Davis, who was considered America's leading nineteenth-century architect. Seven generations of Livingstons and their relatives the Delafields have lived here, and the house is filled with their possessions. The estate offers almost 400 acres of beautiful grounds and gardens with outstanding views of the Hudson and the Catskill Mountains in the distance. (The estate's orchards are particularly beautiful in spring when they are in full bloom, and from mid-June you can pick your own strawberries, raspberries, peaches, and apples here.)

The house and grounds are open daily except Tuesday from 10:00 A.M. to 5:00 P.M. from April through October. In November, December, and March the estate is open only on Saturday and Sunday from 10:00 A.M. to 5:00 P.M. It is closed in January and February. Admission is charged.

Just outside Rhinebeck is **Wilderstein** (Morton Road, Box 383, Rhinebeck, New York 12572; 914–876–4818). Off Route 9, south of Rhinebeck, the mansion is one of the more beautiful of the Hudson estates. At the time of this writing in 1996, it is undergoing restoration. Built in 1852 as an Italianate villa by Thomas Suckley, a wealthy importer, the house was remodeled by his son, Robert, in 1888. Queen Anne-style verandas, gables, and a round tower were added during that renovation.

The park-like grounds were designed by Calvert Vaux, who, with Frederick Law Olmsted, designed Central Park in Manhattan. Joseph Burr Tiffany (a cousin of the famous

Louis Comfort Tiffany) was commissioned to create the interiors, including, of course, numerous stained-glass windows. The last Suckley descendant lived in the house until 1991. The house and grounds are open to the public for tours. From April through October the mansion is open on Thursday through Sunday from noon to 4:00 P.M. The grounds are open daily year-round. Admission is charged.

DAY TWO: AFTERNOON

Lunch

Stop for a simple lunch at **Foster's Coach House** at 9193 Montgomery Street, Route 9 in Rhinebeck (914–876–8052). The fare is plain and hearty, and the ambience is pleasant.

⋘⊙⊙⋙

With renewed energy after your lunch, visit yet another historic site. **Clermont** is the ancestral home of Robert R. Livingston, who lived from 1746 to 1813 and was a chancellor of New York State. The beautiful grounds overlooking the river are open free to the public year-round. You might also consider going to the **Mills Estate**, one of the few mansions along the eastern bank of the Hudson that remained on the river side of the railroad that sliced through other estates in the 1840s and cut off their direct access to the river. At the Mills Estate (formally called Mills Memorial State Park), the lawn sweeps down to the river's edge. The park also boasts a sixty-five-room McKim, Mead and White Beaux Arts mansion and a small (or smaller) mansion known as Hoyt House and designed by Calvert Vaux. The grounds are marvelous for walking and are perfect examples of nineteenth-century romantic landscape architecture.

By the end of the afternoon, no matter what time of year you have come to the Hudson, you won't want to return to contemporary life. Of course, you must, but you can always return. Exploring the Hudson Valley can take years and will give you never-ending delight.

FOR MORE ROMANCE

On your way back to Manhattan, stop on Route 9W in the adorable town of **Nyack**, located on the west bank of the Hudson. It boasts beautiful Victorian houses and many antiques shops. In early autumn, Nyack hosts the "Nyack Septemberfest Street Fair"; later in the fall it holds the oldest antiques fair in the Northeast.

ITINERARY 6
One day

THE GARDEN OF EDEN

*C*entral Park may not look like the Biblical Garden of Eden when you see the bikers and bladers whiz past; you may even suspect there's a rotten apple somewhere amid all this activity. But, for New Yorkers, Central Park is the single facet that actually makes New York City livable. Without it, Manhattan Island might well have been overrun by slums decades ago. It is the City's heart, it's what keeps New York alive. And it is incredibly romantic.

Central Park was designed by landscape artist Frederick Law Olmsted and architect Calvert Vaux in 1858 after decades of fighting among city officials. Even 150 years ago, Manhattan real estate was incredibly valuable and the use of this acreage was a source of great interest to many opposing factions. In the mid-nineteenth century, however, the 843 acres that now make up Central Park were a mishmash of stone quarries, pig farms, swamplands, and shacks inhabited by squatters. One wonders why anyone might fuss over land such as this. Miraculously, the insightful and talented Olmsted turned the land into rolling hills, scenic lakes, and lush meadows (the Sheep Meadow originally had sheep!), while Vaux designed a castle, a dairy, an art museum, a zoo, seven unique cast-iron bridges, and winding roads—all at the height of Victorian romanticism. Later, other benefactors added an outdoor theater, skating rinks, ballfields, and spaces for everything from rock concerts to chess playing.

Thousands of New Yorkers make a beeline for "the Park," as they call it, on weekends. The Park is pretty crowded during the week as well, but join them. There's room for the two of you in New York City's heart.

Practical notes: This itinerary is designed for late spring, but Central Park is marvelous any time of year. Although in winter some of the attractions are closed, you can still bike or roller-blade if there's no snow. Better yet, you can go ice-skating at Wollman Rink.

Since the park is centrally located, you can get to it easily. A taxi can drop you at any park entrance. Subway lines B and C run the length of the park on the Upper West Side with stops at 59th, 72nd, 81st, 86th, 97th, 103rd, and 110th Streets. Lines 1 and 9 on the Broadway line stop at Columbus Circle. Bus routes M1, M2, M3, and M4 run along Fifth Avenue and Madison Avenue on the Upper East Side.

Central Park has three convenient Visitors Centers. **The Dairy** (mid-Park at 65th Street; 212–794–6564) is well worth a visit. An incredibly charming Victorian Gothic structure, it was designed by Calvert Vaux originally as a respite for mothers (or nannies) to provide milk for their young charges. Inside the Dairy is a 12-foot model of the Park and an interactive exhibit about Central Park's history and design. Walking tours often begin here. Equally fascinating is the visitors' center at **Belvedere Castle** (mid-Park at 79th Street; 212–772–0210), also designed by Vaux. From its terraces visitors have unsurpassed views of the surrounding urban buildings as well as the Park itself.

The nearby Turtle Pond is an important habitat for insects and reptiles. The **Charles A. Dana Discovery Center** (110th Street near Fifth Avenue; 212–860–1370) is in the heart of the Harlem Meer and also offers exhibits and tours. The Meer offers a unique waterfront perspective and a view of the more rugged parts of the Park.

If you decide to rent a bicycle or roller blades, stop at one of the scores of rental shops that exist in Manhattan; most shops provide both bicycles and in-line skating equipment. Check the Yellow Pages or ask at your hotel for suggestions. A particularly convenient bicycle and skate concession is located next to the **Loeb Boathouse** at 74th Street and East Park Drive.

A word about safety: No doubt you have heard stories about crime in Central Park. Actually, the Park, especially when it is crowded, is very safe. What's more, it is patrolled by police. Use your good judgment and avoid secluded areas.

MORNING

Start your day in the Park with a picnic of coffee and bagels. In fact, you simply cannot visit New York City without trying an authentic New York bagel. If you are coming from the West Side, pick up your breakfast at **H&H Bagels** (2239 Broadway at 82nd Street; 212–595–8003) or at **Pick-A-Bagel** (1473 Second Avenue; 212–717–4662; and 1083 Lexington Avenue; 212–517–6590).

If you have never explored Central Park before—or even if you think you know the Park well—consider taking a trolley tour. From April through October on Monday through Friday at 10:30 A.M., 1:00 P.M., and 3:00 P.M., the **Central Park Conservancy** offers a tour in a thirty-two-seat trolley. The ninety-minute tour highlights the most popular Central Park attractions, including the Carousel, the Dairy, the Chess and Checkers House, the Mall, Bethesda Fountain and Terrace, Strawberry Fields, the Cascades, Harlem Meer, the Ramble,

Central Park is dotted with famous sculptures, more than fifty in all. Entering the park at Fifth Avenue and 64th Street, you'll see the Delacorte Clock just north of the entrance to the zoo. It chimes every half-hour while musical animals circle the clock playing nursery rhymes. Also, don't miss the famous sculptures of Alice in Wonderland at the north end of the Conservatory boat pond and Hans Christian Andersen on the west bank. Often mentioned in books and films, these two sculptures provide a playful, fanciful mood to the Park. For pure romance, look for the star-crossed figures of Romeo and Juliet, poised for a kiss near the Delacorte Theater at 79th Street.

and the Conservatory Garden. Call (212) 397–3809 for reservations, which are recommended; tickets are $15 for adults.

After you have finished your tour, you simply must take a ride on the Carousel. Stroll through the park toward the Dairy. At the Dairy, stop in to look at the displays and get a map. The Dairy was originally designed as the park's children's center, and it included a Children's Cottage with farm animals and fresh milk to delight the young. The Carousel is just a few hundred yards beyond the Dairy; just follow the sound of the calliope music.

The **Central Park Carousel** is one of the most romantic adventures New York City offers. Built in 1903 and moved to Central Park in 1951, it features some of the largest hand-carved merry-go-round horses in the country. Don't be shy about taking a turn on the Carousel. Also, don't worry that you'll be surrounded only by kids. Passengers include parents, grandparents, nannies, teens, and folks just like you—young at heart! I guarantee that you'll have a spectacular time. And when you finish your ride, get back in line and take it again! Bystanders will envy your *joie de vivre.*

AFTERNOON

Lunch

If you're ready for lunch, indulge in some New York street food. You'll see vendors everywhere offering hot dogs, soft pretzels, Greek souvlaki, ice cream, sodas, and scores of other treats. Take your selections to a park bench and watch the Central Park world go by as you eat.

❧❀☙

Central Park offers scores of activities. If you are so inclined, rent a bicycle or in-line skates and explore to your hearts content. If horseback riding is for you, rent a mount from the **Claremont Riding Academy** (175 West 89th Street; 212–724–5100). To take one of the horses unescorted you must be an experienced English-style rider who knows how to direct the horse to walk, trot, and canter. The cost of the rental is $35 per hour. Miles of lovely bridle paths wind through the park.

For romance, I would particularly recommend seeing the **Central Park Wildlife Conservation Center**—better known as the Children's Zoo. Recently reconstructed, the zoo boasts more than 100 species of animals represented in three climate zones: the Tropics, the Polar Circle, and the California coast. A rain forest with monkeys and birds is featured in the Tropics zone, while close by in the Polar Circle are penguins and polar bears.

Another must-see destination in the Park is formally called the **Conservatory Water**, a lake that hosts model yacht races every weekend. Also, be sure to wander around the Lake and stop by the **Bow Bridge**, one of Calvert Vaux's beautifully designed crossings. It was styled as if it were a bow tying together the two sections of the lake. In the nineteenth century, the lake was used for ice-skating, and a red ball was hoisted from a bell tower on nearby Vista Rock to signal that the ice was safe for skating. To this day, Bow Bridge offers marvelous views of the park.

In the late afternoon, try some boating on the Lake. Rent a rowboat at the **Loeb**

Boathouse. (Boats are available spring through fall on Monday through Friday from 9:00 A.M. to 6:00 P.M. and on Saturday and Sunday until 5:30 P.M. The cost is $7 for a minimum of one hour; a $20 deposit is required.) Lolling on the lake is perhaps the most romantic way to savor Central Park.

EVENING

Dinner

When you've finished boating, have dinner at the bucolic **Boathouse Cafe** (on the lake at East Park Drive at 73rd Street; 212–517–2233). Moderately priced, the Boathouse Cafe is one of New York's most beautiful places to dine outdoors in late spring, summer, or early fall. What's more, it's at its best just as the sun is setting. This is a unique experience—uniquely New York, yet uniquely "far away." The menu is eclectic with a slightly Italian flavor, featuring foccacias, tasty salads, pastas, and fish dishes. The ambience is about as romantic as New York can be.

୧ରତ

After dinner, enjoy another kind of boating experience: take a glide on the lake in the **Daughter of Venice,** a sleek gondola operated by a Venetian-trained gondolier. *The Daughter of Venice,* which seats six people, is available by reservation at the Loeb Boathouse every evening, weather permitting, from April through October on weekdays from 6:00 to 10:00 P.M. and on weekends until 11:00 P.M. It costs $30 for a half hour. Central Park's lake may not be the Grand Canal, but it is every bit as romantic.

And lastly, of course, you cannot visit Central Park without a ride in a **hansom cab**. Pick up a carriage on 59th Street at Central Park South, and end your idyll snuggling up in a horse-drawn carriage. It costs $34 for the first twenty minutes; $10 for each additional fifteen minutes.

The Reservoir

If you enjoy jogging, take a run around the park's reservoir, once used as the city source of reserved water. The 1.6-mile path surrounding the reservoir is designated for jogging. Enter at East 90th Street. Jacqueline Kennedy Onassis, who lived close by, used to jog here. After her death in 1994, the reservoir was named for her. It's a landmark for all active New Yorkers, many of whom used to see Jackie here on a daily basis.

FOR MORE ROMANCE

In addition to the Boathouse Cafe, two "fancier" restaurants are associated with Central Park. If you have been jogging, biking, horseback riding, or whatever during the day, you'll want to return to your hotel and dress before you go to either of these places for dinner.

First, of course, is **Tavern on the Green** (Central Park West at West 67th Street; 212–873–3200; expensive). In summer, the large outdoor Garden Room of this exuberant restaurant is lighted by hundreds of Chinese silk lanterns and decorated with hundreds of flowering plants—not to mention the lush greenery of Central Park. From May through September, there is dancing in the garden from Tuesday through Thursday and on Sunday from 9:00 P.M. to 1:00 A.M. and on Friday and Saturday until 2:00 A.M. You can enjoy the delicious cuisine of one of the best restaurants in New York and dance cheek-to-cheek to live music under the stars.

The second choice is a bit more exotic but is considered one of the most romantic restaurants in New York City. **Nirvana** (30 Central Park South, between 5th and 6th Avenues; 212–486–5700; moderate) sits on the top floor of a skyscraper and serves tasty Indian cuisine. The restaurant's view over the park—especially at sunset—is what makes Nirvana unique.

SATURDAY AT THE MET

*F*irst dates are always tough. It doesn't matter if we're 14 or 44—we're nervous. If it's a blind date, we know we have to make an instant impression. If we're finally spending an evening with someone we've admired, we want to make sure that all goes well, so that, perhaps, romance will blossom.

To my mind, there is no better place in Manhattan for an important first date than the Metropolitan Museum of Art. Even if neither of you is an art aficionado, you are bound to find something fascinating—the Temple of Dendur, the English armor, the Greek statuary, the Impressionist paintings, or perhaps the works of twentieth century art.

A few years back, the Met began staying open on Friday and Saturday evenings until 8:45 P.M. Somehow, even when a major show is in progress, the Met seems to assume a certain quiet calm after 6:00 P.M. Just strolling through the rooms is incredibly romantic. What's more, the Iris and B. Gerald Cantor Roof Garden, which is open from May through October, offers one of the most spectacular views in the city, especially in the autumn when the trees in Central Park are in full color. Then, after you've stimulated your mind and your senses, enjoy a romantic dinner at a nearby restaurant.

Practical notes: Since the Roof Garden is open only from May through October, this itinerary seems intended for warm weather. Nevertheless, the Metropolitan Museum of Art is always a great place for a first date, even in winter. If you go to the Met during the Christmas season, don't miss its fabulous Christmas tree.

Be sure to make reservations well in advance for Erminia. If it is booked, try **Le Refuge** (166 East 82nd Street, between Third and Lexington; 212–861–4505; expensive), which is the French equivalent of the Italian Erminia. It is cozy yet elegant, and the classic country French cuisine is divine. It also has a garden, which is incredibly romantic on a warm, summer evening.

Romance at a Glance

♥ *Have a drink at the Iris and B. Gerald Cantor Roof Garden at the Met.*

♥ *Spend an hour or two exploring the Metropolitan galleries.*

♥ *Dine at Erminia, one of New York's most romantic Italian restaurants (212–879–4284).*

The Evening

Meet at the **Metropolitan Museum of Art** (Fifth Avenue at 82nd Street; 212–535–7710; suggested donation, $7.00 adults, $3.50 seniors) on the steps outside or just inside the doors at the information desk. The Met is so huge, it can be overwhelming. Take a few minutes to plan one or two areas you'd both like to explore. (If you are meeting to see a particular show, this decision will be no problem.) Also, on the way to the gallery of your choice, you will inevitably see other objects and paintings of interest.

The Temple of Dendur is one of the most fascinating artifacts in the museum and almost demands a visit. It is the only complete Egyptian temple in the Western Hemisphere. The temple is a three-room structure built by the Roman emperor Augustus in 15 B.C. along the banks of the Nile in Dendur. Not only is the temple itself incredibly beautiful; it is housed in a pavilion that is spellbinding. When you enter the vestibule in front of the temple (called the *pronaos*), you'll be entranced by the decoration. Only Roman and Egyptian dignitaries were permitted to enter here during ritual occasions. The offering room is beyond. Visiting the temple is something of a spiritual experience.

Another romantic spot is the **Nur al Din Room** on the second floor, originally a winter reception room for a wealthy Syrian family. The room sort of surrounds a small courtyard which features a softly trickling fountain. Then you step under an arch into a raised area where beautiful stained-glass windows allow soft light to filter through.

Both of these exhibits are usually relatively empty, so couples can often linger here alone together, enjoying the art as well as the privacy. (Don't forget that a guard is discreetly posted in the background.) Another area of the museum is not quite so private but offers a host of romantic artifacts, paintings, and furniture—**Medieval Art rooms**. If you come to the Met during the Christmas season, the tree is located in this area.

Sometime during your stay at the Museum, make your way to the outdoor Roof Garden, which is off the second floor. (Ask a guard how to find the elevator to the Garden; it's a little tricky.) Here, you can enjoy a glass of wine or cappuccino while watching the sun set over Central Park. Best of all, marvelous sculpture from the museum's collection are placed strategically around the roof, making the view of the skyline unique. The sculptures change each season, but can include the works of Auguste Rodin, Gaston Lachaise, Jacques Lipchitz, and Henry Moore. What could be more romantic? If you come during colder months when the Roof Garden is closed, you can meet instead in the **Espresso and Wine Bar** off the **European Sculpture Court** or at the **Great Hall Balcony Bar**, which also features music.

Dinner

After you've soaked up all the art you can handle, make your way to **Erminia** (250 East 83rd Street; 212–879–4284; expensive). You can take a cab if it's raining, but it's only a 5-

block (about ten-minute) walk, and the streets in this area of the Upper East Side are lined with lovely town houses.

One of the most charming and romantic restaurants in the city, Erminia is housed in a unique, one-story ivy-covered building. It is rustic in atmosphere, but is, in fact, the ultimate in understated elegance. The food is Italian and, according to some reports, is the closest thing to "real Italian" in Manhattan. Erminia is definitely a restaurant for lovers, with dim lights, candles on the table, a crackling fireplace during the cooler months, and a sense of warmth and intimacy —a perfect place to begin a new relationship.

FOR MORE ROMANCE

The Met often offers concerts in different rooms throughout the museum. Check (212–570–3949) to see if a concert is planned on the evening of your date.

ITINERARY 8
Three days and two nights

ART FOR LOVERS

*W*hen I was in college, I spent my junior year studying art history in Europe. At the time, my idea of the perfect way to travel was to go from European city to European city using the local art museums as the focal point of the tour. (In Europe, of course, the local art museums included the National Gallery in London, the Louvre in Paris, and the Sistine Chapel in Rome. Not bad for reference!)

As it turned out, my boyfriend, who was also my traveling companion, accepted this notion. At first, he was merely game, willing to go along to please me. But being an intelligent young man, it wasn't very long before he became as enthralled with the magnificent art as I was. His enthusiastic companionship made our trips together some of the most stimulating, romantic, and pleasurable I've ever taken.

Today, many experts consider New York City the art capital of the world. It's the place where contemporary art is "happening." What's more, New York houses—and exhibits—the most exquisite examples of world-class art from the beginning of time. This itinerary celebrates the love of art. And I can promise you, it is one of the most romantic ways to explore New York and enjoy each other.

Romance at a Glance

♥ *Stay at the Stanhope Hotel (212–288–5800).*

♥ *Tour the Metropolitan Museum of Art; the Solomon R. Guggenheim Museum; the Whitney Museum of American Art; the Museum of Modern Art; uptown Manhattan galleries; and the Cloisters.*

♥ *Dine at JoJo's, Café des Artistes, and other elegant New York restaurants.*

♥ *Go to New York City Ballet at Lincoln Center.*

Practical notes: A holiday weekend is the perfect time to visit New York for the purpose of viewing art. During non-holiday weekends, museums in New York City are often quite crowded, especially when a special show is in progress. During long holiday weekends, however, many New Yorkers flee to the beach or the countryside, leaving the museums and the restaurants a little more open for visitors from out of town. Memorial Day and Labor Day weekends are terrific opportunities for this itinerary, which you should begin on a Friday evening.

DAY ONE: EVENING

You'll be thrilled when you pull up to the **Stanhope** (995 Fifth Avenue at 81st Street; 212–288–5800; fax: 212–517–0088; expensive: deluxe rooms: $325; suites: $400 to $2,500; packages available from $275 to $550 per night). Not only is the hotel in the perfect location for an art lovers' weekend (it is located across the street from the Met), it is an extraordinary hotel in its own right. Small (only seventy rooms), it is decorated with discreet French antiques and Gobelin tapestries, which create a quiet elegance. The tapestries might easily have been hung in a museum. The large guest rooms are also decorated in period French manner, but they offer every ultramodern amenity. The service is equally discreet and efficient.

After you've settled your luggage in your room, you may want to have a drink at the Stanhope's **Terrace Bar** (on Fifth Avenue in front of the hotel; moderate), which is, hands down, New York's most elegant sidewalk cafe. Hold hands and watch the Big Apple world go by. If the weather is bad, try **Gerard's**, the Stanhope's intimate indoor bar.

If you arrive on Friday night, stroll across the street to the Metropolitan Museum of Art. See "Saturday at the Met" for the ideal way to spend your first evening in the New York art world.

DAY TWO: MORNING

Breakfast

Enjoy breakfast in your lovely room or at one of the hotel's public restaurants. For a hearty American breakfast, head for the elegant **Restaurant at The Stanhope**; or if you prefer a lighter continental breakfast of fruit, pastries, and coffee or tea, try **Le Salon**, which is equally lovely but a bit more intimate.

⤜⟨⟩⤛

After breakfast, prepared to be dazzled. Last night you visited New York City's answer to the Louvre, and you may think you've seen it all, art–wise. The collection at the Met is awe-inspiring but there's more—the Upper East Side of Manhattan is lined with the most important art museums in the world. In fact, Fifth Avenue from about 70th Street (the Frick Museum) to about 88th Street (the Guggenheim) is known as "Museum Mile," and for good reason. The avenues and streets are bursting with art treasures, which you'll have the pleasure of exploring today.

When you leave the Stanhope, turn right and walk 5 blocks north to the **Solomon R. Guggenheim Museum** (1071 Fifth Avenue at 88th Street; 212–423–3500). The Guggenheim is a delight both inside and out. Designed by Frank Lloyd Wright, it is one of the greatest architectural feats of the twentieth century.

On the outside, the building looks like an overgrown snail, but the interior spiral ramp

that gives the museum its snail-like appearance makes a remarkable vehicle for viewing art. The building houses Solomon Guggenheim's incredible collection of twentieth-century art. When you enter, take the elevator to the top, and stroll down the ramp, viewing the ever-changing displays in bays along the way. Don't miss the Justin K. Thannhauser Wing, which displays the Guggenheim's permanent collection, including works by Picasso, Braque, Calder, Kandinsky, Klee, and Miro. Adult admission is $7. The museum is open Sunday through Wednesday, 10:00 A.M. to 6:00 P.M. and Friday and Saturday, 10:00 A.M. to 8:00 P.M.

Stop for coffee and a rest at the cafe, which is operated by Manhattan coffee masters Dean & DeLuca and offers marvelous coffee and pastries in an awe-inspiring Wright-designed dining room.

When you leave the Guggenheim, turn south and walk down Fifth Avenue or Madison Avenue for twelve blocks until you come to the **Whitney Museum of American Art** (945 Madison Avenue at 76th Street; 212–570–3600). Spend the rest of your morning at the Whitney, the foremost showcase for American art created in this century. Founded in 1931 by wealthy sculptress Gertrude Vanderbilt Whitney, it originally opened in her studio in Greenwich Village. It was not until 1966 that this exquisite building designed by Marcel Breuer (also noted for the Breuer chair) was finally completed. Perhaps to pay tribute to the vitality of American art, the only permanent exhibit in the museum is Alexander Calder's *The Circus,* which is located on the first floor. The second, third, and fourth floors offer ever-changing exhibitions that range from debuts of contemporary artists to selections from the Whitney's permanent collection, including Edward Hopper, Jasper Johns, Roy Lichtenstein, Louise Nevelson, and Georgia O'Keeffe, among many others.

Admission at the Whitney is $7 for adults; free on Thursday from 6:00 to 8:00 P.M. The museum is open on Wednesday from 11:00 A.M. to 6:00 P.M., Thursday from 1:00 to 8:00 P.M., and Friday through Sunday from 11:00 A.M. to 6:00 P.M.

Lunch

The Whitney's cafe, called **Sarabeth's at the Whitney**, (lower level of the museum; moderate) offers light lunches daily and brunch on weekends. It's one of the more romantic of the museum restaurants, so you may want to take time for lunch here.

If you want a more substantial repast at a glamorous (and quite romantic) New York restaurant, try **JoJo's** (160 East 64th Street, between Lexington and Third Avenues; 212–223–5656; reservations required; expensive). Owner Jean-Georges Vongerichten is "JoJo," the highly praised French chef who also owns the elegant **Vong**, located a few blocks farther downtown. JoJo's is situated in a bright, warm town house that is at once down-to-earth and elegant. JoJo's specialty is replacing high-fat butter and cream-laden sauces with lighter vegetable sauces. He does this exquisitely. Try his shrimp flavored with carrot juice and Thai lime leaves or his lobster lasagna with truffles and vegetables. The combination of JoJo's unique cuisine and the luxurious yet comfortable surroundings makes this restaurant a real treat.

DAY TWO: AFTERNOON

After lunch, head south to the **Museum of Modern Art** (11 West 53rd Street; 212–708–9696). Admission is $8; on Thursday and Friday from 5:30 to 8:30 P.M., you pay what you wish. The museum is open Saturday through Tuesday, 10:00 A.M. to 6:00 P.M.; Thursday and Friday from noon to 8:30 P.M.; closed Wednesdays.

The Museum of Modern Art, or MoMA as it is known, is to twentieth-century art what the Metropolitan Museum of Art is to all of art history—in other words, it is the most magnificent collection of modern art in the world. It opened in the fall of 1929, only ten days after the stock market crash. To make matters worse, the first exhibit was a flop. Mounted in an office building, it included works by Cezanne, Gauguin, Seurat, and van Gogh, most of whom were not known in the United States at that time. Despite this inauspicious beginning, the museum has survived.

The museum's current main building, one of the first examples of the International Style in the United States, opened in 1939. Later expansions took place in the 1950s, the 1960s, and the 1980s and were designed by the famed architect Philip Johnson, who also conceived the museum's sculpture garden.

MoMA offers an unparalleled view of modern art. Paintings by every major artist since 1889 are on view. Monet's *Water Lilies,* van Gogh's *The Starry Night,* and other remarkable works by Brancusi, Matisse, Picasso, Rauschenberg, Johns, Pollock, and many others will awe you. The museum's photography collection, which spans the entire history of photography, is arguably the best in the world and includes works by Arbus, Atget, Cartier-Bresson, Steichen, Stieglitz, and Weston. One of the most fascinating displays is the architecture and design collection with posters, household appliances, a sports car, and even a helicopter.

Somewhere during your tour, stop for tea or coffee at the cafe overlooking the Abby Aldrich Rockefeller Sculpture Garden, an incredibly beautiful outdoor courtyard with trees, fountains, reflecting pools and sculpture by Matisse, Moore, Picasso, Rodin, and other notables. Concerts are offered here on selected weekends in the summertime. Before you leave, stop at the very special MoMA shop.

DAY TWO: Evening

Dinner

Stroll up Sixth Avenue and through Central Park to the **Café des Artistes** (One West 67th Street between Columbus Avenue and Central Park West; 212–877–3500; expensive; reservations required).

The Café des Artistes, is, to be sure, the most romantic restaurant in New York. Period. I love it! And I'm not alone in that opinion. (It was the restaurant President Bill Clinton insisted upon dining in during an official visit to New York.)

The Café is owned and managed by famed restaurateur George Lang and his wife, Jennifer Lang, a well-known chef and food writer. The Café is located in a remarkable Beaux Arts building called the Hotel des Artistes and is decorated with Howard Chandler Christy's seductive murals of playful nymphs. These along with great vases of beautiful fresh flowers and other romantic touches create an ambience at once sophisticated and intimate. Because the Café is popular with celebrity residents of the Upper West Side, you may well see some famous faces at the next table! The huge menu is basically French with hints of George Lang's Hungarian heritage. Lang's passion for asparagus in season is often evident in several dishes—order one in his honor!

The Café des Artistes is known for its desserts, so allow yourselves the tantalizing pleasure of delayed gratification: Leave now to catch the ballet at Lincoln Center, then return here to satisfy your passion for sweet delights.

To me, ballet is the perfect performing art for those who are visually inclined. A visual feast, it endeavors to elevate human interaction to an impossibly graceful, higher-than-earthly sphere through its integration of movement, music, and sometimes narrative. I particularly recommend seeing the **New York City Ballet** (The New York State Theater, Lincoln Center, Broadway and 64th Street; 212–870–5570), which is a five-minute walk from the Café.

The New York City Ballet features the unsurpassed choreography of its founder George Balanchine, as well as the marvelous works of Jerome Robbins and former dancer, Peter Martins. Even if you are not a lover of dance, you'll appreciate this world-renowned company.

After the ballet, be sure to view the Chagall paintings at the Metropolitan Opera House at Lincoln Center, then head back over to the **Parlor at the Café des Artistes** for dessert. The menu offers such a heavenly range of desserts, you'll have trouble deciding. Think seriously about the Original Ilona Torte, a chocolate delicacy named for Mr. Lang's mother. You'll find that the thin-crust raspberry tart, the frozen mocha praline, or the strawberries with crème fraîche are hard to resist. The Café also offers a remarkable selection of cordials with which you can toast one another as the day ends.

DAY THREE: Morning

Enjoy a leisurely breakfast in your lovely room, then head uptown to one of New York City's greatest treasures: **The Cloisters** (Fort Tryon Park, 192nd Street between Riverside Drive and Fort Washington Avenue; 212–923–3700; closed Mondays). You can reach the Cloisters by subway, bus, or taxi. The subway is quicker (it will take about 30 minutes) but the hour-long bus trip will give you a fascinating tour of upper Manhattan. If you choose the subway, take the A train, which runs up Eighth Avenue, and get off at 190th Street. Take the elevator up to the street and turn right onto Fort Washington Avenue, then head through

Fort Tryon Park to the museum. If you choose the bus, take the uptown M4 bus, which goes up Madison Avenue and is marked "Fort Tryon Park—the Cloisters." You can also take a taxi, but it will be an expensive ride—probably about $20.

Located in Fort Tryon Park overlooking the Hudson, the Cloisters houses a vast majority of the Metropolitan Museum of Art's medieval art collection. The works of art are housed in a collection of buildings gathered in Europe and recreated here in 1938 by Charles Collen from parts of twelfth– and thirteenth–century French and Spanish monasteries, chapels, and cloisters. Clustered in a unified manner on land donated by John D. Rockefeller, Jr., the Cloisters owe a great part of their romance to the beautiful grounds and vistas of Fort Tryon Park. Before or after you have taken in the beauties of the museum, be sure to explore the paths in the park itself. If the weather permits, walk north past the Cloisters Museum and into Inwood Park, and follow the paths down to the Hudson River. The walk will be deliciously romantic, and at the northern tip of Manhattan the Hudson River begins to reveal its spectacular beauty.

Rivaling the landscape, however, is the breathtaking nature of the Cloisters themselves and the marvelous medieval art treasures located within them. On view is extraordinary medieval sculpture, exquisite illuminated manuscripts, marvelous works of gold and silver (including the famed silver gilt "Monkey Cup"), incredible stained glass, and fascinating curiosities like a complete set of playing cards, circa 1470.

The most renowned treasures at the Cloisters are the famed Unicorn Tapestries, which are among the Metropolitan Museum's most highly prized works of art. Woven in Brussels around 1500 and once owned by Jean, Duc de Berry, brother of the King of France, these five tapestries depict the quest and capture of the mythical unicorn. Although they are 500 years old, they appear incredibly fresh and modern.

The Medieval Gardens are as fabulous as the art. More than 250 varieties of plants grown in the Middle Ages can be found in the Cloisters gardens. The Bonnefont Cloister has

If the weather permits, pack a picnic lunch to take with you to the Cloisters. In keeping with this beautiful place, give your picnic a French flavor and take along a few baguettes, perhaps some pâté de campagne, chevre cheese, strawberries, and a bottle of Beaujolais or Champagne. After you've explored the grounds of the Cloisters, find a quiet place and enjoy a romantic petit déjeuner. Ask your hotel to prepare the picnic for you or find a nearby gourmet food shop (many line upper Madison Avenue, just one block from the Stanhope) that will prepare such a repast.

herbal, medicinal, and culinary plants, while the Trie Cloister features plants shown in the Unicorn Tapestries.

At some point as you explore the Cloisters and Inwood Park, you may want to relax and enjoy a cup of tea or a quick bite to eat. If so, stop at the **Unicorn Cafe** inside the Museum. If you wish to extend your stay and learn more about the Cloisters, consider taking a guided tour of the museum at 3:00 P.M.

FOR MORE ROMANCE

If you come to New York over a long holiday weekend or can extend your art-lovers' stay an extra day, spend some time in SoHo. (See "X-Rated" for more details about this area.) While you're there, be sure to visit the **Guggenheim Museum SoHo** (575 Broadway at Prince Street; 212–0423–3500). Housed in a nineteenth-century landmark building in the SoHo Cast-Iron Historic District, this dramatic site houses changing exhibits. Open Sunday and Wednesday through Friday from 11:00 A.M. to 6:00 P.M., Saturday from 11:00 A.M. to 8:00 P.M. Closed Monday and Tuesday.

SUMMER

ITINERARY 9
Three days and two nights

A HONEYMOON IN JUNE

*T*his idyllic weekend is styled for those people who have decided to throw radicalism, funkiness—and probably quite a lot of money—to the wind and celebrate their love the old-fashioned way: with a classic June wedding followed by an extravagant honeymoon in New York City. I've suggested New York classics together with *la crème de la crème* of New York restaurants, walks, and, of course, accommodations. This should result in memories that will last for your lifetime together. Congratulations and warm wishes for a life of love!

Practical notes: Since you'll be staying at the Carlyle, you could not be in better hands. Your every expectation, wish, and need will be anticipated and taken care of. Don't hesitate to ask—and don't be surprised if every bellman and waiter knows your name!

Obviously, this itinerary is planned for the month of June. But nothing in this itinerary is limited to summer enjoyment. If you get married in November, you can have an equally delightful experience.

DAY ONE: EVENING

After your long and special wedding day—and possibly a bit of traveling—you are probably exhausted. Prepare now to be pampered beyond your wildest dreams. You'll arrive at New York's most beautiful hotel, **The Carlyle** (Madison Avenue at 76th Street; 212–744–1600; outside of New York State, call toll-free: 800–227–5737). Accommodations here are expensive: one-room apartments are $310 to $420 per day; suites with living room begin at $500 per day.

Every room in the Carlyle is subtle and elegant. Famed decorator Mark Hampton is responsible for much of the decorating, and his signature quiet, comfortable lushness is evident. Big, soft chairs and sofas and exquisite chintz curtains and spreads make each room feel like a home. Of course, every room includes every sort of modern convenience: dedicated telephone lines, stereos, cassettes, CD players, your own service pantry, and refrigerator.

Romance at a Glance

♥ *Stay at The Carlyle (212–744–1600 or 800–227–5737).*

♥ *Dine at New York's most magical restaurants, including Restaurant Daniel, La Goulue, Barbetta's, and Windows on the World.*

♥ *Stroll hand-in-hand while exploring Manhattan's classic treasures: Central Park, Fifth Avenue, the Empire State Building, Times Square, Broadway, and the Statue of Liberty.*

Dinner

Once you've settled in your room, plan to have dinner at **Restaurant Daniel** (20 East 76th Street between Fifth and Madison Avenues; 212–288–0033; very expensive). Restaurant Daniel sits conveniently right across the street from the Carlyle, but you are treating yourselves to dinner here simply because it is considered one of New York's best restaurants. It is owned and operated by Daniel Boulud, considered one of New York's most innovative chefs by such respected gastronomic lights as Patricia Wells. The menu is classic French with a twist. The subtlety of the cuisine is reflected in the restaurant's decor. The walls, carpets, tablecloths, and other furnishings are all in a warm beige. This soft elegance serves as background for lush floral arrangements, exquisite Limoges china, and sparkling crystal and silver. The food, too, is almost disarming in its quiet power. Building on a classic French home-style base, Boulud takes even a simple salad or a light codfish in broth to exquisite heights.

However, even Daniel Boulud may not be able to entice you on your wedding night. If you're not interested in dinner, save this delight for another time, and simply close your door and enjoy each other.

DAY TWO: MORNING

This is your honeymoon, so I haven't even bothered to plan anything for this first morning of your married life. Just luxuriate together. You have all the time in the world, so when you finally rouse yourselves, take a leisurely, warm bath or shower. If you need fortification afterwards, order tea or coffee and some sweet pastries from room service.

When you decide to go out, stroll south down **Madison Avenue**. Peek into all the marvelous shops, one after the other.

Lunch

Stop for lunch outside at **La Goulue** (746 Madison Avenue between 64th and 65th Streets; 212–988–8169; expensive). This is a French place with a certain amount of Big Apple Attitude, but just laugh off its way of taking itself seriously and enjoy its wonderful food. Try to sit at the tables near the street, and as you hold hands, watch the fanciest New Yorkers walk by.

DAY TWO: AFTERNOON

After lunch, stroll over to **Central Park** (See "Garden of Eden," page 55, for more details). At 64th Street, you will find yourselves very near the Children's Zoo, so stop by and watch the polar bears romp or the monkeys play. Or venture a short distance into the park and take a turn on the carousel or a short ride in a hansom cab.

Come out of the Park on Fifth Avenue and walk south. Just go with the flow. Stop wherever your hearts desire. Try on a few luxuries at **Bergdorf Goodman**, **Tiffany & Co.**, or the stores of **Trump Tower** (all located around Fifth Avenue and 57th Street). Walk south a few more blocks to **St. Patrick's Cathedral** and **Saks Fifth Avenue** (50th and Fifth).

Don't forget to walk around Rockefeller Center, still the center of midtown Manhattan. For a brief respite, stop by **Paley Plaza** (3 East 53rd Street between Fifth and Madison Avenues), an unexpected spot of greenery amidst New York's blaring taxi horns and rushing throngs. Snuggle up together and listen to the sound of the waterfall.

Continue walking south on Fifth Avenue and when you get to 34th Street, you'll find yourself at the foot of the edifice that makes New York, New York: **The Empire State Building.** Take the elevators up to the 86th floor and make believe you're Cary Grant and Deborah Kerr in *An Affair to Remember.* Actually, these lovers never quite made it to the top of the Empire State Building, but their effort to do so served as a symbol of their love. Take photos of each other and record this moment as an emblem of your devotion.

If you have the time and the inclination, think about catching a taxi to 12th Avenue and taking the delightful ride on the **Port Imperial Ferry** (West 38th Street and 12th Avenue at the Hudson River; 800–533–3779; $4 each way). This delightful ferry shuttles others from Manhattan to Weekawken, New Jersey. (And back, of course.) On the New Jersey side, you can stop for a drink at **Arthur's Landing** (at the Ferry Pier, Weehawken, New Jersey), catch the Manhattan skyline at one of its most remarkable vantage points, then return in time for dinner, the theater, or both.

In preparation for your wedding, you've probably done a lot of shopping and received a number of beautiful gifts. Still, be sure to buy each other a little something that will remind you always of your honeymoon. Tiffanys', for instance, has a great selection of small silver pieces—like key chains, necklaces with Elsa Perretti hearts, or small frames that could hold a photo of the two of you.

DAY TWO: EVENING

Dinner

Have dinner at **Barbetta** (321 West 46th Street, Restaurant Row; 212–246–9171; expensive). Snooty New Yorkers label this gorgeous Italian restaurant "old-fashioned" and turn up their noses at the food, but, in my opinion, they're wrong. The food is marvelous (especially the traditional pastas, fish dishes, and desserts), but the atmosphere is, in my opinion, the most romantic in all Manhattan. Yes, Barbetta's has been here a long time (I celebrated a special wedding anniversary here more than twenty years ago), but, like fine wine, Barbetta's just gets better. If the weather is balmy, try to dine in the garden, with its beautiful central fountain. If it's cold or rainy, you'll be happy inside, too, regardless of whether you are placed upstairs or down. All the rooms have working fireplaces, including a small private room where you'll receive especially intimate service.

If it's Thursday, Friday, or Saturday night, you could make Barbetta's your entire evening. On those evenings, Barbetta's offers ballroom dancing to live Hungarian and Russian music.

If a Broadway play is more to your liking, leave the restaurant early enough for the curtain. Broadway is especially alive these days with everything from marvelous comic musicals to serious dramas. The choice is yours.

After the play, you'll probably be ready to return to the Carlyle, but you might consider one last romantic pause: Stop at **The View**, the restaurant and lounge on top of the New York Marriott Marquis (1535 Broadway between 45th and 46th Streets; 212–398–1900; expensive.) The bar revolves very slowly, and you can sip a Drambuie or other nightcap and watch the twinkling lights on the Great White Way below you.

DAY THREE: MORNING

Today you'll be touring the sights of New York's majestic harbor. Exploring the Statue of Liberty and Ellis Island takes several hours and these museums tend to get crowded, so start the day early. Order breakfast in your room, then try to catch the first ferry (9:30 A.M.) to Liberty Island. You'll remain downtown all day and you'll be having dinner at Windows on the World, a rather formal restaurant where jackets and ties are required for men and reasonably dressy garb is required for women, so don't dress in blue jeans or shorts. It would be a long and time-consuming trek back to your hotel in the late afternoon, so go prepared.

Ferrying around New York's harbor is one of the world's most romantic adventures. A visit to the Statue of Liberty and Ellis Island (where more than 12 million immigrants were processed between 1892 and 1954) is a requirement for all visitors. Head off as early as possible by taxi or the #1 subway to South Ferry and go to **Castle Clinton National Monument** in **Battery Park**, where you'll buy your tickets for the ferry to both the Statue of Liberty and Ellis Island. (The ferries depart daily every thirty minutes between 9:30 A.M. and 3:30 P.M. Tickets are $7, which includes admission to both sites.)

The ferry stops first at Liberty Island, where you can disembark to explore the island and the **Statue of Liberty** and then catch a later ferry for Ellis Island. Exploring the statue, the exhibits, and Liberty Island itself takes a couple of hours, so on this trip you may simply want to enjoy the majesty of the Statue from afar and return to Liberty Island another time. The

Ellis Island Immigration Museum does a wonderful job of telling the immigrants' story through displays, artifacts, photos, interactive devices, and film. It takes at least two hours to tour the museum, but the time and energy you expend will be worth it.

Lunch

Enjoy lunch at the Immigration Museum's cafeteria. The best of American fast food with a multiethnic flair is offered here. Choose from Italian pizzas, German hot dogs, and other ethnic dishes. On a warm day, you can "picnic" on the delightful patio overlooking downtown Manhattan.

If the menu here fails to attract your interest, finish your tour, then catch a ferry back to Battery Park, and walk just a few blocks north along the water's edge. If the day is balmy and beautiful, have late lunch outdoors at a cafe table at one of the numerous pubs and elegant fast-food places surrounding the yacht basin at the World Financial Center.

DAY THREE: AFTERNOON

Stroll through the **Winter Garden at the World Financial Center**. The Winter Garden is New York's "crystal palace" filled with towering palms trees overlooking a lovely esplanade that offers beautiful views of the river and the harbor. Off the Winter Garden are scores of shops and restaurants. Browse for something special as a memento of your visit.

Go south along Broadway until you come to Wall Street. At the top of Wall Street is famed **Trinity Church**, which was designed by Richard Upjohn and consecrated on Ascension Day in 1846. In those days before skyscrapers, the spire on Trinity Church defined the Manhattan skyline. Turn east and walk down Wall Street. Stop for a moment and chat with **George Washington** himself—that's him on the pedestal in front of the Federal building. Directly across the street is the famous New York Stock Exchange. Turn west again and walk up Wall Street and continue west on Rector Street for one block to Church Street; turn north and head back to the **World Trade Center Plaza**.

After you've explored the interior of the Winter Garden, head back outdoors toward the yacht basin. Walk toward the river's edge and then turn north and walk through the new parks that line the water's edge in this area. Wend your way out of the park and head east along Barclay Street or Park Place two blocks until you come to Broadway. Turn south (or right). Between Vesey and Fulton Streets on Broadway, you'll come to **St. Paul's Chapel**, a lovely Georgian chapel built in 1766, the only pre-Revolutionary church extant in the city. George Washington worshipped here during the Revolutionary War. It's also interesting to note that the Hudson River flowed just behind the chapel prior to landfill.

Allow yourselves to wander in these streets, but pay enough attention so that eventually you end up back at the **World Trade Center Plaza**. Atop #2 World Trade Center is a fabulous observation deck, as well as a sort of mini-amusement park known as "Top of the World." You can take a simulated helicopter ride around New York, order food in a diner modeled on a subway station, snuggle up in a spot modeled on Central Park, or have your photo taken on a simulated SoHo stoop. It's sort of corny, but ride up and enjoy the fun.

DAY THREE: EVENING

Dinner

For your last evening of your Manhattan honeymoon, there's no better place for cocktails and dinner than **Windows on the World** (107th Floor, 1 World Trade Center; 212–938–1111; very expensive; jackets required). The restaurant has been one of New York's (and maybe the world's!) favorites since it originally opened in 1974. It was closed for three years after the 1993 bombing of the World Trade Center, but it reopened in 1996 and is now more marvelous than ever.

One restaurant critic called dining at the "new" Windows on the World a "transforming experience," and the first transformation you'll experience is the incredible (I mean quite literally unbelievable) views from the restaurant. From the bar (modestly called "The Greatest Bar on Earth"), you can look down on the Statue of Liberty and the tiny-appearing harbor vessels; from your table you can see traffic jams (auto and airplane), but you're in position to experience them as if they were twinkling holiday lights.

The views are just the starters. Windows on the World features what its creators call a "World View Cuisine." The menu represents virtually every cuisine in the world but not in that mishmashy way many "nouvelle" restaurants tend to do these days. For example, Mexico is represented not by tacos and enchiladas but a wonderfully aromatic veal shank slathered in spices and roasted in parchment. Scandinavia shows off with shrimp grilled on skewers and served with a sauce of crème fraîche, aquavit, and caviar.

After dinner take a taxi back to your hotel and catch the late show at **Cafe Carlyle** before you slip back into your perfect nest. Frankly, you simply can't spend your honeymoon at the Carlyle Hotel without seeing and hearing Bobby Short perform. Have no fear, if Bobby is not appearing, Dixie Carter, Barbara Cook, or Eartha Kitt probably is. In any case, you won't be disappointed. The cabaret in the Cafe Carlyle is the epitome of New York sophistication.

FOR MORE ROMANCE

If you are spending more than three days in New York City, you'll undoubtedly want to explore Greenwich Village (see "Whatever Happened to Tio Pepes," page 177 for details) or the East Village and SoHo (see "X-Rated," page 189 for details).

To have a full taste of the choicest of New York living, spend a few days of your honeymoon at the beach on Long Island, where New York natives go to relax. (See "The

Hamptons à Deux," page 89.) After your urban explorations, you'll probably welcome some leisurely days on the beach.

ITINERARY 10
Three days and two nights

THE HAMPTONS À DEUX

*I'*m a beach person. There is nothing I love more than lying in warm sand on a beautiful beach and soaking up the sun (no matter what my dermatologist says). OK, that's not entirely true. The fact is, the only thing I like better is lying in the warm sand on a beautiful beach soaking up the sun with the man I love.

As I came to write this itinerary, I tried to think of some adjectives to describe the Hamptons, a string of elegant beach towns located on the eastern tip of Long Island. Chic? Legendary? Fabulous? Breathtaking? All the superlatives are true, yet none alone really sums up this area's magic. So, it's The Hamptons, without adjective, *à deux*—just for the two of you. After you've explored the region, you'll undoubtedly agree that there's simply no better place to lie in the warm sand on a beautiful beach and soak up the sun with the one you love.

Practical notes: For this weekend, you'll need a car. To get to the Hamptons, take the Long Island Expressway (LIE) to exit 70; when you exit the expressway, drive south for three miles until you reach the Sunrise Highway (Route 27), and head east. Follow Route 27 east to Southampton.

Starting at Memorial Day weekend and through Labor Day, the Hamptons are very crowded, especially, of course, on weekends. The traffic from the Midtown Tunnel in Manhattan until you reach Montauk (120 miles) is usually bumper-to-bumper from 4:00 P.M. on Friday afternoon until midnight Sunday evening. To enjoy a more romantic trip, think about taking this getaway during the work week when the natives are slaving in their offices in steamy Gotham City.

Romance at a Glance

♥ *Stay at The Mill-Garth (516–267–3757).*

♥ *Dine at Sapore di Mare, the American Hotel, and other Hamptons night spots.*

♥ *Spend a day exploring Shelter Island.*

♥ *Explore the various Hamptons villages.*

If you want to take public transportation to the Hamptons, you can take the Long Island Railroad. For information on its regular service to the Hamptons, call (718) 217–LIRR or (516) 822–LIRR. You can also take the Hampton Jitney (212–936–0440 or 516–283–4600), which provides regular service from Manhattan and local service from Southampton to Montauk.

As with weekends in New York City, make your hotel and restaurant reservations well ahead of time. In summer, these places are heavily booked, and you don't want to be disappointed.

DAY ONE: MORNING/AFTERNOON

Start your trip no later than mid-morning. (If you are driving out to the Hamptons on a weekday morning, it should take you about two hours. If you are leaving on a late Friday afternoon, count on three hours or more.) Although the Long Island Expressway is not exciting, as soon as you head south from the Expressway toward Route 27, you'll begin to smell and feel the salt air and see the legendary potato fields of Long Island.

Follow the signs to **Southampton**. As you drive into the village, you'll know you've arrived someplace special. Southampton was discovered well before the likes of Billy Joel or

Liz Smith arrived. As a matter of fact, it was founded in June 1640 by colonists from Lynn, Massachusetts, and was the first English settlement in the State of New York.

Lunch

Stop for lunch at **The Old Post House** (136 Main Street, Southampton; 516–283–1717; moderate). Sit outside on the porch or patio, enjoy a tasty seafood salad or sandwich, and soak up the atmosphere.

⌀⌀⌀

After lunch, take a short visit to the Old Halsey House, the oldest existing frame house in the state, or stroll down Main Street for a look in the restored Silversmith Shop, which first opened about 1750. You might also want to browse through the beautiful—and pricey—antiques and fashion shops on Main Street and Job's Lane.

Before you head toward your Inn, drive around Southampton for a view of a few of the town's legendary mansions. The best roads for viewing are parallel to the ocean on Meadow Lane and Gin Lane and on their intersecting streets, which are called "Necks"—Halsey Neck, Cooper's Neck, and First Neck. As in Newport, in a sort of reverse snobbism, the homes here are called "cottages." Also, if you haven't seen the beach and the crashing sea yet, pull up to the town beach on Meadow Lane and feast your eyes on one of the most beautiful beaches in the world.

Now return to Route 27 and drive on. As you cruise east you'll pass through several small villages. Among these are Water Mill, named for its signature windmill, and Bridge-hampton, which has a main street of quaint shops. If you want to explore a bit, turn south (or right) and drive down a few of the back roads that run between Route 27 and the sea. The houses, estates, and winding roads are marvelous.

Drive through Easthampton for the moment—you'll return, believe me—and on to Amagansett. Although not quite as luxe as Southampton or Easthampton, Amagansett is very charming. Of all of Amagansett's remarkable lodging places, **The Mill Garth** (516–267–3757; $135 per night for a room in the inn to $275 per night for the mini-cottages) is the best choice for an intimate, romantic getaway. To reach the inn, turn left at the Mobil Station (this is the first left after the Bayberry Nursery) onto Windmill Lane. The Mill Garth is just one-half block from the highway on the left side of Windmill Lane.

The 150-year-old main house is lovely and offers about ten guest rooms. For the most privacy I recommend the "Top O'Stairs," the "Terrace Suite," or "The Hampton Suite." These rooms are let for $135 per night.

If it fits your budget and your mood, try to book one of the small cottages located in the complex of lawns and gardens surrounding the larger inn. Each is filled with lovely antiques, including four-poster beds, and each offers warm ambience and marvelous privacy. I particularly recommend "The Dairy House," the "English Ivy Cottage," or "The Garden Cottage," which has its own fireplace. Each has its own bath (with deep Turkish toweling robes) and kitchenette. The cottages rent for $275 per night. (By the way, the Mill Garth does not have a restaurant or offer room service, so stop at the local shops and markets for breakfast fixings, wine and cheese, or whatever other foodstuffs you may require.)

From the Mill-Garth, it's only about a half-mile to the beach. You can walk, borrow bicycles from the innkeeper, or drive. To me, coming to the beach is pure bliss. Once you've settled yourself in your cottage, you should make your way down to the ocean. If you can still catch some sun, great. If it's late in the afternoon, buy a bottle of wine at a local shop and have your pre-dinner cocktails on the beach.

After your sojourn on the beach, dress up a bit and head to Easthampton. Drive down Main Street first in order to get your bearings, then drive down Ocean Avenue to see Easthampton's row of "cottages." Unless you're related to the Vanderbilts or the Rockefellers, you'll probably be awestruck. Drive back into the center of town, and stop at the **East Hampton Chamber of Commerce** at the corner of Main Street and Newtown Lane for a free walking guide and other information about the area.

Easthampton is another of Long Island's "east end" settlements founded more than 300 years ago. (In fact, many of the original descendants proudly remain in the neighborhood.) Most of the older houses have been designated historic landmarks, and each one has a story to tell. For example, **The Studio**, the second house from the V where Woods Lane becomes Main Street, was the home of Thomas Morn, a noted watercolorist. Two doors down, at 217 Main Street, is the former summer White House for President John Tyler. Among other interesting houses is the Winthrop Gardiner saltbox called **Home Sweet Home**, a 1750 home once owned by John Howard Payne, who wrote the song "Home Sweet Home." Nearby is **Mulford Farmhouse**, built in the 1650s; its surrounding acreage was a working farm until the late 1940s.

Like Southampton, Easthampton also boasts scores of wonderful boutiques and shops, most of which are on either Main Street or Newtown Lane. Enjoy them if you have the time—or come back in the morning.

DAY ONE: Evening

Dinner

Even out here in the country, there is a nightlife in the Hamptons, and one of the most popular eateries is **Sapore di Mare** (Route 27, Easthampton; 516–537–2764; expensive). Rustic yet elegant, Sapore di Mare offers interesting and tasty Northern Italian fare, including special pizzas, risotto, and, of course, seafood. The wine list is terrific. On a Friday or Saturday night, it will be bustling. Because it's a haunt of the rich and famous, you may well find yourselves at a table next to someone well known.

If you still have energy after your long day, catch a film at the movie house located on Easthampton's Main Street.

A serious sunburn could spoil romance completely, so be careful as you enjoy the beach and islands. Try a sunblock massage before you go out, and when you return, soothe any sun-kissed spots by massaging each other with some fragrant oils. Think about it!

DAY TWO: Morning

You might like to sleep late this morning, cuddle up with your honey, and forget about being a tourist. If you're eager to shop and see the sights, however, go into Amagansett, Easthampton, or even Bridgehampton.

Brunch

Have a late-morning brunch at the **Honest Diner** (74 Montauk Highway, Amagansett; 516–267–3535; inexpensive), a kitschy 1950s diner where you can have some great scrambled eggs or any other kind of big all-American breakfast your hearts desire.

DAY TWO: Afternoon

If I were you, I'd be on the beach by 11:00 A.M. You decide on the timing that's best for you. In any case, you can't come to the Hamptons without getting in some serious beach time. Drive or bike down to the Amagansett beach (formally called Atlantic Avenue Beach, informally called Asparagus Beach), or, if you'd like to, try a couple of other locations. For example, head down fancy Ocean Avenue to Easthampton's town beach, or drive west to Bridgehampton and take the Sagaponack road to the Bridgehampton town beach. (Ask your innkeeper for specific directions to these beaches; find out how you can get passes if necessary.) It almost doesn't matter on which beach you decide to park your blanket. The Long Island beaches are some of the best in the world.

When you've had your fill of sun and sand, head back to the Mill-Garth and take a long, leisurely shower together.

DAY TWO: EVENING

In early evening, head north on Route 114 right across the south fork tine, to the quaint town of **Sag Harbor**. (It's about a fifteen-minute drive; ask your innkeeper for exact directions.) Sag Harbor was once a major American port in the late eighteenth and early nineteenth centuries and was one of the best-known whaling centers in America. If you have some time before dinner, try to stop at the **Sag Harbor Whaling and Historic Museum** (corner of Garden Street and Main Street; 516–725–0770), which will tell you more about Sag Harbor's history. Take a few minutes and walk down Main Street and look at the lovely early American houses, still inhabited by happy New Yorkers who have managed to get the best of urban and small-town life.

Dinner

The American Hotel (Main Street, Sag Harbor; 216–725–3535; moderate to expensive) is a must for dinner. The hotel looks like something right out of a nineteenth-century novel, and it is. It's well over 100 years old, and the ambience is cozy, warm, and elegant. The food is sort of Continental-American, specializing, not surprisingly, in fish as well as some game (like Long Island duckling). Dining at The American Hotel is the ideal accompaniment to a visit to Sag Harbor.

I'm lazy; after a day at the beach and a nice dinner, I'm ready for bed. (That's also, perhaps, the most romantic suggestion.) However, if you want to try something more active, try **East Hampton Bowl** (71 Montauk Highway; 516–324–1950). Located just west of East Hampton the bowling alley and bar stay open well past midnight every night. It will cost each of you $2 for the shoe rental and $3.50 per game to bowl. On Saturday nights, the bowling alley features "Rock–'n–Bowl," with music and a bit of dancing. This is tremendous fun—after all, foolishness is one way to be utterly romantic. Really!

For a "nightcap," go back down to the beach and snuggle up together while listening to the waves crash against the shore.

DAY THREE: MORNING

Grab a quick breakfast at the Honest Diner, then spend today exploring beautiful **Shelter Island**. Shelter Island really is an island and is named, appropriately, for its sheltered position in the middle of the two tines of Long Island's fork. It is thought by some to be a bit less chic than the Hamptons, but many upper-crust New Yorkers actually prefer the privacy that Shelter Island affords. To get there, take the ferry from North Haven. (To get to North Haven, drive through Sag Harbor and follow the signs. The ferry takes cars, bikers, or pedestrians; fee varies according to type of vehicle and number of passengers.)

Shelter Island was first settled by Quakers in 1652, and later was thought to be an important hideout for pirates, including the likes of the infamous Captain Kidd. But before the Quakers or the pirates, Shelter Island had long been the home of the Mashomack Indians. In fact, one of the "must-do" activities on Shelter Island is the **Mashomack Preserve** (Route 114, just north of the South Ferry; 516–749–1001), which is a beautiful nature preserve run by the Nature Conservancy. Stop at the visitors center when you get off the ferry. Browse for a few minutes in the gift shop, pick up a map, and spend a couple of hours walking through.

This breathtaking preserve offers a unique look at salt marshes, tidal creeks, fields, woodlands, and ocean coastline. The preserve offers four walking trails of varying lengths. You'll be awed by the scenery and diversity of this beautiful refuge.

After you've explored the Mashomack Preserve, get back in your car and continue north up Route 114 to "The Shelter Island Heights," the town center of Shelter Island. As you drive along, you'll see that in some ways Shelter Island is more like New England than Long Island. Huge oaks hang over the road, and the island is quite hilly in places.

When you get to Shelter Island Heights, you'll be charmed by sedate Colonials as well as by a number of gingerbread-trimmed Victorians. Here, too, you'll find interesting shops and several places to stop for a bite of lunch.

Lunch

Many Shelter Island natives frequent **The Dory** (Bridge Street, Shelter Island Heights; 516–749–8871; moderate). It looks like a typical beach bar, but the food is tasty and fresh. Try to get a table on the back patio overlooking Chase Creek, then order one of the especially good fish dishes. Steamed mussels in ginger-lemon grass broth or fried calamari are two nice choices.

∽⊙⊙∾

One of the best ways to see Shelter Island is by bicycle. After lunch, rent a bike at

Piccozzi's (516–749–0045), just down Bridge Street from The Dory. Get a map from the gas station or one of the gift shops and spend the afternoon biking around the island. One great route leads east from The Heights to Little Ram Island and Big Ram Island, two lovely areas connected by a causeway to the main island. The round trip is about 10 miles. Stop along the way at the **Ram's Head Inn** (108 Ram Island Drive; 516–749–0811) for a rest, a drink, and a view of charming Coecles Harbor.

If biking is not your thing, explore the shops in The Heights, then tour the island by car. Don't be afraid if you get lost. Shelter Island isn't that big; you'll always find your way back to the center.

Head home by way of the North Ferry, which will take you from Shelter Island to Greenport, then head west through the charming rural towns along the North Fork and back to that Big Island, Manhattan.

FOR MORE ROMANCE

If you have more than three days to spend in the Hamptons, be sure to trek all the way to the end of Long Island to **Montauk**. Quite different in atmosphere from the rest of the Hamptons, Montauk is, in fact, the sandy tip of Long Island. The scrub-covered terrain includes miles of white dunes. Visit the magnificent Montauk Lighthouse, one of the last of its breed.

ITINERARY 11
Three days and two nights

ALL THAT JAZZ!

*J*azz is sexy. There's no doubt about it. It's the musical perfection of Ella Fitzgerald. The sultry sadness of Billie Holiday. The heat of Louis Armstrong. The cool of Miles Davis. It's the hesitation followed by the sense of surprise. Regardless of whether you're listening to Dixieland or bebop, jazz evokes smoke-filled rooms, late nights, and, yes, a certain kind of freewheeling sexuality.

Writer F. Scott Fitzgerald labeled the free-spirited 1920s the "Jazz Age," but jazz began long before the 1920s and has lasted long after. In fact, it is perhaps one of the few truly American art forms, a gift that emerged to a great degree from the African American culture. Jazz was actually born in New Orleans and ripened in Kansas City and Chicago before it came to New York City. By the 1920s, jazz had migrated to Manhattan, and its center remains here to this day.

There's no sexier way to enjoy New York City than to follow the beat of the jazz greats to the many fascinating crevices of this town. Enjoy yourselves!

Practical notes: This itinerary is appropriate for any time of year, but New York City pays special tribute to jazz every year in late June at the **JVC Jazz Festival** so you might consider planning your trip at this time. In a ten-day period, jazz is presented in scores of venues throughout the city, including Lincoln Center and Carnegie Hall. For details call the JVC Festival New York (P.O. Box 1169, Ansonia Station, New York, New York 10023) at (212) 787–2020.

Other popular jazz festivals are presented annually and are well worth attending. Among them is the **Greenwich Village Jazz Festival**, usually held in August; call (212) 242–1785 for details. **Jazz in July**, presented by the 92nd Street YM/YWHA (1395 Lexington Avenue, New York, New York 10128) is equally good; call (212) 996–1100 for details.

Try to see the exuberant new Broadway musical *Bring in 'Da Noise, Bring in 'Da Funk*— it is fabulous. If tickets are not available, check out what's playing at City Center, Carnegie Hall, or Lincoln Center. All of these centers offer jazz-related concerts. If you come during JVC Jazz Week or during one of the other special jazz festivals mentioned above, you will have no trouble finding suitable entertainment on Friday evening.

Romance at a Glance

♥ *Stay at the Paramount (212–764–5500).*

♥ *Dine at an array of "jazz"-evoking New York eateries, including Jezebel, The Empire Diner, and Sylvia's.*

♥ *Tour New York's downtown jazz clubs; attend jazz concerts.*

♥ *Tour Harlem and attend a Sunday Gospel service.*

DAY ONE: EVENING

Plan to arrive at your hotel in late afternoon. Jazz is hip, and one of the "hippest" hotels in New York is the **Paramount** (235 West 46th Street between Broadway and Eighth Avenue; 212–764–5500; $160–$210, double; $350–$450, suite). Designer Philippe Starck has designed three hotels in Manhattan: Morgan's, the Royalton, and the Paramount. The Paramount is the least expensive of the three, but like the other two it is sleek and fanciful. The rooms are tiny but amusingly decorated like ship's cabins, including fabulous swivelling armoires and unique headboards. Most of all, it's fun.

Dinner

To get you into a "jazz" mood, have dinner at **Jezebel's** (630 Ninth Avenue at 45th Street; 212–582–1045). Jezebel's offers Southern cuisine at its very best: Southern fried chicken, spicy chicken wings, baked ham, smothered pork, barbecued ribs, sweet yams, mashed potatoes, fresh green beans, collard greens, and a fabulous selection of desserts. The decor is sultry, with lace-covered lamps and lots of chiffon curtains—rather like a New Orleans bordello. If you are not worried about spilling barbecue sauce on your new silk blouse or tie, consider snuggling up as you enjoy your dinner in one of the several hanging porch swings that serve as seats at many of the tables.

⋘⋙

If you can get tickets, see *Bring in 'Da Noise, Bring in 'Da Funk,* the highly praised Broadway musical conceived and performed by Savion Glover a 23-year-old tap dancing genius. (Ambassador Theater, 219 West 49th Street, 212–239–6200). The show is structured around the history of black jazz music, especially as it relates to percussion and tap dancing. The music and especially the dancing are breathtaking. This is currently one of the hottest shows in New York, so be sure to order tickets well ahead of time.

After the show, chances are good that you'll be wired. In fact, you may just want to dance yourself! If you are five minutes over the age of twenty-five, however, tap dancing is probably not the best way to calm you down, so head east as you leave the theater and walk just two blocks to Rockefeller Center. At **Rainbow and Stars,** part of the famed Rainbow Room group, located on the 65th floor of the GE Building at 30 Rockefeller Plaza (212–632–5000; expensive) you'll reach the height of intimacy and glamour. Although patrons who want to eat dinner must order before 10:00 P.M., you can show up as late as 10:30 and simply order champagne during the later hours as you soak up incomparable music from the likes of Tony Bennett, Rosemary Clooney, Maureen McGovern, or others who appear here regularly. There is a $40 per person cover charge, but it's worth it. Reservations are necessary, even for the late show.

If you just want to enjoy each other and avoid the cover charge, go directly to the **Rainbow Promenade Restaurant and Bar**. The bar, featuring the same marvelous art deco decor as the Rainbow Room next door, runs along the south side of the 65th Floor with windows overlooking the Empire State Building, the Statue of Liberty, and the full expanse of southern Manhattan island. In addition to champagne, the bar will also serve a number of other intoxicating concoctions with such tantalizing names as "Between the Sheets." You might just try a classic Manhattan. Viewing the Empire State Building from this bar is considered by some people to be better than standing atop the skyscraper itself. In fact, New York City offers no more romantic spot to end a jazzy—and incredibly romantic—evening.

Before you head back to your hotel, you may want to stroll down West 52nd Street between Fifth Avenue and Sixth Avenue. This is known as "Swing Street" and was for years the center where all the great New York jazz clubs clustered. The only remnant of this glittering past is **The "21" Club** (21 West 52nd Street; expensive), which was in its heyday one of the chicest speakeasies in New York. It remains a revered grand gentleman of a place, and you might want to stop into the downstairs bar for a nightcap and a bit of nostalgia.

DAY TWO: MORNING

Sleep in—make this your holiday. This is going to be a long day, so you may need the extra rest. Tonight's itinerary calls for some serious club crawling downtown.

In order to get "south," you'll spend the day touring one of the most vital neighborhoods in Manhattan: Chelsea. (This little side trip is not about jazz, but it's a marvelous romantic interlude before your jazz evening.) From West 42nd Street, you can take a subway (Broadway line #2 or #3), bus, or cab to 23rd Street. If you feel energetic, you can walk. It's about 1 mile.

Brunch

Manhattan is sprouting diners in every neighborhood these days, but the **Empire Diner** (210 Tenth Avenue at 22nd Street; 212–243–2736) remains the quintessential New York diner. It was immortalized in Woody Allen's movie, *Manhattan,* where its sleek black, white, and silver lines were filmed in equally luscious black-and-white film. The Empire is open twenty-four hours a day and serves a complete menu of delicious diner-style standards but brunch—with eggs any way you like them, omelettes of all types, and various lunch platters and sandwiches—is probably its best meal. Order favorites like lox and bagels or French toast and share the bounty. If the weather is warm, sit at the tables outside. The street life is great.

DAY TWO: AFTERNOON

After fortifying yourself at the Empire Diner, take the afternoon to stroll around the streets of Chelsea. For decades, Chelsea has been a popular place to live for New York natives. Basically the neighborhood is bordered by 6th Avenue on the east, the Hudson River on the west, 23rd Street on the north, and 14th Street on the south, but Chelsea blurs a bit with the Gramercy/Flatiron district to the east and the upper West 20s to the north.

Chelsea's beautiful residential streets are lined with exquisite and notable houses, some of which remain private residences. Most, however, have been carved up into apartments, albeit very charming ones. Stroll down West 20th Street between 9th Avenue and 10th Avenue for a particular treat, especially numbers 202 through 206. While you are on this block, stop in the churchyard at the **General Theological Seminary**. It adds a bit of verdant lushness to an already beautiful block.

Since you've seen the Empire Diner and the spectacular Chelsea residential buildings, you can't leave without taking a peek at the famous **Chelsea Hotel** at 222 West 23rd Street between Seventh and Eighth Avenues. Another of New York City's most notable architectural and literary landmarks, it is rather down-at-the-heels these days, but its multiple gables, dormers, cast-iron balconies, and other architectural gewgaws make it fascinating to look at. Many writers have lived there at one time or another. Mark Twain, William Dean Howells, Thomas Wolfe, Mary McCarthy, Arthur Miller, Brendan Behan, Vladimir Nabokov, and Dylan Thomas are among the famous former tenants. Andy Warhol added to its wild reputation by portraying the hotel—in all its degeneracy—in his movie *Chelsea Girls*. The hotel had fifteen more minutes of fame in the late 1970s when Sid Vicious, lead singer of the punk rock group, The Sex Pistols, was indicted for murdering his girlfriend in the Chelsea.

If shopping is your thing, Chelsea offers some extraordinary choices. It is home to the original **Barney's** (106 Seventh Avenue), **Loehmann's** (next to Barney's), a spectacular **Barnes & Noble** superstore (675 Sixth Avenue at 22nd Street), **Bed, Bath, and Beyond** (620 Sixth Avenue at West 18th Street), and several other large retailers. Best of all, don't miss the **Antique and Flea Market** that is open on Saturdays and Sundays at 26th Street and Sixth Avenue. The market not only attracts a remarkable array of antique dealers but an equally fascinating array of celebrity shoppers.

If you wish to wile away a few hours in a pool hall, check out **Chelsea Billiards** (54 West 21st Street; 212–989–0096.) It's a place popular with the twenty-something crowd, but anyone can go and have a fun—even a romantic—time.

DAY TWO: Evening

This is going to be the ultimate Manhattan jazz evening—at least downtown-style jazz. (There's an uptown jazz scene, too. You'll see a bit of it tomorrow, but catching all of New York's jazz takes weeks!) Jazz clubs are notorious for their bad food, so before you settle in for some serious music or wild dancing, you may want to have dinner at a spot noted for food and atmosphere and then move on to the musical treats.

Ella

Ella Fitzgerald is universally considered America's leading lady of jazz. Although Ella was born in Virginia (in 1918), her early success occurred in New York. When she was sixteen, she went on stage at the Harlem Opera House Amateur Night after losing a bet with friends. She sang "The Object of My Affections" and won three encores and $25. She soon became well known around Harlem, and her first recording, "A-Tisket, A-Tasket" was a huge hit. For the next sixty years, until her death in 1996, she reigned as queen among female jazz vocalists.

Dinner

You will no doubt have noticed that Chelsea is lined with terrific restaurants. For a touch of romance and intimacy, however, I strongly recommend **Alley's End** (311 West 17th Street between Eighth and Ninth Avenues; 212–627–8899; moderate.) Just getting there is a bit of an adventure; the restaurant is located at the end of an alley, as you may have guessed. When you enter, you'll find yourself next to a tiny, friendly bar. Whether you sit in a booth or at a table, the rooms are warm and friendly, yet somehow quiet. The menu varies and is remarkably creative with especially tasty salads and marvelous grilled fish dinners. It's also reasonably priced. What more could you ask for?

❧❧❧

Get ready to test New York's downtown jazz scene. Jazz comes in all types and styles, and New York's jazz clubs are equally various. You could go for the "Grand Dads" of downtown clubs: **The Village Vanguard** (178 Seventh Avenue South; 212–255–4037); **The Blue Note** (131 West 3rd Street; 212–475–8592), or **The Bottom Line** (15 West 4th Street; 212–228–7800). These clubs offer two shows nightly, and they charge for cover, tickets, and drink minimums. Call ahead for details. The Village Vanguard and the Blue Note are both small spaces, but all feature well-known performers. The intimacy is just part of the fun. I once sat so close to Lionel Hampton, I could feel his breath.

For the younger and more hip (or younger-at-heart and just as hip), many possibilities exist. **CBGB and OMFUG** (which originally stood for Country, Bluegrass, Blues, and Other Music for Uplifting Gourmandisers) has been around for twenty years at Bowery at Bleecker Street (212) 473–7743. It now hosts mostly loud rock bands. **The Knitting Factory** (74 Leonard Street at Church Street, TriBeCa; 212–219–3055) has emerged as one of Manhattan's most popular jazz clubs. Better-known jazz and rock acts appear "upstairs." Downstairs, the AlterKnit room features performance artists, poets, and others. The **Mercury Lounge** (217 East Houston Street; 212–260–4700) offers an eclectic mix of songwriters, country bands, pop-rock groups, and alternative rockers.

If you want to dance, try either **Tramps** (51 West 21st Street, 212–727–7788), which offers both performers and dancing, or **The Tunnel** (220 12th Avenue at 27th Street; 212–695–4682), reported in the *New York Times* to be "the New York City department store of discotheque." Both these places are jam-packed, particularly on weekends, and therefore are not private, intimate haunts. If sweaty dancing and noise appeals to you, these two discotheques are perfect destinations.

After you have cruised the clubs and listened to fabulous music, you may find that you want to stop for a 4:00 A.M. snack. The best place—especially since you're already downtown—is **Florent** (69 Gansevoort Street, between Greenwich and Washington Streets; 212–989–5779). Florent is Paris in Manhattan in the heart of the meat-packing district. (Don't get worried when you see the neighborhood.) In the dead of night, you can get anything from soup to *steak frites.* You'll also be surprised at the clientele.

Take a taxi back to the Paramount.

Midtown Jazz

Michael's Pub (*211 East 55th Street between Second and Third Avenues; 212–758–2272*) *is not particularly convenient for this downtown-based itinerary. But if you have the time, it's a great place to listen to music. If you are in New York City on a Monday night, Woody Allen may be playing his clarinet.*

DAY THREE

Sleep late. When you finally get up, treat yourself to a tour of Harlem, home for almost a century to most of America's great jazz musicians. (See "Harlem Dreams," page 233, for details.) Be sure to have lunch at Sylvia's. It's the best way to end your jazzy—and romantic—weekend.

FOR MORE ROMANCE

The Academy Award-winning documentary, *A Great Day in Harlem,* depicts the day in 1958 when famed photographer Art Kane managed to pull together about 100 jazz greats for a photo for *Esquire* magazine. They gathered on 126th Street in Harlem. Never before had so many famous jazz musicians been together in one place. The film is available on video. Rent it after your trip, cuddle up, and relive your hot days and nights in New York.

ITINERARY 12
One day and one night

FIREWORKS!

*T*he Fourth of July is America's birthday. It celebrates the day the Founding Fathers signed the Declaration of Independence, declaring their release from Britain's rule. For most Americans, it also connotes picnics, swimming, fireworks—and a strong feeling of security, excitement, and love. Why not celebrate Independence Day with a little *inter*dependence, lolling on a boat in New York's historic harbor and watching fantastic fireworks with someone you love?

Practical notes: Both the South Street Seaport and the activities surrounding the Fourth of July are very popular. Be sure to book well ahead of time, both for your hotel, your lunch, and for your dinner aboard the ship.

If the Seaport Inn is booked, try **Manhattan Seaport Suites** (129 Front Street; 800–427–1788; 212–742–0003; fax: 212–742–0124; studio suite: $195 per night; deluxe one-bedroom suite: $235 per night). This is a European-style apartment hotel; each room has its own kitchenette. While not particularly romantic, it is conveniently located to the Seaport, and is safe, clean, and convenient.

MORNING

Check into the **Best Western Seaport Inn** (33 Peck Slip; 800–HOTEL–NY or 212–766–6600; $99–$155 per night). You won't be able to get into your room before 1:00

Romance at a Glance

♥ *Stay at Best Western Seaport Inn, 800–HOTEL–NY or (212) 766–6600.*

♥ *Explore the South Street Seaport Historic District, New York's original historic port, now restored.*

♥ *Lunch at the River Cafe, one of New York's most beautiful spots.*

♥ *Watch the fireworks from aboard a launch in New York's harbor.*

P.M. but you can leave your bags at the hotel. The Seaport Inn is not a particularly deluxe hotel, but it makes up for what it lacks in luxury with its idyllic location and its quiet, unpretentious charm. The Inn is located in a beautifully restored nineteenth-century building at the heart of the revitalized South Street Seaport. Every room has all modern amenities, including a refrigerator, safe, and personal hairdryer. Some rooms have a whirlpool or steambath. Once you have checked in, begin to explore the **South Street Seaport Historic District**. Walk one block south of your Inn, and you'll be there.

The South Street Seaport is the largest concentration of early commercial buildings surviving in New York City. Now a national historic district that covers an 11-block area near the East River piers south of Brooklyn Bridge, these Georgian, Federal, and Greek Revival brick and granite buildings evoke the period when New York was the leading port in North America and these mercantile buildings were erected to serve the needs of expanding shipping interests. After years of neglect and deterioration, the buildings were restored and rehabilitated in the early 1980s by the Rouse Corporation, the same architectural group that revived Baltimore's seaport and Boston's Quincy Market.

The Seaport is buzzing with activity year-round—and never more so than over the Independence Day weekend. Performance artists, jugglers, competitive in-line skaters, dancers, singers, acrobats—you name it—they are all here. Also of interest are the scores of shops and museums.

Start at **Schermerhorn Row**, located in the heart of the seaport on the south side of Fulton Street. This block of buildings forms the architectural centerpiece of the Seaport and houses the **Museum Visitor's Center**. Founded in 1967, the South Street Seaport Museum celebrates old New York and describes South Street when it was known as the "Street of Ships." At the Visitor's Center, you can find maps and buy tickets to ships, tours, and exhibits.

You may want to take a guided tour, but if you choose to browse through the seaport on your own, don't miss the **Fulton Market Building**, across the plaza from the Visitor's Center. This building, which was redesigned to look like New York City food markets of the nineteenth century, still houses the Fulton Fish Market on the east side and a modern food market on the west end. The upper floors of the Fulton Market feature shops, two restaurants, and a small craft museum. After you've explored the Market building, head over to Pier 17 Pavilion, modeled after the great recreation piers of old New York. Its three floors are filled with shops, food stores, pushcarts, and restaurants.

AFTERNOON

Lunch

If you're caught up in the excitement of the Seaport and just want to catch a quick bite, you'll see scores of places, both with outdoor seating (or with tables overlooking the cobblestoned streets of the Seaport) or inside the Fulton Market Building or Pier 17. It will be crowded, however, and therefore not very intimate. Try **Gianni's** (15 Fulton Street; 212–608–7399; moderate), which serves Northern Italian dishes, many of which, not surprisingly, are centered on seafood. Best of all, Gianni's offers seating that is ideal for people-watching. For something a bit less elegant, try **Fulton Street Cafe** (Fulton Street in

the Market Building; inexpensive), which features sandwiches, salads, and more great people-watching.

You may want to find a quieter place to just be together, but you'll have to plan a bit to do so. My suggestion: Have a *late* lunch at the **River Cafe** (1 Water Street, Brooklyn Bridge; 718–522–5200; expensive). The most efficient way to get there would be to swim (just look across the East River: The River Cafe sits on a barge at the base of the Brooklyn Bridge on the Brooklyn side), but, of course, that's out of the question. You could also take a subway, but you'll have to walk miles on both sides of the bridge to make your connections. I suggest you take a taxi, which will cost about $5.

Be sure you book reservations at the Cafe well in advance; plan to get there about 1:30 P.M. Since the earlier diners have cleared, you can ask for a window seat and linger over a delicious lunch, a bottle of good wine, and each other. The Cafe offers a seasonal menu, and I suggest anything with fish. Walk back to the Seaport by way of the Brooklyn Bridge. (See page 215 for directions to the Bridge entrance.)

⚬⚭⚬

It takes about an hour to walk across the Bridge and make your way back to the Seaport. You may also be thirsty, so stop for a quick beer or soda at the **North Star Pub** located in the same complex with the Visitor's Center. This real English pub (and like British pubs, it's "standing room only") is one of the most popular in the Seaport. Then head back to the Seaport Inn to dress for dinner.

EVENING

It probably won't surprise you to learn that on the Fourth of July evening, the harbor begins to teem with boats of every size, shape, and color. Even if you know nothing about boating, you will definitely want to join the party. And you'll have many choices.

For a full evening's entertainment, including dinner, dancing, and watching the fireworks, go for **World Yacht Cruises** (Pier 81, West 41st Street at the Hudson River; 212–630–8100). Reservations must be made well in advance and charged to a major credit card which must be shown when picking up boarding passes. Cruises depart nightly at 7:00 P.M. The cost is $62 per person Sunday through Friday and $75 on Saturday for dinner and dancing. For just the cruise and dancing (no dinner), you pay $25 each. Jackets are required for men; patrons tend to dress up. Take a taxi to and from the Seaport.

The best place to sit on the yacht is on the upper level—but the lower level isn't bad either. Live music for dancing begins the moment the boat leaves the dock and continues throughout the evening. You can nibble at dinner, dance cheek to cheek, or escape the dance floor for a few private minutes out on the deck. The sophisticated menu offers such delights as roulade of guinea hen stuffed with wild mushrooms, chicken supreme served with cheese sauce, and a nice variety of pastas with fish or vegetable sauces. The ship glides down the Hudson River, around the tip of Manhattan, under the Brooklyn Bridge, and up the East River. Then it turns around and heads into the harbor for a close-up view of the Statue of Liberty. Last, it returns to Pier 81. (Take a taxi to and from the pier.)

Another choice for a romantic way to view the fireworks is from **The** *Petrel* (212–825–1976), which embarks from the south end of Battery Park. The fare is $25 per person for a two-hour sail; reservations and advance payment are required. This handsome launch is a magnificent teak and mahogany sailboat built in 1938. The notion of sailing under billowing sails around Manhattan harbor is utterly thrilling and romantically reminiscent of the experience of the eighteenth–century sailors who once made New York City's harbor famous. The *Petrel* accommodates about thirty-five passengers, so alas you won't be entirely alone. But I dare say, you won't mind.

Still another option is a sail aboard the schooner **Pioneer** (Pier 17, South Street Seaport; 212–748–8786; $16), the historic ship owned and operated by the Seaport Museum. The *Pioneer* offers special Fourth of July cruises beginning at 8:00 P.M. just in time for the show.

Many other commercial ferries and cruise ships are available at Pier 17 at the Seaport. If the World Yacht cruises, the *Petrel,* or the *Pioneer* are fully booked, you'll have no trouble finding another way to watch the fabulous fireworks from the water's edge. The best vantage point is from the FDR Drive, which closes to traffic for several hours before sunset. This is hardly the most romantic venue, but you'll get a good view. For other viewing tips, check the newspaper or call Macy's (212–695–4400), which sponsors the display.

If you've selected one of the cruises that does not serve dinner, you may need some fortification after the big show. (Even if you have had dinner, you still should follow this plan.) If you're starting from the Seaport walk west across Fulton Street to Church Street and then two blocks south to the World Trade Center. (If you're coming from one of the other launches, ask a taxi driver to drop you at the World Trade Center.) Take the elevator to the top of 1 World Trade Center, and then ask for a table near the window in the bar—known modestly as **The Greatest Bar on Earth** (1 World Trade Center, 107th Floor; 212–938–1111.) Not only is this in fact, "the greatest bar on earth," it's the greatest *view* on earth! And not only is the view breathtaking, but the food is spectacular, too. If you have not had dinner, share some marvelous hors d'oeuvres. If you have already eaten dinner, just order some old-fashioned port, and enjoy the view.

Happy Birthday, America!

More Fireworks

Bring along—or buy at one of the many shops in the Market—a dozen scented votive candles. Take them back to your room, and then, after your evening celebrating America's birthday, light all your candles in your room and create your own fireworks amid their warm glow.

FOR MORE ROMANCE

The Fourth of July weekend, which is usually a three- or four-day holiday, is a terrific time to visit Manhattan. Although you've undoubtedly caught a few glimpses of the Statue of Liberty, Ellis Island, and historic lower Manhattan during your forays into New York harbor, visiting them at closer range is also a must.

If you are staying for three or four days, be sure to take a side trip to Brooklyn Heights. (See "Romance? In Brooklyn? Who Knew?" on page 205 for more details).

FRENCH KISS

I suspect that most people, when asked to name the most romantic city in the world, would instantly say Paris. New Yorkers aren't really defensive about that judgment, but they are quick to point out that almost everything that is admirable about Paris—marvelous cuisine, spectacular art, world-class shops, an urban river view, and fascinating street life—can also be found in New York.

Okay, so New York may not be as beautiful as Paris, the City of Light, but where Paris has elegance, New York has electricity; where Paris has refinement, New York has verve. Still, if it's a "Paris state of mind" that you crave, New York is big-hearted enough to accommodate you—with first-class French hotels, restaurants, art, and shopping.

This is a weekend for Francophiles—especially those folks who love France but can't fly to Paris at the moment. I believe you'll be astonished at all the Parisian delights to be found in Manhattan. But even if you don't feel like you're in Paris, I guarantee that you will find *amour* during your days and nights in the "City of *Electric* Light."

Practical notes: When I planned this itinerary, I thought of it as a summer holiday to celebrate Bastille Day (July 14). The fact is, you could have a "French Kiss" weekend in New York any time of year.

I must confess that the French peasants storming the Bastille would never have been able to indulge in this itinerary: It is extremely expensive. The Hotel Plaza Athenée is very special, but if it is a bit beyond your means right now, you will most likely be quite content at the Hotel Elysée.

DAY ONE: EVENING

If it's within your budget, stay at the **Hotel Plaza Athenée** (37 East 64th Street; 212–734–9100; $284–$395 per night for a double; $590–$900 per night for a suite). Hotel Plaza Athenée, sister hotel to Paris's Hotel Plaza Athenée and the venerable Georges V, has won many awards and is considered one of the best hotels in New York—in fact, in the world. It is also one of the most romantic, both in location and ambience. Situated on a quiet, residential street, it offers luxe eighteenth-century decor. You will think you're in Paris!

Elegant both inside and outside, the Plaza Athenée is a relatively small hotel with only 153 rooms, including thirty-six suites. (Some of the deluxe suites feature terraces and solariums; request one of these so that you can enjoy intimate midnight cocktails overlooking Manhattan or a delightful terrace breakfast.) All the rooms are beautifully decorated with luxurious carpeting and rich fabrics. Most rooms feature individual pantries, and all have every necessity.

For those readers of more modest means, I recommend the less expensive **Hotel Elysée** (60 East 54th Street; 212–753–1066; fax: 212–980–9278; standard room, $245 per day; suites, $275 to $375 per day). Of all the hotels I researched for this book, the Elysée was my personal favorite. (That's partly because I am not a millionairess and partly because the Elysée also has an appealing literary tradition, having served over the years as home to Tennessee Williams and other writers—as well as celebrities like Ava Gardner, Vladimir Horowitz, and Dame Margot Fonteyn.) Not only does the Hotel Elysée exude discreet European style but its French country decor helps to create a quiet elegance that is, at once, warm and sophisticated. It's also a very friendly place, serving afternoon tea daily in the second-floor sitting room—and wine and cheese from 5:00 to 8:00 P.M.

Dinner

After you've settled into your room, take a taxi or, if the weather is fine, walk south on Madison or Fifth Avenue to **Lespinasse** (in the St. Regis Hotel; 2 East 55th Street; very expensive). In the introduction to this book, I stated that I searched hard for restaurants that offered both romance and culinary excellence. Lespinasse is without question one that delivers both. First, the decor is magnificent: high ceilings, beautiful murals, plush carpeting, and widely spaced tables. Second, the service is impeccable.

But the menu, which chef Gray Kunz changes with the seasons, is more dazzling than the decor, and for several years, Lespinasse has enjoyed four-star status from the *New York Times* and other arbiters of the cuisine of Gotham. The menu focuses on the French tradition but has many Asian elements. For example, you might try rack of lamb on a curried eggplant tart with carrot emulsion, seared arctic char with a fricassee of shiitakes, ramps, and pickled daikons, or crisp rice cake with saffron-yogurt emulsion. It also offers a vegetarian tasting menu along with a more conventional chef's tasting menu. The tasting menus are $105 per person—this price seems astronomical even by New York standards, but it's worth every penny. Desserts are equally as delicious as the main courses, ranging from a traditional chocolate soufflé with raspberry coulis to quince mille-feuille with lemon-buttermilk ice cream.

⌀⌀

You'll want to linger over dinner. At Lespinasse, dining is a rather theatrical experience, even for jaded New Yorkers. When you feel ready to move on, take a taxi uptown and catch the late show at **Iridium** (44 West 63rd Street; 212–582–2121; moderate to expensive), a trendy jazz club opposite Lincoln Center. (While you're near Lincoln Center, be sure to stop to admire the beautifully lit Chagall paintings that you can see from the plaza in front of the Metropolitan Opera House. Chagall paintings also decorate L'Opéra in Paris). The decor at Iridium is ultramodern, and the clientele is ultra-chic and ultra-European. While not intimate, it features great jazz and a taste of New York at its most cosmopolitan.

After the show, catch a taxi back to your hotel.

DAY TWO: MORNING

When you awaken, luxuriate in your room a while by ordering breakfast from room service. Then prepare to *shop*.

You wouldn't go to Paris without spending a morning perusing the shops, and this is no less true in New York. New York offers many of the choicest of Parisian designers, including **Chanel** (5 East 57th Street, between Fifth and Madison; 212–355–5050), which has wonderful accessories like scarves and gold-and-pearl classic earrings; **Hermès** (11 East 57th Street; 212–751–3181), especially for its signature scarves and ties; **Yves St. Laurent Femme** (855 Madison Avenue; 212–988–3821) and **Yves St. Laurent Homme** (859 Madison Avenue; 212–517–7400), which offers some of the choicest clothing in the world; and **Givenchy** (954 Madison Avenue at 75th Street; 212–772–1040) for gorgeous dresses and accessories.

If you're looking for crystal, china, silver, or jewelry, there's **Baccarat** (625 Madison Avenue between 58th and 59th Streets; 212–826–4100), where you can buy exquisite wine

Some of my favorite French restaurants in New York City have proven to be particularly romantic as well as delicious. In addition to those already mentioned in this itinerary, consider: Lutèce, La Caravelle, Raoul's, Provence, La Grenouille, and La Luncheonette.

My very favorite French restaurant and, to my mind, the most romantic, is Bouley—and it is closed. Chef/owner David Bouley is building an even grander restaurant (and cooking school) near his original Duane Street location. He's also involved in the renovation of the Russian Tea Room with Warner LeRoy, owner of Tavern on the Green. In a funny way, waiting for Bouley's reopening is the most romantic of notions—that is, if you agree that romance includes the idea of ineffable longing. I had the most memorable meals of my life at the original Bouley, and I long to return. Alas, it will never happen. In any case, the new Bouley is sure to be a remarkable restaurant, and if it has debuted by the time you read this, don't miss it.

goblets that range from $60 to $2,500 a stem, and **Lalique** (680 Madison Avenue between 61st and 62nd Streets). Lalique started out as a jewelry designer, but when he was asked by Coty to create a bottle for their scent, he became a glassmaker.

Christofle (680 Madison Avenue at 62nd Street; 212–308–9390), the premier French silversmith since 1830, created the exclusive silverware used by Louis Philippe (emperor from 1830 to 1840) and French aristocrats. Known for its timeless, sophisticated designs, the firm's New York base reflects its reputation. As Christofle says, it is French *"couture pour la table."* Stop also at **D. Porthault** (18 East 69th Street between Fifth and Madison Avenues; 212–688–1660). Inspired by the Impressionist painters, Madelaine Porthault began in 1925 to silk-screen lush floral designs onto bed linens. The store occupies a landmark town house just off Madison Avenue. All are 100% cotton and are woven in the firm's factories in France.

If serious art is your pleasure, visit the **Wildenstein Galleries** (19 East 64th Street; 212–879–0500). This five-story town house, located very near your hotel, was constructed especially for gallery use. Its elegant architecture and decor includes a crystal chandelier, grand staircase, parquet floors, and Louis XV consoles topped with vases of fresh flowers. Together these details set off the very serious and very expensive French masterpieces that are for sale here.

Lunch

When you've had your fill of shopping, take time for lunch. One of my favorite French restaurants—especially for lunch—is **La Côte Basque** (60 West 55th Street; 212–688–6525; prix fixe, expensive). For years, La Côte Basque was on East 55th Street; about two years ago, it moved a block west. La Côte Basque regulars worried that much of the luxurious yet comfortable charm of the old restaurant would be lost. Not so. Like an old friend, it's nearly unchanged. Every element—most particularly the wonderful Basque murals—remains as it always was, and so does the wonderful classic French menu. La Côte Basque is everything a French interlude should be, regardless of whether you're in New York or Paris.

DAY TWO: AFTERNOON

Just as you wouldn't dream of going to Paris without venturing to the Left Bank, you shouldn't come for a weekend in Manhattan without visiting New York's bohemian enclaves: Greenwich Village and SoHo.

Flag down a taxi and ask the cabbie to drop you at the Washington Square arch. If you're interested in the Village of writer Jack Kerouac, painter Robert Rauschenberg, and choreographer Merce Cunningham (by the way, Merce still lives on Bethune Street; if you stop in the local greenmarket, you just may meet him), head west. (See "What Ever Happened to Tio

Pepe's," page 177, for details.) If you want to mingle among young artists in SoHo, head south through the park. (See "X–Rated," page 189 for details.)

Spend the afternoon strolling through the streets (like Paris, New York is a city for walking), shopping in the hundreds of fascinating shops, and exploring the various galleries. If you want to rest and revive yourselves with an espresso or a café au lait, stop in at **Le Gamin Cafe** (50 MacDougal Street between West Houston and Prince Streets; 212–254–4678). Le Gamin is perhaps the most French cafe in New York. It opens at 8:00 A.M., serves typical French cafe fare, and allows patrons to sit for hours. (You can even smoke cigarettes; in fact, you can smoke a Gauloises if you so desire.)

DAY TWO: EVENING

Dinner

Have dinner at one of downtown's most sophisticated French restaurants, **Chanterelle** (2 Harrison Street, between Greenwich and Hudson Streets; 212–966–9690; very expensive; reserve at least one month in advance). The fact is, by any account—French or not—Karen and David Waltuck's Chanterelle is not to be missed. The decor is a bit on the austere side, but the food is incredible. The menu changes regularly, but some of the delights include tomato consommé over Louisiana shrimp with caviar, steamed squash blossoms filled with chicken and wild mushrooms, sauteed soft-shell crabs with ginger and tomato, pan-roasted striped bass with a sweet corn coulis. The desserts are delicious, but even better is the delectable cheese course.

෴

Just as Paris has *les bateaux-mouches,* New York has World Yacht Cruises. As in Paris, you'll glide down the city's famous river; in New York, it's the Hudson and a bit of the East River. The boat passes the Statue of Liberty and the Brooklyn Bridge, and then it circles back to the

> *If at some point you find yourself near the New York Public Library at 42nd and Fifth, stroll behind the large library building and rest for a few minutes in Bryant Park. Few places in New York are more like Paris than the refurbished Bryant Park. With the overhanging trees, the darling Parisian cafe chairs, and the lively ambience, you'll think you're in the Tuilleries or perhaps an intimate corner of Luxembourg Gardens.*

pier. Every bit as romantic as *les bateaux-mouches*, this is a special way to appreciate New York. You can dine aboard ship or just go for the cruise and dancing.

Reservations for **World Yacht Cruises** (Pier 81, West 41st Street at the Hudson River; 212–630–8100) must be made in advance and charged to a major credit card that must be shown when picking up boarding passes. Cruises depart nightly throughout the year at 7:00 P.M.

If an evening on the water doesn't appeal to you, walk just two blocks west of Chanterelle to the Hudson River Esplanade. Stroll south, along the river, of course, to the World Trade Center and have a drink at The Greatest Bar on Earth atop Number 1. By now, you'll probably be ready to return to the Plaza Athenée. Hail a taxi in front of the Vista Hotel at the bottom of the World Trade Center to take you back to your hotel.

DAY THREE: MORNING

Brunch

You can't stay at the Hotel Plaza Athenée without enjoying brunch at the hotel's celebrated restaurant, **La Régence**. Brunch at La Régence has been rated the Best Brunch in New York. For lunch and dinner as well, La Régence is considered one of New York's premier French restaurants, featuring the acclaimed cuisine of chef Marcel Agnez. Like the rest of the hotel, La Régence is beautifully decorated. Its twelve-foot-high vaulted ceiling, handwoven carpets, hand-painted walls and ceilings, and eighteenth-century French appointments create a marvelously romantic setting.

You can either start your brunch with the appetizer buffet or make the appetizers your entire meal. The buffet features steamed lobster, other seafood, a variety of salads, and several pâtés. If you prefer a proper entree after the appetizers, you can select such dishes as rack of veal with mustard sauce, fettuccine with seafood, apples, and red pepper, or eggs Benedict.

⋐⋙⋑

The Plaza Athenée is located in the heart of **New York's Museum Mile**. Spend the rest of Sunday exploring some of them. (See "Art for Lovers," page 67, for details.) Most importantly, visit the **Metropolitan Museum of Art** at 82nd and Fifth Avenue (if weather permits, stroll up Fifth Avenue next to Central Park) and explore the French Impressionist collection. You'll be impressed!

Bonne chance!

FOR MORE ROMANCE

Many people who visit Paris take a day to venture outside the city to the smaller city of Versailles and the palace built by Louis XIV. New York State's "palace" stands about 25 miles north of Manhattan along the Hudson River; it belonged to one of America's kings of commerce, John D. Rockefeller, who, incidentally, gave nearly $3 million to France in the 1920s, partly to restore the Versailles palace and park to its original splendor.

The Rockefeller estate is called **Kykuit**, and the loveliest way to get there is to take a day trip by boat. Call **NY Waterway Sightseeing Cruises** (800–533–3779) for reservations and details. Boats depart from Pier 78 at West 38th Street and Twelfth Avenue. The boat trip to Kykuit is almost as pleasurable as the tour of the estate. However, the unique Rockefeller mansion, its playhouse, its remarkable gardens decorated with museum-quality sculpture, and the art and antiques that fill the house are quite extraordinary. The experience is breathtaking—it's about as close to royalty as we republicans get.

ITINERARY 14
One afternoon and one evening

SCORIN'!

*T*aking a crowded subway train to a baseball game in the South Bronx or central Queens may not sound particularly romantic, but one of the best dates I ever had was at a night game at Yankee Stadium. My boyfriend at the time was a Boston Red Sox fan, and the Yankees and the Red Sox were vying for the pennant that year. My friend insisted on wearing his Red Sox cap, and I was certain a rabid Yankee fan would beat him up—(no one did). One truly memorable part of that night was that we were being treated to box seats, and while my boyfriend sat on one side of me, Norman Mailer sat on the other.

As you know, baseball games are the most American of American traditions and a baseball game in New York City is the most New York of New York traditions. But more, with the chants, the characters, the occasional brawls, the hot dogs, the organ music—it's fun! And to my mind, one of the most pivotal components of romance is laughter. This evening will provide its share—and more.

So go, enjoy yourself—and know that by the seventh-inning stretch you'll be in love—if not with your date, then with America's favorite pastime.

Practical notes: An outing to a baseball game must be planned between April and

Romance at a Glance
♥ *Attend a baseball game at Yankee Stadium or Shea Stadium.*
♥ *Have dinner at John's, an old-fashioned Italian restaurant.*
♥ *Have a nightcap at the Temple Bar.*

October when baseball is in season. If October arrives and either the Yankees or the Mets are in the pennant race or the World Series, tickets will be virtually impossible to get. For ticket information for the Mets, call **Shea Stadium** (718–507–TIXX); take the #7 subway to Shea Stadium. For ticket information for the Yankees, call **Yankee Stadium** (718–293–6000); take the #4, C, or D trains to Yankee Stadium.

Although I am a loyal Mets fan, if you are going to the ballpark for a sense of baseball history, I would recommend a Yankee game. Yankee Stadium, "the House that Ruth built," is one of the last of the old great ballparks in the United States. What's more, if George Steinbrenner has anything to say about it, the stadium's days may be numbered. If you have time, walk through Monument Park, where Yankee legends are commemorated.

You can decide to go to a game an hour or two before game time. Take the subway to the ballpark, and buy a ticket at the stadium. Bleacher tickets are very affordable; box seats are expensive, but they are usually sold out to season ticket holders and corporations.

It you don't know much about baseball, you should at least be aware that Yankee fans and Mets fans are two very different breeds. For starters, the "Bronx Bombers," as the Yankees are known, consider themselves to be the elite of baseball, and the fans are pretty snobby as well. On the other hand, Mets fans, many of whom are descendants of Brooklyn Dodger fans, are a bit more down-to-earth.

I'm assuming that one or both of you is a baseball fan, so I'll leave it to you to sort out the fine points of the game.

THE AFTERNOON

Take the subway to either Yankee or Shea Stadium. Don't worry about finding the stadium when you get to the end of the line. You'll be pulled along by the rowdy throngs. For this itinerary, I've planned an afternoon game so that you'll have time to have a real dinner afterwards. However, if, like my boyfriend, you consider a beer and a hot dog to be seductive fare, attend a night game.

If you've never been to a baseball game, ask your date—or your neighbors in the stands—for information. Diehard fans love to flaunt their knowledge. The Yankee fans may be slightly patronizing, but let them have their fun. Before the fourth inning, you'll have singled out your favorite players—and then you'll be hooked. For the sake of romance, give your date an enthusiastic hug whenever your favorite fielder makes a double play.

When the game is over, you'll be either elated or depressed. It doesn't matter—on your way out of the stadium you'll be pushed and shoved back to the subway entrance, so by the time you get on the train, you'll just be annoyed. Once aboard, you will probably have to stand all the way back to midtown, but you can take the opportunity to lean against each other as a buffer to the pressing crowd.

THE EVENING

Dinner

Make your way by subway down to the Union Square station. (It will probably take close to an hour, regardless of which stadium you've left.) When you come out of the station, walk south to 12th Street and east to Second Avenue. Just east of Second is **John's of 12th Street** (302 East 12th Street; 212-475-9531; moderate), one of the oldest Italian restaurants (1908) in the city and one of the most comfortable and friendly. Although the decor is simple (note the candles in the Chianti bottles in the back dining room), the food is bountiful, delicious, and inexpensive. If you indulged in hot dogs at the game, you may want simply to share a pasta salad. Even if you are starving, the portions are enormous. Somehow, like the baseball game, this family-style restaurant is as romantic as it is down-to-earth.

༺ৡৡৡ༻

If you aren't exhausted—or just can't bear to end this happy day—go for a nightcap at the Temple Bar. You'll have to walk a few blocks, but you'll probably feel like a stroll after sitting at the game and eating all that pasta. **The Temple Bar** (332 Lafayette Street at Bleecker Street) is about 10 blocks south and 2 blocks west of John's. Sophisticated and hip without being precious, it's also a serious—and sexy—drinking bar. So, if you can handle it, lift a glass to Ruth and DiMaggio—and to each other.

FOR MORE ROMANCE

If your romance develops with enthusiasm, you may want to take a weekend and go to the Baseball Hall of Fame in Cooperstown, New York. Not only is Cooperstown one of the prettiest Victorian towns in America, the drive through the Catskill Mountains is enchanting.

ITINERARY 15
Three days and two nights

LA DOLCE VITA

*W*hen we try to recall the original settlers of New York City, most of us think of the Dutch, forgetting that an Italian, Giovanni da Verrazano, was actually the first explorer to arrive in New York harbor in 1524. (The Verrazano Narrows Bridge was named for him.) From the beginning, natives of Italy have been a primary ingredient in New York's savory melting pot. At first the Italian population was small but included such well-known figures as Lorenzo da Ponte, who wrote the librettos for several of Mozart's operas, and Giuseppe Garibaldi, the great Italian political leader. Between 1880 and 1910 more than two million Italians moved to the United States, and today New York City is still home to the highest concentration of people of Italian descent in the country.

Anyone who appreciates all the marvelous qualities of the Italian way of life and the contributions of Italian-Americans to the culture of the United States—brilliant cuisine, beautiful music, incredible art and literature—will enjoy this itinerary. And exploring New York from an Italian point of view is one of the most romantic ways to get to know the city.

Practical notes: Like the other ethnic itineraries in this book, much of the romance of Little Italy is nostalgic. Visiting here means catching a glimpse of a tiny, crooked street that exudes just a whisper of what life must have been like for beloved ancestors decades ago. If you are of Italian descent, you may learn something here—like why baking *pizzelles* at Christmas is a must, or whether or not Angelo's meatballs come even close to the ones your grandmother used to make.

For the sake of romance, I've suggested a hotel that is located in uptown Manhattan, quite far from the Italian enclaves. In Little Italy, the hotels reflect little or nothing of Italian culture, but if you would rather stay nearer the neighborhood, try the **Holiday Inn Downtown** (138 Lafayette Street; 212–966–8898; doubles: $125–$175 per night). The rooms are clean and well-appointed but not particularly romantic; add some Italian romance of your own with a bottle of Barolo or Pinot Grigio, some cheese, bread, and fresh fruit. Some Vivaldi, Verdi, or even some Tony Bennett or Frank Sinatra on tape or CD may add some atmosphere as well.

Romance at a Glance

♥ *Stay at The Mayfair (212) 288–1088.*

♥ *Dine at several of New York's favorite Italian restaurants, both classic and trendy.*

♥ *Tour historic Little Italy and Italian Greenwich Village.*

♥ *Enjoy a classic Italian opera.*

♥ *Tour New York harbor and Ellis Island.*

Little Italy is a fascinating area to explore any time of year, but it is at its most festive in September during the Feast of San Gennaro, in mid-October over the long Columbus Day weekend, or in early summer when Greenwich Village celebrates its *Festes Italianas.* At Christmastime, Little Italy is decorated within an inch of its life, making the holiday season a delightful time to visit. Whenever you decide to come, be sure to bring comfortable shoes for this itinerary, since you'll be doing a fair amount of walking.

DAY ONE: Evening

As soon as you arrive at **The Mayfair** (610 Park Avenue at 65th Street; 212–288–0800 or 800–223–0542; fax: 212–737–0538; rooms, $275–$410; suites, $440–$1,700; special weekend rates and packages available), you'll immediately realize that although this lovely hotel bears a decidedly Anglo-Saxon name, it has the luxurious feeling of a Roman villa. (In part, that may be due to the fact that the general manager, Dario Mariotti, is of Italian descent.)

The lobby is lined with Palladian-style arches and filled with lush carpets, antique furnishings, and huge bouquets of fresh flowers. The Lobby Lounge is incredibly romantic, an ideal place to enjoy a quiet breakfast, afternoon tea, or cocktails. The rooms are all decorated in soft, yet luxurious buff and coral tones, against luxe furnishings. Many of the rooms have working fireplaces; ask for one of these when you book your hotel. Of course, all the rooms have the necessary modern amenities like multiple telephone lines and cable television. In addition, the Mayfair offers a state-of-the-art fitness center. If you wish, you can even have exercise machines brought to your room.

The Mayfair prides itself on its impeccable European-style service. The white-gloved elevator operators are discreet, friendly, multilingual, and at your service twenty-four hours a day. Umbrellas, newspapers, and shoeshines are all thoughtfully provided daily, and the hotel even offers a special "Pillow Bank," with a selection of twelve different pillow types to suit your specific need. They even supply chicken soup for any guest with a cold. (Let's hope that neither of you need this pampering!)

Dinner

After you've settled yourselves in your room, head out for a marvelous Italian dinner at one of the most romantic Italian restaurants in New York: **Felidia** (243 East 58th Street; 212–758–1479; expensive.) From the Mayfair, you can easily walk to Felidia. (Turn south on Park Avenue and then east on 58th Street. It should take you about fifteen minutes.)

Felidia is located in a charming brownstone, and its atmosphere is intimate, a bit rustic (with rows of copper pots, open wine racks, and brick walls), yet subtle and elegant. Felidia offers traditional Italian regional fare, but the dishes tend to be predominantly Northern Italian, highlighting the flavors of Venice and Trieste. Try any of their fresh pastas or risottos, or for a special treat, try the *gnocchi al' Ortolana*. Felidia also boasts a marvelous wine list, and at times offers "tasting menus" featuring a particular wine or port. You'll be transported.

⋙⋘

Stroll back from dinner through the streets of the lovely East Side of Manhattan to the Mayfair. Just for the fun of it—it has nothing to do with being Italian *except* that it is fun—stop and take a turn on the **Roosevelt Island Aerial Tramway** (Tramplaza, 59th Street and Second Avenue; 212–832–4543; every fifteen minutes from 6:00 A.M. until after midnight; $1.40 per person each way). This adorable little hanging car looks a bit like a ski gondola and travels from Manhattan to Roosevelt Island, a planned community rather fascinating in its own right. You can ride, snuggled up together, for about five minutes over the East River, witnessing the spectacular New York skyline from the little red cabin, then turn around and come back.

Have a nightcap in the Lobby Lounge, and then retire to your beautiful room.

DAY TWO: MORNING

Start your day with a very light breakfast. (I'm afraid you'll be eating frequently during your tour through Little Italy—or at least you'll want to.) Then, as early as possible, go downtown to Little Italy, the place where millions of Italian immigrants began their lives in America. Take a taxi or take the Lexington Avenue IRT subway (#4, 5, or 6) from 59th Street to Chambers Street/Brooklyn Bridge.

Today, Little Italy is bounded to the north by Houston Street, to the east by Mulberry Street, to the south by Canal Street, and to the west by Broadway. For this walking tour, however, begin at the corner of **Mulberry and Worth Streets**. (When you exit the subway,

check one of the many maps posted near the station or ask directions to Worth and Mulberry, which is just a few minutes walk from the subway station.) As you face north from the corner, you will see a park on your left called **Columbus Park**, which may be the only visible hint that you are in an Italian area—or that this was once an Italian neighborhood. Today, this section is the heart of Chinatown, which will be very visible.

Actually, this area was once called **Five Points**, named for the intersection of five streets: Mulberry Street, Anthony (now Worth) Street, Cross (now Park) Street, Orange (now Baxter) Street, and Little Water Street, which no longer exists. Originally the area was a swamp, but it was filled in 1808, creating a posh neighborhood for rich New Yorkers briefly known as Paradise Square.

By 1820, however, Paradise Square had begun to sink and become foul-smelling. The lovely homes crumbled, and the prosperous residents moved uptown, leaving the decaying houses and taverns to sailors, prostitutes, and, of course, the very poor. For decades during the nineteenth century Five Points was the most disreputable slum in New York. By the 1890s, it was overrun by Irish and Italian gangs led by former prizefighter Paul Kelly (born

Paolo Antonio Vaccarelli), Al Capone, and Lucky Luciano, and others who later became prominent in organized crime. Today, this area is known as Foley Square and forms the heart of the city's legal and political activity.

As you make your way north along Mulberry Street, you'll see many civic buildings as well as Chinese shops and restaurants. (For the past century, Chinatown has been centered on Mott and Mulberry Streets below Canal while Little Italy has centered on Mulberry Street north of Canal.) As soon as you cross Canal, you'll quickly realize that you've come into the Italian neighborhood. The Chinese restaurants instantly disappear, and instead you'll see such Italian delights as Sambucca's Cafe, Luna, and La Bella Ferraro.

Make your way up Mulberry Street. One of the first landmarks you'll come to is the rear entrance to the **Precious Blood National Shrine of San Gennaro**. The church is actually located on Baxter Street, and it is worth the short walk around the block to take a closer look inside this lovely shrine. Every September the annual San Gennaro Festival is held in honor of this patron saint of Naples. Mulberry Street from Columbus Square to Spring Street is strewn with bright lights and lined with vendors selling Italian sausages, pizza, and zeppole.

Over the past fifteen years, Little Italy has undergone an incredible transformation, changing from a rather down-at-the-heels neighborhood to a trendy adjunct to neighboring SoHo. The facades of many of the restaurants have been modernized, but they remain much the same. You may recognize **Umberto's Clam House** (129 Mulberry Street) where in 1972 the organized-crime figure Joey Gallo was shot to death during a family dinner in a famous gangland shoot-out. Or, if you lived in New York when you were a kid, you'll no doubt recognize **Puglia's** (189 Hester), still a great place for a "cheap date."

At the corner of Grand and Mulberry, be sure to shop for some of the best Italian foodstuffs in the city. On that corner alone, you'll find **The Italian Food Center** (186 Grand), **Alleva Dairy** (188 Grand) and **Piemonte Home Made Ravioli, Inc.** (190

Grand). You'll find a delectable array of meats, sausages, cheeses, and pastas. And, of course, don't miss **Ferrara's** (195 Grand Street), which has been serving the best cappuccinos and pastries for more than 100 years. It has been "glitzed" up a bit, but you may want to stop for a bite.

On the block between Grand and Broome, you'll see several other favorite restaurants like **Taormino's** (147 Mulberry), **Paolucci's** (149 Mulberry), and **Angelo's** (146 Mulberry). You may want to take a quick side-trip to visit the **Parisi Bakery** (198 Mott Street), a venerable Manhattan Italian bakery. Near the corner of Mulberry and Broome, stop for a peek inside—and maybe a beer—at **Mare Chiaro** (176½ Mulberry). Mare Chiaro is one of the last of the old-fashioned neighborhood *bars* in Little Italy. While the other places appeal to tourists, Mare Chiaro is content to please the natives. Or, if you prefer something a bit more romantic, go up to the corner and stop for a cappuccino and pastry at **Caffe Roma** (385 Broome Street).

Like the Lower East Side and Chinatown, Little Italy was never really isolated from other ethnic neighborhoods (although, to a great extent, the various nationalities kept to themselves). While enjoying a cappuccino in Caffe Roma while I researched this book, I witnessed the true meaning of the phrase "melting pot": The Italian and Spanish waitresses at the cafe ordered a Chinese take-out lunch which was eventually delivered by a black man. In the late nineteenth- and early twentieth-centuries, these neighborhoods were predominantly Jewish and Irish with smaller Italian and Chinese populations. Today, the Chinese population is the largest ethnic group in the area, and large numbers of Spanish-speaking (mainly Puerto Rican) immigrants make this home as well. The numbers of Jewish and Italian residents, on the other hand, grow smaller every year.

When you arrive at the corner of Broome and Mulberry, walk east for two blocks to **Elizabeth Street**. On the northeast corner of Broome and Elizabeth, note the red brick building. Constructed as the **Knickerbocker Ice House** (324 Broome) in the early

twentieth century, it provided ice for individuals and businesses in the era before refrigeration. The term "iced" (that is, murdered) was coined here. Mobsters kept their victims on ice here until a safe disposal could be arranged.

Stroll north on Elizabeth Street, which lacks the touristy charms of Mulberry but perhaps better illustrates the true life-style of the early denizens of Little Italy. Along the west side of Elizabeth are the remains of several nineteenth-century tenements, typical of the sort of housing most immigrants had to inhabit. Walk north another block and note the fascinating building at **166 Elizabeth**, at the corner of Elizabeth and Kenmare Streets. The walls of this tenement building are adorned with sculptures of Roman goddesses, the work of skilled Italian stonecutters who lived in the neighborhood.

Lunch

If you haven't utterly spoiled your appetite with cappuccinos, pastries, and other Italian treats, stop for lunch at what is arguably the best pizzeria in New York City: **Lombardi's** (32 Spring Street, between Mott and Mulberry; moderate). Lombardi's is one of the oldest pizzerias in the city, and Mr. Lombardi, a descendant of the original owner, still runs the place. Recently, it has been revamped into a charming haunt and serves mouth-watering thin-crust, coal-oven pies that are delectably garlicky (you have to share). Try the "white" pizza with clams. Fabulous!

DAY TWO: Afternoon

After lunch, walk west on Spring, then turn north on Mott one block. Notice the 14th Ward Industrial School of the Children's Aid Society, a marvelous example of Victorian Gothic-style architecture that was built in 1889 to aid indigent children. This school instructed young Italian immigrant children in reading, writing, and arithmetic as well as mechanical arts, with the effort focusing on educating them in a trade.

Directly across the street is **Old St. Patrick's Cathedral and cemetery**. Built between 1809 and 1815 by Irish Catholics, it served as the main diocesan cathedral until the new St. Patrick's Cathedral on Fifth Avenue was completed in 1879. Originally, the church had a more elaborate Gothic architecture, but after a fire in 1868, it was restored more simply due to lack of funds. It is still quite lovely, and to my mind, the wall surrounding the cathedral is one of the most romantic edifices in Manhattan.

The fascinating, if rather disturbing, fact surrounding Old St. Patrick's Cathedral is that it was considered to be an Irish church, and Italians were not permitted to worship here. (Bitter fights, especially between Irish and Italian gangs, erupted around St. Patrick's.) Efforts to set up a Roman Catholic parish for Italians began as early as 1858, long before the largest immigration of Italians to New York. **The Church of St. Anthony of Padua** (163 Sullivan Street) was formed in 1866 by Franciscans of the Province of the Immaculate Conception, and its current Romanesque church was finally dedicated on June 10, 1888.

Walk west along Prince Street. You will leave what today is known as Little Italy as soon as you cross Lafayette Street; however, in the 1920s the Italian neighborhood occupied the entire region bounded to the north by West 4th Street, the east by the Bowery, the south by Five Points, and the west by the Hudson River, incorporating much of what is known today as Greenwich Village. Genoans, Calabrians, and Sicilians settled the older section, while Piedmontese, Tuscans, and Neapolitans settled in the Greenwich Village area.

Continue walking west along Prince Street. You'll be walking through SoHo. Before it became one of the choicest parts of Manhattan, this neighborhood housed many businesses involved in the garment industry. Italians gravitated to this neighborhood because many of them, like many of their Jewish neighbors, worked in the garment trade.

For a bit of nostalgia, be sure to stop at **Raffetto Ravioli** (144 West Houston Street; 212–777–1261), which features every kind of ravioli and pasta you could wish for and also sells the right sort of Arborio rice to make the perfect risotto. This still-popular shop has been a Village staple for decades.

When you get to West Broadway, turn north. As soon as you cross Houston Street, West Broadway becomes **La Guardia Place**, named after one of New York's most famous mayors—and most famous son of Italy—Fiorello La Guardia. Stop by and look at the charming statue of the "Little Flower," as La Guardia was known. (Also, notice the fabulous community garden on this block. It's not particularly Italian, but it's worth a look while you're here.)

Walk north into Washington Square, also once a swamp like Five Points. Check out the statue of Garibaldi, an important Italian freedom fighter, linger in the square to absorb its unique ambience, then exit at the southwest corner. Walk south on MacDougal Street, and turn right at Minetta Lane. (During Prohibition, these narrow alleys were lined with speakeasies that later became legitimate cabarets; today they are off-off Broadway playhouses.) When you emerge at Sixth Avenue (also called Avenue of the Americas), you'll be on Father Demo Square, entering the parish of the **Church of Our Lady of Pompeii** (25 Carmine at the corner of Bleecker), the center of the Greenwich Village Italian community. The church, which was founded in 1926, was the parish of Mother Francis Xavier Cabrini, America's first saint, who often prayed and worked with the poor here. The church also holds a *Festa Italiana* in June.

Walk along Bleecker and savor the many Italian food specialty shops, especially **Zitos Bakery** (259 Bleecker Street), **Faicco Pork Store** (260 Bleecker Street), and **Ottomanelli's**

Meat Market (281 Bleecker Street). For anyone who lives in the Village, Italian or not, these shops are mainstays and make life worth living. Stop to rest your feet at **Rocco's** (243 Bleecker Street) or **Bleecker Street Pastry** (245 Bleecker Street), both classic Village Italian cafes.

DAY TWO: EVENING

Dinner

No doubt, you've noticed that the streets of Manhattan, especially those in these neighborhoods, are peppered with Italian restaurants. Maybe you've seen a place you want to return to for dinner. If you haven't decided, you must now. Do you want an old-fashioned Italian restaurant that offers traditional Italian/American fare? Or do you want a 1990s chic Italian spot that mixes Italian gastronomic delights with some fancy modern touches? Do you want an expensive restaurant or a reasonably priced one? In any case I'm sure you want something relaxing and romantic—of course.

The very best Italian restaurant in the Village is, by all accounts, **Il Molino** (86 West 3rd Street between Thompson and Sullivan Streets; 212–673–3783; reservations required; expensive). The food at Il Molino is classic and exquisite, particularly their pastas. Their fettuccine Alfredo is absolutely sinful, and anything else you order is sure to please you. Although the tables are a bit close, the lights are low and the dining room is intimate.

For something classic but a bit less expensive, try any of the restaurants along Thompson or Sullivan Streets. I can't help but recommend my personal favorite of these: **The Grand Ticino** (223 Thompson Street, between Bleecker and 3rd Streets; 212–777–5922; moderate).

If you opt for something more trendy, you have some marvelous choices in the Village area. On the pricey side is **Barolo** (398 West Broadway between Broome and Spring Streets, 212–226–1102; expensive). In addition to an innovative Northern Italian menu (please try the spinach flan with creamed fontina and truffle paste), Barolo has one of the most beautiful—and romantic—courtyard gardens in the city. If it's a warm evening, Barolo is a must and worth the wait to get a garden table.

For a delightful chic-yet-warm atmosphere and quite delicious contemporary Tuscan fare, try **Savore** (200 Spring Street at the corner of Sullivan; 212–431–1212; moderate). The cuisine is light and creative, and the atmosphere is equally friendly and fresh.

My favorite Italian restaurant in the Village is the Il Cantinori (32 East 10th Street; 212-673-6044; expensive). It, too is Tuscan, exudes elegance in a casual way, and, to my mind, is one of the most romantic restaurants in New York. Oh, and the Tuscan fare is marvelous, too.

ᥱᥩᥢᥩᥢᥩ

After dinner, think seriously about going to the **Amato Opera Theater** (319 Bowery at 2nd Street; 212–228–8200. Reserve tickets in advance). For a very reasonable price, you can listen to Italian opera classics—Puccini, Rossini, Verdi—presented in a tiny, old-fashioned theater. It's not the Metropolitan Opera, but it's not meant to be. In fact, the Amato is probably much like the opera your ancestors enjoyed in precisely the same neighborhood.

After the opera, take a taxi back to the Mayfair. Relax in your room and reflect on the sights of Italian New York that you've just explored.

DAY THREE: MORNING

Sleep late, then order breakfast in your lovely room. When you finally rouse yourselves, head downtown again. The fact is, you can't have an Italian New York weekend without touring the **Statue of Liberty**, **Ellis Island**, and **New York Harbor**. (For details on the Statue of Liberty and Ellis Island, see page 160.)

Take a taxi or the Lexington Avenue subway (#4 or 5) to the Bowling Green stop. Head for Castle Clinton National Monument in Battery Park, where you'll buy your ticket for the ferry and the monuments. (Call 212–363–3200 for information.)

Ellis Island is the portal through which millions of Italians entered the United States.

FOR MORE ROMANCE

Of course, Italian culture—music, opera, literature, art, and cuisine—is one of the richest in the world, and New York City has benefited greatly from the fruits of that culture. To remind you of just one of these contributions, attend the Opera at Lincoln Center (see "Moonstruck" for details) or take an afternoon to explore the Renaissance rooms at the Metropolitan Museum of Art.

Autumn

GLITTERING LITERATI

*N*ew York City is the literary capital of the United States—and the book publishing capital of the world. Writers and editors flock to New York, at least for some part of their lives, to drown themselves in the urban poetry of Gotham. There's hardly a neighborhood in Manhattan (or the outer boroughs) that doesn't have a literary tale to tell. What's more, New York's literary history is not only broad but deep—that is to say, it's old. Almost from the moment the Dutch offered their trinkets to the Algonquins, New York City has had some form of literature.

You can't possibly explore all of New York's literary byways in one weekend. So instead of a novel, you'll have what I hope is a perfect short story—and a romantic one, at that. Edith Wharton, John Cheever, Anne Beatty, and hundreds of others would be pleased that you came along for the tour.

Practical notes: When is the best time to come to New York for a glittering literary holiday? Anytime, actually, but, in my opinion, New York is definitely at its literary finest in the autumn. Writers, and those who worship writers, get excited in the fall; it's kind of like going back to school. To add to the pleasures of this weekend, I suggest that you buy Marcia

Romance at a Glance

♥ *Stay at the historic Algonquin Hotel (212–840–6800).*

♥ *Explore the main branch of the New York Public Library; the Morgan Library, and some of New York's best bookstores.*

♥ *Tour Greenwich Village and other New York spots famous for their writers.*

♥ *Stroll through literary Central Park.*

♥ *Drink and dine at writers' haunts, including The White Horse Tavern and The Cedar Tavern.*

Leisner's wonderful book about literary New York. Entitled *Literary Neighborhoods of New York* (Washington and Philadelphia: Starrhill Press, 1989), it provides fascinating information on the famed novelists, playwrights, and other authors who lived and worked in Gotham.

DAY ONE: EVENING

For a literary weekend in New York, there is only one choice for a hotel: **The Algonquin** (59 West 44th Street; 212–840–6800; fax: 212–944–1419; double room, $240 per night; suites, $375–$550 per night). Anyone interested in American literary tradition knows about The Algonquin, made famous by writers Robert Benchley, Dorothy Parker, Robert Sherwood, and Alexander Woollcott, who in the 1920s formed the most famous lunch club of all time, The Algonquin Round Table. (Other members included Edna Ferber, George S. Kaufman, Heywood Broun, George Jean Nathan, and Marc Connelly.)

The Algonquin itself opened in November 1902 in the heart of what was then the chicest part of the city. (At the turn of the century, the neighborhood comprising the East and West 30s and 40s was the SoHo of its day, the place where fancy people lived and artists worked and played.) The most exclusive clubs—Harvard, Yale, and New York Yacht among them—lined 44th Street.

Compared to other hotels suggested in this book, The Algonquin is not the most luxurious. Although it was recently renovated and is certainly comfortable and offers every amenity, its great charm is its history—and its unique personality. Indeed, in 1994, it was declared by the *Historic Traveler* magazine to be one of the ten best historic hotels in America. To this day, it remains a favorite haunt of writers, playwrights, actors, and artists.

When you arrive, you may feel that you've stepped back in time. The Algonquin lobby is still the heart and soul of the hotel. It buzzes with excitement and activity, but it also has comfortable chairs and sofas artfully arranged to provide sites for intimate conversation. (If you like, you can have a chat with Matilda, the Algonquin cat, or any of the literary ghosts who hover around the place.) The Oriental carpeting, soft lights, warm oak paneling, and faintly down-at-the-heels antiques (the grandfather clock, the bells on the table) will make you feel as though you're walking into your great-grandmother's living room (before she had it done over). It's so very welcoming, comfortable, and *intelligent*. Pay attention to the framed drawings by James Thurber and Al Hirschfeld that decorate the rooms and halls, and enjoy the complimentary copies of *The New Yorker*.

Dinner

After you have settled in your room, have dinner in **The Rose Room** at the Algonquin Hotel (off the lobby; moderate). This was the room where those wits met daily for lunch and traded quips around one of these round tables. The cuisine is good, straightforward American fare, served in an elegant setting—an ideal atmosphere for contemplating literature and each other.

⋘⊙⋙

After dinner, catch the show in the hotel's Oak Room, which offers some of the best jazz in the city. (These can include Harry Connick, Jr. and Andrea Marcovicci. If Steve Ross is performing, don't miss it—no matter what.) Then, enjoy a nightcap in the lobby or at The Blue Bar. (The Blue Bar, when it used to be a makeshift coat closet at the front of the lobby, was one of my favorite bars in New York. It was more than romantic; it was downright sexy. Today, the Blue Bar is not quite so "blue"; still it's pleasant and intimate.)

And now, after your evening absorbing the delights of the historic Algonquin, to bed.

DAY TWO: MORNING

When you rouse yourselves, have a simple breakfast of pastry and coffee in the lobby.

Then head out, and east to Madison Avenue and south to the **J. Pierpont Morgan Library** (29 East 36th Street at Madison Avenue). The Morgan Library houses one of the world's greatest collections of illuminated books, manuscripts, and drawings and offers a full calendar of changing exhibitions of special parts of the collection. Constructed at the turn of the century under the direction of McKim, Mead and White, the magnificent building is itself a beautifully kept monument to the life of *la crème de la crème* of New York society in the late nineteenth and early twentieth centuries. The museum was recently renovated—quite beautifully, I might add. The library's lovely, glass-roofed atrium is the perfect spot to relax over a cup of tea or coffee, and the elegant gift shop may provide the perfect gift for someone you love.

When you leave the Morgan, head north on Madison, then west on 40th Street. You'll find yourself face to face with the main branch of the New York Public Library (Fifth Avenue between 40th and 42nd Streets). The majestic Beaux Arts building was completed in 1911 on land that once contained the Croton Reservoir, New York City's water supply, which was moved up the Hudson River when library construction began. The two lions, named Patience and Fortitude by Mayor Fiorello La Guardia, have become symbols of New York's literary life.

When you enter the library you'll immediately see the Gottesman Exhibition Hall. It also hosts special exhibitions, so look around if you see something of interest. Then stroll down the south hall into the DeWitt Wallace Periodical Room, named after the founder of *Reader's Digest*. The lovely murals that line its walls celebrate the New York publishing world. Finally, go upstairs to the reading rooms. This library building does not lend books, but

permits researchers and all other visitors to peruse their phenomenal collection in any of the reading rooms on the third floor. The main lending library is located across the street at 40th Street and Fifth Avenue.

Lunch

When you're finished exploring the library, have lunch at the **Bryant Park Grill** (Bryant Park, 40th and Fifth Avenue behind the library; 212–840–6500; moderate). Located directly behind the library, Bryant Park, named after the poet William Cullen Bryant, has gone through several incarnations from potter's field to squalid hangout for drug addicts and the homeless. In the late 1980s, however, the park was totally renovated and is today one of the most attractive spaces in Manhattan. Its lovely landscaping, lighting, and scores of benches and tables make it reminiscent of Parisian parks.

The Bryant Park Grill is a pleasant restaurant, definitely at its best on the patio outdoors on a warm day. It couldn't be a more romantic place for your first New York literary lunch. (If the weather does not cooperate, don't worry; the indoor restaurant is almost as charming.) You can also bring take-out from any number of nearby eateries to the park to eat at one of the park's tables.

DAY TWO: AFTERNOON

After lunch, stroll up Fifth Avenue. Stop at the famous spots: Rockefeller Center, well-known stores like Cartier and Tiffany, and Trump Tower. Most of all, focus your attention on the various bookshops, particularly **Gotham Book Mart** (41 West 47th Street), one of New York's most famous new and used bookstores.

Continue all the way up Fifth until you get to the entrance to Central Park at 59th Street. If the mood strikes you, go into the park at 59th Street, and follow the East Drive to The Mall which is also known as **Central Park's Literary Walk** (from 67th to 70th Streets leading to Bethesda Terrace and Fountain). This is one of the most romantic lanes to stroll in the entire park. Two rows of stately American elms form a natural canopy above it, and busts of poets and writers line the sides. The walk is especially lovely in the fall when it is framed by a carpet of gold and red leaves.

Continue to walk north. Stop by the Bethesda Fountain, then follow the paths to the north end of the Conservatory Water, and stop for a few minutes by the famous sculpture of Alice in Wonderland, commissioned by publisher George T. Delacorte. Then, go on to the west bank of the pond where you'll find another literary statue, a likeness of Hans Christian Andersen reading from his story "The Ugly Duckling." This spot has another literary connection as well; it is here that J. D. Salinger's character Holden Caulfield comes to tell the ducks his troubles in the novel, *The Catcher in the Rye*.

Still more fabulous bookstores line Madison Avenue. If the mood hits you, stop by **Books & Company** (Madison Avenue between 75th and 76th Streets). Books & Company is at once the most up-to-date literary bookstore in the city and a real old-fashioned neighborhood independent bookseller, one of the finest of a dying breed. It's very special.

DAY TWO: EVENING

Dinner

Depending upon where you end up in your wanderings, either walk to or hail a taxi to take you to **The Four Seasons Restaurant** (99 East 52nd Street; 212–754–9494; expensive) for drinks and dinner. Aside from being one of New York's premier restaurants, The Four Seasons is still the favorite lunch spot for the titans of publishing. Many a seven-figure deal has been put together over a table in the Grill Room. But that's on weekdays. On weekends—and especially for a romantic dinner—the place to be is the serene, airy pool room where, it won't surprise you, the indoor trees by the pool change with the seasons.

The Four Seasons, by the way, offers a pre-theater dinner seating as early as 6:00 P.M. The staff will smoothly get you off in time to catch a show if you let them know you have those plans. For appetizers, try prosciutto di Parma with fresh figs or a salad of hearts of palm with smoked duck. For a main course, consider veal scaloppine garnished with a chanterelle ragout, or try tuna in a pepper coating with Swish chard. Don't forget that the wine cellar at The Four Seasons is world class.

Many "literary" plays are on Broadway these days, authored by some of America's greatest playwrights, including Edward Albee, Sam Shepard, and Eugene O'Neill. The choice is yours. Take a taxi from the Four Seasons to the theater.

Since the Algonquin is located in the heart of the theater district, you can probably walk back to the hotel. For fun, you might want to have a nightcap at the Royalton (44 West 44th Street; 212–869–4400; expensive). The Royalton is considered by some people to be New York's hippest hotel. The bar crowd is incredibly chic. Join in the fun for as long as you wish, then cross the street to the Algonquin.

At the end of your day, luxuriate in the sound of each other's voices. Read aloud from one of the many books you've undoubtedly purchased during your adventures. Woo your lover with the sweet music of poetry and literature. It's a unique and romantic way to become more intimate.

DAY THREE: MORNING

Breakfast

In the morning, leave the Algonquin before breakfast and either catch a taxi or take the subway (IRT #1, 2, or 3 to the Christopher Street/Sheridan Square stop) to Greenwich Village. Where else? Greenwich Village has a long, rich history, but it is best known for its writers and artists, among whom are such notables as Henry James, Edgar Allen Poe, Jack Kerouac, and Calvin Trillin. Have the cabbie drop you at the corner of Waverly and Grove Streets at **Les Deux Gamins** (170 Waverly Place; 212–807–7357). Les Deux Gamins is very French and very bohemian and, therefore, ideal for breakfast in the Village. Enjoy the most authentic café au lait and croissant or baguette this side of Paris to fortify you for your tour of the neighborhood.

❧

The Village is a great place to walk. When you have finished breakfast, walk east along Waverly Place, cross Sixth Avenue, and continue along Waverly Place until you come to Washington Square Park. Washington Square is the center of Greenwich Village and was (and continues to be) the haunt of many writers.

When you reach the Square look (or walk) south. The colonial building (New York University Law School) across from the southwest corner of the square was once **60**

Washington Square South, the site of the so-called "genius houses," studios inhabited at various times by such writers as Theodore Dreiser, O. Henry, and Stephen Crane. Willa Cather, who also lived here (as well as in several other Greenwich Village locations, including 5 Bank Street), set a love story called "Coming, Aphrodite" in these surroundings.

Novelist Henry James (1843–1916) was born at **21 Washington Place**, just east of Washington Square. At the time of James' birth, Washington Square was considered one of the most fashionable addresses in New York City. The upper-crust residents eventually moved steadily uptown, but from the 1830s to the 1860s the Greenwich Village, Union Square, and Gramercy Park neighborhoods were the center of posh Manhattan.

Although Henry James set most of his novels in Europe, he did place some in the United States. Washington Square, of course, served as the name of one of his most famous novels. (*Washington Square* also provided the plot of the famous movie and play, *The Heiress.*) His heroine, Catherine Sloper, lived in one of the beautiful town houses that line the north side of the square east of Fifth Avenue. She was courted by her dubious lover on a bench inside the square.

If you're in the mood, take a short detour to the **Old Merchant's House** (29 East 4th Street, between the Bowery and Lafayette Streets), which may have served as food for thought for James when he wrote his novel *Washington Square*. A well-to-do merchant named Seabury Tredwell lived here with his family from 1835 through the turn of the century. His daughter, Gertrude, fell in love with an unacceptable suitor whom she was forbidden by her father to marry. As a result, Gertrude chose not to marry at all and, after her father's death, resolved to maintain the family home just as her father would have liked it. You can tour the house and imagine upper-middle-class family life as it was lived in New York City in the 1830s.

The James family also included Henry's brother, William, who was a philosopher. William wrote many books, one of which served as inspiration for contemporary novelist

Caleb Carr, who wrote the recent bestseller, *The Alienist*. Based on William James' theories, much of the action in *The Alienist* takes place along Broadway between Grace Church (where the weddings in many of Edith Wharton's novels are held) and Union Square.

After you've explored the Park and/or the Old Merchant's House, make your way to Broadway, then turn north toward the beautiful **Grace Church** (East 10th Street and Broadway). Just past Grace Church is the **Strand Bookstore** (Broadway and 12th Street), a not-to-be-missed stop for literary gluttons; it's one of New York City's literary landmarks and the largest used bookstore in the nation. As a bibliophile, you'll undoubtedly spend many hours—and many dollars—in the Strand.

After indulging yourself, head south one block, then west one block to the corner of East 11th and University. At **Dean & DeLuca** (11th Street and University Place), you may want to rest a while over a cappuccino and look over your literary wares.

When you leave Dean & DeLuca, walk west along East 11th Street. These elegant brownstones are the sorts of buildings often described (albeit disparagingly) by Edith Wharton. Newland Archer, the hero of *The Age of Innocence,* and his family lived in a similar brownstone house along West 11th Street. By the 1870s, the time *The Age of Innocence* is set, lower Fifth Avenue and the Washington Square area had settled into a quiet upper-class neighborhood, which it remains to this day. The nouveau riche had moved farther uptown.

When you get to Fifth Avenue, turn south and view one of the many residences of Mark Twain. Twain leased the house at **14 West 10th Street** for one year in 1900 when he was at the pinnacle of his success as one of the most famous writers and most fashionable celebrities in the world. In 1904, he returned to New York and rented another showplace at 21 Fifth Avenue at the corner of 9th Street, but that brownstone is now demolished. It had been designed in neo-Gothic style by James Renwick, the architect who also designed Grace Church. Today a plaque marks the spot. Although Twain's masterpieces, *The Adventures of Huckleberry Finn, The Adventures of Tom Sawyer,* and *Life on the Mississippi* reflect his

Midwestern roots, Twain was a Gilded Age celebrity at the end of his life.

Walk west on 10th Street, cross Sixth Avenue, and in the middle of the next block, you'll find Patchin Place, a charming mews nestled behind beautiful iron gates. Poet e. e. cummings (1894–1962) lived at **4 Patchin Place** from 1924 until the end of his life. You can walk in and look around. Although it is not architecturally grand, it is secluded and as such is one of the most romantic spots in the city.

Lunch

Continue west, turn left at Greenwich Avenue, and turn right at Christopher Street. Continue west along Christopher until you come to **The Lion's Head Tavern** (59 Christopher Street, near Seventh Avenue. Not long ago, you could have stopped here for a light lunch, but in the fall of 1996, it closed its doors forever. This bar was for decades one of the great literary hangouts in the city. Poets, sports writers, editors, literary agents, and journalists congregated here. Its death was a painful one. To ease the pain, cross Seventh Avenue, walk north along 4th Street to 11th Street, then turn left and walk west to Hudson.

At Hudson, see the **White Horse Tavern** (corner of West 11th Street and Hudson Street, 212–243–9260; moderate). The White Horse, once a longshoreman's bar, joined the "literary establishment" when the Welsh poet Dylan Thomas decided it would become one of his favorite drinking holes. The White Horse has lost a bit of its working-class patina, now offering outdoor tables during warm weather and something more than a classic bar menu. Nevertheless, they still deify Dylan, and it's definitely a place for paying homage to the Welsh bard—and to literary New York.

On the other hand, you might want something a bit more romantic—in the conventional sense. Since we're in a bohemian mode, I suggest you walk just a few more blocks west to **The Black Sheep** (311 West 11th Street; 212–242–1010; moderate), which offers a delicious brunch. The food is a mixture of styles but has a decidedly French flair, and the wine and the desserts are good, too. During the colder months, blazing fireplaces make this already-romantic restaurant even more so.

DAY THREE: AFTERNOON

After lunch, make your way to Bedford Street. Walk until you find number 75½, the "narrowest house in New York," also known as the Millay House, since poet Edna St. Vincent Millay (1892–1950) lived here for a short time. In the 1920s Millay symbolized bohemian Greenwich Village. A native of Maine, Millay graduated from Vassar College in 1917 and immediately came to the Village, where she lived with her sisters. Edna and her sisters were known as great beauties and did not hide the fact that they had many lovers. Edna finally married at age thirty-one and moved with her husband to an upstate New York farm. Although she symbolized the bohemian culture of 1920s Greenwich Village, she remains one of America's greatest poets.

Continue a bit farther down Bedford Street and take a look in **Chumley's** (86 Bedford Street between Grove and Barrow Streets; 212–675–4449; moderate) a well-known speakeasy and hangout for 1920s bohemians like Millay. Stop for a beer and check out the autographs on many of the tables.

As you end your literary weekend, you'll be "lost" in the center of Greenwich Village. To my mind, nothing could be more romantic. Spend your last hours here wandering the streets, enjoying each other and the best of literary New York.

FOR MORE ROMANCE

Brooklyn has as strong a literary tradition as Manhattan. If you have time during your visit to New York, spend a day on the opposite end of the Brooklyn Bridge. (See also "Brooklyn, Romantic? Who Knew?" for details.)

CROSSING DELANCEY

*I*n the charming film, *Crossing Delancey,* Amy Irving plays Isabelle, a modern, uptown single girl whose "Bubby" (grandmother) is concerned because "such a pretty girl" has reached the age of 33 and has not yet found a husband. Bubby still lives on the Lower East Side, and in keeping with an old Yiddish custom, she hires a matchmaker who produces Sam the "pickle man" (played by the adorable Peter Riegert). Sam is the heir to Guss's Pickles, the famous pickle store on Essex Street, and is committed to carrying on the tradition of the place. Of course, Isabelle resists—and, of course, the two fall in love.

But the film, like the Lower East Side itself, is imbued with another kind of romance—a kind of sadness for the fading institutions, values, and life-style of the first Jewish immigrants. It is this nostalgia that makes this itinerary so romantic. One can walk along the streets of the Lower East Side and almost hear the banter of the ghosts from a century ago. Their voices tell us of backbreaking work and certain heartache, but they also speak of hope and love. The fact that these ghosts can still be heard is just a hint of the colorful life that once inhabited these streets. These people are not really gone; in fact, in a few short decades, their offspring escaped the poverty and moved on, in many cases, to astonishing success and affluence. But as one walks down Essex, Hester, or Ludlow Streets, one can still see vestiges of those romantic days. One can still hear the chatter of hundreds of Jewish bubbies.

Practical notes: For an itinerary that features the Lower East Side, it is difficult to suggest a romantic hotel. The most convenient hotel to the area is the **Off Soho Suites** (11 Rivington Street; 212–979–9808). Rooms are moderately priced, clean, and well-appointed, but they are not particularly fanciful or sexy. I would suggest providing a bit of your own romance by adding flowers and scented candles.

For a more glamorous (and romantic) downtown alternative, try the **Millennium** (55 Church Street; 212–693–2001). The Millennium is expensive and is designed to appeal to business people. To insure romance (and avoid a room looking into the side of the World Trade Center), ask for a room that offers a view of the river or the churchyard of St. Paul's Chapel.

This itinerary suggests (actually, *requires*) a fair amount of walking, so come prepared with good walking shoes. The ideal season for touring the Lower East Side is during the spring or fall.

Romance at a Glance

♥ *Stay at Holiday Inn Downtown or another convenient downtown location.*

♥ *Dine at the famous Ratner's Dairy Restaurant, Katz's Delicatessen, Sammy's, Ludlow Street Cafe, and other famous spots on the Lower East Side.*

♥ *Explore the Lower East Side and other downtown areas.*

DAY ONE: MORNING

Before touring the Lower East Side itself, it seems natural to explore Ellis Island where all immigrants who arrived in America between 1892 and 1924 had to be processed into the country. Head off as early as possible for **Castle Clinton** (in Battery Park), where you'll buy your tickets for the ferry to the Statue of Liberty and Ellis Island. (The ferries to Ellis Island depart every 30 minutes between 9:30 A.M. and 3:30 P.M. Tickets are $7, which includes admission to the Statue of Liberty and Ellis Island.)

Castle Clinton was built in 1807 as a defense post but was enclosed in 1824 and became a fashionable theater known as Castle Garden. From 1855 to 1896, it served as the city's immigration center and processed over seven million people into the country. In 1896, it was remodeled and became the city's aquarium. It is now a monument and the main visitors center and departure point for the Statue of Liberty–Ellis Island Ferry.

The ferry stops first at the **Statue of Liberty**, where you can disembark and explore Liberty Island and the Statue itself. The elevator taking you up to the observation decks within the Statue is very small and lines are often long. As a result, it can take several hours to visit the Statue. Viewing the inside of Lady Liberty is quite fascinating, but if time is short, you may simply want to enjoy the majesty of the Statue from afar and continue on to Ellis Island.

The Ellis Island Buildings were lying in ruin until the mid-1980s when more than $150 million was spent to renovate the edifice and turn it into the what is now known as the **Ellis Island Immigration Museum**. During its years as a processing center (1892 to 1924), more than 15 million immigrants passed through these buildings. The exhibits chronicle both the history of the island and its buildings as well as the history of the peoples who immigrated to America. Most of the first floor, which was a baggage storage area, features a moving pile of antique baggage of the sort brought by immigrants. Throughout the rest of the floor are several bright, easy-to-understand displays explaining America's cultural diversity. The second floor features the emotionally moving Great Hall, which was the central waiting room, while the third floor offers an exhibit entitled "Treasures from Home," which includes displays of items brought by many different nationalities to the new world. The items brought by Russian Jews are fascinating.

Don't miss the documentary film, "Island of Hope, Island of Tears" shown every half hour throughout the day, which describes the physical tests, financial and criminal checks, and other issues immigrants had to face. (The film is free, but the complimentary tickets must be obtained prior to your admission to the theater.)

If you can work it in on this visit to New York, head to The Jewish Museum *(1109 Fifth Avenue at 92nd Street; 212–423–3230). The Jewish Museum is dedicated to presenting the scope and diversity of Jewish art, history, and culture. Housed in the original 1908 Warburg Mansion, it was renovated and reopened in 1993. The exhibit entitled "Culture and Continuity: The Jewish Journey" is not to be missed. The museum is open every day from 11:00 A.M. to 5:45 P.M. and until 8:00 P.M. on Tuesday. Admission is $7 for adults and $5 for students and seniors.*

Lunch

Enjoy lunch at the Museum's cafeteria. It combines the best of American fast food with multicultural choices like Italian pastas and pizzas, German wursts (also known as hot dogs), Chinese fare, and other ethnic dishes. On a warm day, you can picnic outdoors on the delightful patio overlooking downtown Manhattan.

DAY ONE: Afternoon

Finish your tour, then catch a ferry back to Battery Park.

If you have more time and energy—and the weather permits—take a stroll along the Battery Park waterfront up to the recently renovated Esplanade by the World Financial Center. It offers a spectacular view of the waterfront, the yacht basin, and usually a few art shows, jazz concerts, and performance artists. Take a look at the glass-enclosed Winter Garden, which is the focal point of the Financial Center. If something can be classically romantic, this stroll will be the most conventionally romantic part of your weekend. Stop for a glass of wine—and enjoy each other.

DAY ONE: EVENING

Dinner

What would an evening in Jewish New York be without dinner at **Sammy's Famous Roumanian Jewish Steakhouse** (157 Chrystie Street, between Delancey and Rivington; 212–673–0330; reservations required; moderate).

Like the rest of this itinerary, Sammy's is not exactly noted for hearts and flowers. Instead of rosebuds on the table, you'll find a pitcher of chicken fat, but it's a Jewish institution—and part of the romance of crossing Delancey. In fact, although it is not kosher, it is considered to be the best Jewish restaurant in the city. The portions are huge—and the menu is heart-rending—literally. Consider chicken livers with cracklings, shredded black radishes, and onions. Or how about Rumanian tenderloin steak or boiled beef with gravy coupled with *kasha varnishkes.* Sammy's also offers entertainment. Okay, so it's not Bobby Short, but you'll love it. Would I lie?

⚜

If you don't feel like lingering over dinner, **The Ludlow Street Cafe** (165 Ludlow Street; moderate, no cover charge) is a hot spot with the Generation X crowd that features rock and roll or blues every night. In fact, this cafe is one of the signs of fresh, new life in this old Jewish neighborhood. For that reason alone, it's worth dropping in for an after-dinner drink and some music.

DAY TWO: MORNING

Breakfast

After last night's dinner, you may just want a cup of weak tea for breakfast. However, if

your stomach can take it, you may want to go to **Katz's Delicatessen** (205 East Houston Street at Ludlow; 212–254–2246). You can either be waited on at the tables or order at the counter. Katz's boasts an unlikely piece of romantic film history: It was in Katz's that Meg Ryan (Sally) performed her famous orgasm demonstration to Billy Crystal (Harry) in the comedy *When Harry Met Sally*. If you want to ensure that you get your fair share of romance, just ask the man behind the counter if you can have what she had.

Now walk over to the **Lower East Side Tenement Museum** (90 Orchard Street, between Delancey and Broome; 212–431–0233.) This original tenement building has been restored to show how immigrants lived at the turn of the century. The museum features a gallery of exhibits on the immigrant experience and offers several guided tours, ranging in price from $7 to $12. Orchard Street itself was the center of the Jewish Lower East Side. The pushcarts that once lined the block are long gone, but the shops selling fashionable merchandise at discount prices remain. Although the Jewish cultural element has almost vanished, most of the stores are closed on Saturday, the Jewish Sabbath, and Sunday is the traditional shopping day. You can take one of the museum's tours or follow these directions. Walk south on Orchard, and turn left at Grand Street. If bagels and bialys are your thing, take a slight detour to **Kossar's Bialystoker Kuchen Bakery** (367 Grand Street; 212–473–4810) for the best bagels in New York. Then, head back to Essex. Make your way to the site of **Guss's Pickle Products** (35 Essex Street), the shop featured in the film *Crossing Delancey*. Barrels of delectable pickles are outside, and people line up to buy them to this day. Continue south on Essex until you reach Hester Street, and turn right. You'll run into **Kadouri Imports** (51 Hester Street), a terrific source of dried fruits, nuts, and lots of spices. Next door is **Gertel's Bakery**, an old Jewish bakery offering some of the best Jewish bread and pastry in New York—all kosher. You might want to stop at Gertel's for a cup of coffee and some of the pastry. (My guess is that you won't be able to resist.)

Stroll west along Hester Street, crossing Ludlow, Orchard, and Allen Streets. Try to imagine what it must have been like when the streets were teeming with pushcarts, noisy urchins, and tenement residents meeting on their front steps. Another film, *Hester Street,* portrayed this life beautifully. Turn left at Eldridge Street, and continue south until you reach the **Eldridge Street Synagogue** (12–16 Eldridge Street; 212–219–0888), built in 1886 by Polish Jews. This was the first synagogue built by East European Jews in America and stood as one of the major synagogues until the 1930s when it closed due to dwindling membership. (The synagogue offers several fascinating tours each Sunday on the hour from noon to 4:00 P.M.; $5 donation.)

Continue down Eldridge Street, turn left at Canal, and go over to Allen Street which was one of the main thoroughfares of the Jewish Lower East Side. Allen Street in the late nineteenth and early twentieth century was much narrower than it is today, and the Second Avenue elevated train roared overhead. Dark, dirty, and noisy, Allen Street acquired a sordid reputation for being a red-light district. Today, the elevated is gone and Allen Street is a brighter, more pleasant thoroughfare.

Just along Canal Street is the **Jarmulowsky Bank**, established by Sender Jarmulowsky, a Jewish immigrant who arrived in the early 1870s. Jarmulowsky's bank attracted Jewish immigrant patrons, who felt more secure placing their money in a bank owned by a Jew and staffed by people who spoke Yiddish. Soon his became one of the most successful immigrant banks in New York, leading the banker to construct this edifice completed in 1912.

At the end of Canal Street is **Straus Square**, named for businessman and philanthropist Nathan Straus, a co-owner of the famous department store, Macy's. Straus is most famous for establishing facilities to distribute purified baby milk on the Lower East Side and in poor neighborhoods throughout the country.

Head to the right to the corner of East Broadway and Rutgers Street to the **Wing Shing** restaurant. Until the mid-1980s, this was the **Garden Cafeteria**, a twenty-four-hour coffee shop and diner frequented by some of this century's most renowned revolutionaries and intellectuals. Bukharin, Trotsky, and Castro all came here to eat cheap food and to make their plans to overthrow their home governments. Writer Isaac Bashevis Singer also came here frequently.

Just past the Wing Shing is the ***Daily Forward* Building** (175 East Broadway), built in 1912. The *Forward,* founded by Abraham Cahan in 1897, was the leading Yiddish newspaper during the heyday of the Jewish Lower East Side and featured a strong Socialist and pro-labor editorial stance. By the 1920s it had a circulation of more than 200,000. Note the Yiddish word *Forverts* adorning the top of building.

Just beyond the *Forward* Building is the **E. B'way Bakery**, the only surviving Jewish bakery on the street. Stop in for some delicious Russian black bread or classic Jewish pastries. Continue on East Broadway to Jefferson Street. On the north side of East Broadway stands the **Seward Park Branch** of the New York Public Library. Built in 1910, it was the most heavily used library in all New York City until World War II. Unable to study in their overcrowded tenements, immigrants both young and old came to the library, which stayed open from 6:00 A.M. until 1:00 A.M.

Stroll west along the north side of East Broadway and then turn north on Essex Street. This end of Essex maintains a bit of its Jewish character. Stop by the **Bezalel Jewish Art**

Gallery (11 Essex Street) and take note of other shops selling religious goods, like **Zelig Blumenthal** (13 Essex Street) and **Weinfeld's Skull Cap Mfg.** (19 Essex Street), which is more than 100 years old and is the oldest such factory in the neighborhood. In times past, these sorts of shops lined the streets of the Lower East Side.

Lunch

When you get to Delancey, turn right and head for **Ratner's Dairy Restaurant and Bakery** (138 Delancey, between Norfolk and Suffolk Streets; 212–677–5588), one of the most famous Jewish dairy restaurants in New York. Like Katz's and Sammy's, Ratner's may look a bit old-fashioned, but it is not to be missed. Its blintzes and onion rolls, as well as its mushroom barley soup, are the best.

DAY TWO: AFTERNOON

If you haven't already succumbed, spend an hour or two shopping, especially along Orchard Street. Although the goods are no longer piled on pushcarts, a Sunday afternoon on Orchard Street still has the atmosphere of a bazaar, with dresses, coats, sweaters, shoes, purses, linens, and fabrics hanging on clotheslines or piled on tables right on the street. More than 300 stores line Orchard and the surrounding streets from Houston to Canal. Check out **Anna Z** (143½ Orchard) for women's sportswear, **Fine & Klein** (119 Orchard) for handbags and other accessories, and **Beckenstien's** (125 Orchard) for fabrics.

In some ways, shopping on the Lower East Side has lost some of its fascination. Now most shops and department stores throughout the city are open on Sunday, and in some cases the discounts in the neighborhood shops are no better than the sales in more conventional stores. Since the shops themselves and their merchandise changes, this is a place to browse, not to look for something in particular.

George Burns, George Raft, Al Jolson, Fanny Brice, Sophie Tucker, Raphael Soyer, Ben Shahn, Irving Berlin, Meyer Lansky, Bugsy Siegel, George and Ira Gershwin, and Mae West are just a few of the famous personalities that began their lives in the tenements of the Lower East Side. But remember, the Lower East Side was not just Jewish—it was a hodgepodge of many nationalities. In fact, Irving Berlin summed it up best. He said that when he was starting out as a young Jewish singer and musician, he played in an Italian restaurant in Chinatown owned by an Irishman.

When you've had your fill of blintzes and bargain-hunting, head back to your hotel. If weather and time permits, stroll through Chinatown and Little Italy, and again, try to imagine life in the late nineteenth and early twentieth centuries, when all sorts of ethnic groups piled together created the most colorful melting pot in the world. It may not have been so romantic for your forebears, but it will certainly be romantic for you.

You might want to end your afternoon at the **10th Street Baths** (268 East 10th Street between First Avenue and Avenue A; 212–473–8806). These Russian (and Turkish) baths are not exactly as sybaritic as those you'll find at an elegant spa, but as the last remaining bathhouse in an area (the Lower East Side and the East Village) that once had scores of them, it's a thrilling experience. They still heat up enormous boulders in the basement and, when they are red-hot, throw water on them to release penetrating wet heat. They also feature a *platza* rub, done with softened oak branches tied together in the old Russian style and applied with soap. Turkish baths or saunas are also available.

The baths are open daily from 9:00 A.M. to 10:00 P.M. In deference to their cultural heritage, coed baths are available only on Monday, Tuesday, Friday, and Saturday. Wednesdays are for women only; Thursdays and Saturdays (the Sabbath) are for men only.

FOR MORE ROMANCE

If you want to add an evening at the theater to your itinerary, think about going to one of the remaining theaters on Second Avenue, once known as the Yiddish rialto, since it was lined with scores of Jewish theaters. Try the **Orpheum** (126 Second Avenue between East 7th Street and East 8th Street; 212–477–2477), a former Yiddish playhouse, or **The Jewish Repertory Theater** (344 East 14th Street; 212–505–2667), where *Crossing Delancey* premiered. The **Variety Arts Theatre** (110 Third Avenue at 14th Street; 212–239–6200) is another choice; it is housed in a marvelous vintage theater and offers popular off-Broadway productions. Call for information.

MOONSTRUCK

*R*emember the marvelous Academy Award-winning film *Moonstruck*? Cher plays a middle-aged Italian widow, Loretta, who lives in Brooklyn Heights. Her mama's-boy gentleman-friend, Johnny, played by Danny Aiello, proposes to her, but Loretta is clearly not in love with him. She considers herself unlucky in love, however, and concludes that a nice, passionless union with this sweet man is her last and best chance at happiness. She agrees to the marriage, and Johnny immediately departs for Sicily to visit his supposedly dying mother. Before leaving, Johnny asks Loretta to help him make amends with his brother, Ronnie, played by Nicholas Cage.

There's bad blood between Ronnie and Johnny. Ronnie is a baker, and lost his hand in a nasty accident: Johnny distracted him as he was operating a bread-slicing machine. As a result of his maiming, Ronnie's fiancée left him for another man. Ronnie blames Johnny for his ruined life, but thoroughly enjoys wallowing in his own misery.

Loretta and Ronnie have the good luck to meet under a *bella luna,* a magnificent full moon, and, after a tumultuous first meeting, they fall madly in love and passionately into bed. Loretta insists they take their moment of fire "to their coffins," but Ronnie makes one last request: that Loretta go with him to the opera to see *La Bohème.* The evening cements their relationship forever.

Well, this all sounds very melodramatic—dare we say operatic? Actually, it's hilarious. This *Moonstruck* itinerary, fashioned after Ronnie and Loretta's first date, can be enjoyed for anything from your own special first date to your milestone wedding anniversary celebration. We can't promise this date will ensure passionate love and lifelong commitment, but you can be certain it will be a delightful—and delectable—evening!

Romance at a Glance

♥ *Have dinner at The Grand Ticino (212–777–5922), a famous Greenwich Village restaurant.*

♥ *Go to the opera at the Metropolitan Opera House at Lincoln Center. Ideally, see Puccini's* La Bohème.

♥ *After the opera, enjoy a coffee or a brandy at an old-fashioned Italian coffeehouse.*

Practical notes: Opera tickets are hard to come by if you are not a season subscriber. Opera buffs usually hold season tickets, so most of the seats at many performances are reserved. What's more, opera tickets at the Met are outrageously expensive. If one of you is a buff and you already have tickets, then you are set. If you are trying to buy tickets for a single performance, however, you'll have to be a little creative. It is almost guaranteed, for instance, that any performance of *La Bohème* will be sold out. You can get around this by arriving at the theater about forty-five minutes before the performance to negotiate with any of the several guaranteed-to-be-there scalpers, or you can try to get standing room tickets ($10) at the back of the house. Admittedly, standing for three hours is not exactly romantic unless you are as passionate about opera as you are about each other. (Some aficionados suggest buying standing-room tickets and then begging an usher for any unused seats reserved for season ticket-holders in the Grand Tier.)

Finally, you can break out your Gold Card (tickets can be as high as $230 a seat on weekends; more than $100 on weeknights) and spring for orchestra seats, which are almost always available at the last minute.

Even if you have never been to an opera before, don't worry. *La Bohème* is one of the best-known operas of all time, and you'll probably recognize some of the arias. (Some of them have even been recast into popular songs!) Also, the story line is laid out in the program notes, and the Metropolitan Opera House at Lincoln Center now has computerized screens at each seat that displays the words as the artists sing. You'll have no trouble following the story.

With regard to your attire, anything goes. In Old Guard New York, one would not think of going to the opera in anything less than a Worth gown and white tie and tails. Today, you can show up in denim, and no one will blink an eye. I would suggest striking a happy medium between formalwear and jeans—a festive, silky outfit for her and a business suit for him.

Finally, if you wish to turn this date into a more unhurried adventure, schedule the opera for a Saturday matinee and follow it with a leisurely dinner.

THE EVENING

Dinner

Depending upon where you live or are staying, walk or take a cab to the **Grand Ticino** (223 Thompson Street, between Bleecker and West 3rd Street; 212–777–5922; expensive). The Grand Ticino has been a well-loved Village Italian spot since 1919. The food is not nouvelle or chic, but it is the best of old-fashioned Italian fare. The fish and the desserts are especially good, or if you want to keep in a *Moonstruck* mood, order a steak. (Before he seduces her—or perhaps to seduce him—Loretta fixes Ronnie a steak "to eat bloody to feed his blood.") Regardless of what you order, the Grand Ticino atmosphere is intimate, warm, and romantic.

Curtain time is 8:00 P.M. so you'll have to schedule an early dinner (about 6:00 P.M.), and leave for the theater no later than 7:15. Your taxi ride from Greenwich Village to Lincoln Center should take about twenty minutes at this time of day and will cost about $10).

La Bohème

La Bohème *is the tale of the poet Rodolfo and his love affair with the doomed Mimi, Bohemians living in the Latin Quarter of Paris in 1830. It is a story of young love, the joys of pursuing art, women, and wine—and finally, the deep responsibilities of life and the inevitability of death. Puccini's opera was first performed at La Scala in Milan in early 1895 and initially received terrible reviews. One critic said: "Poor Puccini! This time he's on the wrong track! This is an opera that won't have a long life …" Today it is considered Puccini's most popular opera and one of the greatest works in the entire Italian repertory.*

Your taxi will drop you right in front of the plaza of **Lincoln Center** (70 Lincoln Center Plaza at 64th Street and Broadway; for information, call Events at 212–875–5400), of which the magnificent Metropolitan Opera House is the focal point. Lit up like a Christmas tree with its elegant chandeliers, its lobby features massive Chagall paintings. With the bubbling fountain outside on the plaza in front of the lights and glass, the entire sight will go to your head like champagne. You'll see patrons pouring into the Opera House—and you'll be thrilled to know that you are going there, too. Critics have both praised and criticized Lincoln Center. (Loretta, in *Moonstruck,* calls the Chagall paintings a "bit gaudy.") But whether or not you find the paintings, the miles of red carpet, and the glass chandeliers gorgeous or garish, they create a thrilling effect. And the opera itself may inspire you to hold hands or steal a kiss.

After the opera, you'll want to unwind (or prolong the evening) over a glass of wine or a late-night coffee or dessert. If you are heading back downtown, hail a cab and head for **Caffe Vivaldi** (32 Jones Street between Bleecker and West 4th; 212–929–9384). This is one of the great coffeehouses of Greenwich Village, and the background music is, naturally, well-known arias. However, if you want to go somewhere within walking distance of Lincoln Center, nothing exceeds the charm and romance of the **Café Des Artistes** (1 West 67th Street; 212–877–3500; expensive). The Café offers a delectable after-theater dessert menu.

If this is a first date, end your evening with one of the great lines from *Moonstruck:* "Oh thank you, you have such a head for knowing." (It won't matter who says it to whom.) If this is a special anniversary or just an evening with someone you love, end with a kiss and one of the great lines of all time:

"Ti Amo."

FOR MORE ROMANCE

If you are visiting New York during the summer months, check out "Met in the Park," which are outdoor performances of various operas by artists from the Met, staged in various parks in the New York metropolitan area. Performances are usually scheduled in Central Park (Manhattan), Pelham Bay Park (Bronx), Juniper Valley (Queens), and Prospect Park (Brooklyn). Best of all, these performances are free. For information, call (212) 362–6000.

Encore

The music of La Bohème *is so spectacular, and the film* Moonstruck *is so enchanting, you may want to recreate your marvelous evening at home electronically—perhaps to celebrate the anniversary of your first date. Prepare a simple pasta and light salad, open a great bottle of wine, play a CD or tape of* La Bohème *as you enjoy your dinner, then curl up and watch* Moonstruck *on your VCR.*

ITINERARY 19
Three days and two nights

WHAT EVER HAPPENED TO TIO PEPE'S?

*T*his itinerary is for the young at heart. It's for those of you who perhaps lived in Greenwich Village in the 1950s or 1960s (or wanted to) and considered yourselves, depending upon your age, to be "beat" or "hip"—and, most especially, "literary" or "artistic." But, like most of us, you ended up getting married, moving to Scarsdale, Westport, or even Columbus, having kids, and getting caught up in the *sturm und drang* of everyday life. Still, you dream of those days when you stayed up until dawn listening to music, drinking cheap Chianti, and arguing about Kerouac or Pollock.

I must confess that I, too, was once young in New York. During that period (the late 1960s), I spent many a Saturday night with my equally young husband having dinner at what I considered to be an "exotic" (okay—I grew up in Ohio) Mexican place on West 4th Street called Tio Pepe's. Not long ago, I was at a party of the stodgy grown-up variety, and a man I was chatting with said, "So, what ever happened to Tio Pepe's?" We looked at each other and laughed.

Well, guess what? Tio Pepe's is still thriving—and so are we. So plan a getaway with your graying honey and relive those bohemian dreams. This itinerary represents a hodgepodge of reflections, but for anyone who spent the days of their youth in the Village, it should ring some bells.

DAY ONE: EVENING

Check into the **Washington Square Hotel** (103 Waverly Place; 212–777–9515; 800–222–0418; fax: 212–979–8373; $90–$100 per night). Your hearts will pound as you arrive at your hotel, because one of the best features of the Washington Square Hotel is its location, which is, not surprisingly, right off Washington Square. (Yes, that is the famous Washington Square Arch halfway down the block.)

The entrance and the lobby to the Washington Square are charming, but the rooms, I'm afraid, while comfortable are quite small. In a way, that's part of their charm. Remember when you lived in the Village, and you were forced to pay a small fortune for a tiny space? Your "pad" was probably a fifth-floor walk-up, too. And when you began your lives together, you may well have rolled around in a single bed for months before you could afford a double. So, look at it this way: You've moved up in the world! The Washington Square does have very comfortable queen-sized beds, fully appointed bathrooms, and a reliable elevator.

After you've settled in your room, you'll want to go out and explore.

Dinner

For the sake of posterity, you may want to have dinner at **Tio Pepe's** (168 West 4th

Street; 212–242–9338; inexpensive), still a very festive spot for classic Mexican and Spanish fare from tapas to the classic paella Valenciana. (Remember the thrill when you first learned how to make paella—or, as in my case, when you first learned what paella was?) Tio Pepe's also features a skylight roof garden that is rather romantic.

As you scan the scene at Tio Pepe's, reality may rear its graying head. You'll quickly see that the restaurant is jam-packed with what look like kids. Since you may well have similar young adults at home and may be eager to escape them for the weekend, I would suggest that you wend your way through the streets of the West Village and have a more sophisticated dinner at a classic Village French restaurant.

Au Troquet (328 West 12th Street at Greenwich Street; 212–924–3414; moderate) is one of those Village restaurants that looks as though it has been tenderly plucked out of Paris' Left Bank and lovingly placed on a discreet corner on far west Greenwich Street. Not only is it romantic in the old-fashioned sense, the food is authentically French and quite delicious. The staff is French, and will not only oblige your every whim but make you feel at home. You won't encounter a 1990s New York attitude here. In fact, you may want to wile away the evening at Au Troquet.

Or, for old times' sake, you just might want to catch the late show at the **Village Vanguard** (178 Seventh Avenue at West 11th Street; 212–255–4037; call for show times and current entertainers). After all these years, the Vanguard still offers the best jazz in the city, and many of those people whom you loved so thirty years ago are still playing.

After the show, maybe you just want to linger over coffee at **Cafe Borgia** (185 Bleecker Street at MacDougal Street), a coffee bar that was a coffee bar when coffee bars were coffee bars—and then considered "bohemian." (If Cafe Borgia is full, try **Le Figaro**, right across the street at 184 Bleecker Street.) Sit outside if the weather permits, hold hands, and watch today's Village life go by.

Again for old times' sake, you may want to peek into **Cafe Wha?** (115 MacDougal Street between West 4th and Bleecker Streets; 212–254–3706). If you're a 60s person, Cafe Wha? will mean a lot to you. I guess I have aged, however—it's too much for me now!

When you've absorbed enough Village street life, walk back to the hotel and snuggle up together—just the two of you.

DAY TWO: MORNING

Spend the morning checking out the East Village. If you spent time here back in the sixties, you won't recognize the place. Abby is gone; Phoebe's is closed; Tompkins Square is all cleaned up; and you don't smell nearly as much pot on the street. That cheap tenement apartment you may have lived in (the one with the tub in the kitchen and the world's largest cockroach colony), probably looks reasonably habitable these days (and probably is!—at a rather high price).

Brunch

Start with brunch at **Danal** (90 East 10th Street between Third and Fourth Avenues; 212–982–6930; moderate). Danal reminds me of restaurants I used to love in the Village—but which, for the most part, have utterly disappeared. It's cozy with fireplaces and an eclectic array of furniture, including comfy sofas where you can sit together in relative privacy as you enjoy brunch. The food is yummy—especially brunch, which includes salads, tasty herbed omelettes, and delicious muffins and scones.

৩৬৩৩৩

After brunch, spend a couple of hours strolling along the streets of the East Village. When you leave Danal, turn right and walk east to Third Avenue, then turn south for one block, then east again along **Stuyvesant Street**. This elegant block formed the center of the homestead (or *bouwerie*) that once belonged to Peter Stuyvesant, New York's first governor, in the seventeenth century. Formally known as St. Mark's Historic District, two of the houses along the street, the **Nicholas William Stuyvesant House** (44 Stuyvesant Street, built in 1795) and the **Nicholas and Elizabeth Stuyvesant Fish House** (21 Stuyvesant Street, built in 1803) are architecturally important and quite fascinating. They were built during a building boom in the late eighteenth century when Petrus Stuyvesant, the great-grandson of the Dutch governor, subdivided the family land into building lots.

Continue down the block to Second Avenue, then turn right, or south. The lovely church on the corner of Second Avenue and 10th Street is **St. Mark's-in-the-Bowery**, the second oldest church building in Manhattan after St. Paul's. It is built on land that once was the site of Peter Stuyvesant's private chapel. Stuyvesant himself is buried in the churchyard. Of course, if you were politically active in the 1960s, you'll remember St. Mark's as one of the most socially committed and politically liberal centers in the city at that time. The St. Mark's Poetry Project was established here to explore artistic, social, and political concerns, and the church still offers many performances in music, dance, poetry, and theater.

Continue south one more block until you come to **St. Mark's Place**. For veterans of the 1960s hippie revolution, St. Mark's Place should evoke some nostalgia. It was on this block that New York hippies congregated and the Flower Children blossomed. **The Electric Circus** (25 St. Mark's Place) was one of the centers of hippie night life. Originally a Polish meeting hall, the building was converted by artist Andy Warhol into a multimedia happening featuring Lou Reed's Velvet Underground and the legendary—and incredibly noisy—Electric Circus.

Explore the shops along St. Mark's Place, many of which bear a strong resemblance to the funky stores of the sixties. Then head east again across East 7th Street. At **206 East 7th Street** between Avenues B and C is one of Allen Ginsberg's 1950s pads, also inhabited at various times by William Burroughs and Jack Kerouac. It's not much to look at but is typical of "homes of the poets" of the 1950s and 1960s. Backtrack to Avenue B, then turn north, and walk up to Tompkins Square Park and East 10th Street. The block between Avenues A and B along the Park is incredibly lovely, and Tompkins Square Park, after having gone through several incarnations, is a charming urban center.

Backtrack along Avenue A one block to 9th Street and walk west. Today 9th Street is lined with some of the funkiest shops, a real pleasure to explore. Check out **Angelica's Herbs** (147 First Avenue) and **Enchantments** (343 East 9th Street) for special herbal delights and **Mascot** (328 East 9th Street) for fascinating custom-made frames and other unique painted objects. To me, today's 9th Street is not much like it was thirty or forty years ago, but it is what the Village used to be. See if you don't agree.

Lunch

You may not want a big lunch after a large brunch at Danal, but you might want to stop for a drink and to rest your feet at **The Cedar Tavern** (82 University Place between 11th and 12th Streets; 212–929–9089; moderate). The Cedar Tavern, which you'll probably remember, was a favorite haunt of artists (Jackson Pollock) and writers (Ginsberg, et al.)

Actually, the original Cedar Tavern was two blocks down University, but the bar has retained an un-touristy Village atmosphere.

If you prefer a cappuccino or espresso instead of a beer, go across the street to the **Dean & DeLuca Cafe** (75 University Place; 212–473–1908; moderate) for a light salad, sweet roll, and coffee. The high ceilings, great open windows, and chic decor make this a great place to rest and restore yourselves.

DAY TWO: AFTERNOON

Spend the afternoon wandering around in the West Village. Walk west along 11th Street, cross Fifth Avenue, and stop for a moment at **18 West 11th Street**. You'll quickly notice that this house looks a bit different from the other nineteenth-century town houses on the block; this one has a very modern, angled, bay window on the front. In 1970, members of the radical Weathermen, a left wing political group, had started a bomb factory in the basement, and one of the bombs had exploded. One of the bomb builders died, and the others escaped, living underground for years afterward.

When you reach Sixth Avenue, turn left and spend a few minutes in **Balducci's** (Sixth Avenue and 9th Street; 212–673–2600), one of the best gourmet food shops in the city. It features imported and domestic Italian and American specialties. After exploring Balducci's, cross Sixth Avenue and head west along **Christopher Street**, then turn left along **Gay Street**. This curved street is lined with small rowhouses all built about 1810. It has known several incarnations—as a black neighborhood, then a strip of speakeasies, and finally a popular street for artists and writers. Ruth McKinney wrote *My Sister Eileen* in the basement of 14 Gay Street, and Howdy Doody, the famous 1950s puppet, was designed in 12 Gay. At the end of Gay Street, turn west on Waverly Place and walk back to Christopher Street and **Sheridan Square**.

Cross Seventh Avenue and pick up Grove Street. Follow Grove Street from Sheridan

Several restaurants, cafes, jazz clubs, and playhouses still exist in the Village after decades. The list, happily, remains quite extensive, offering visitors and natives alike the chance to savor the romance of the good old days. Among those you might remember are: Seville, John's Pizzeria, David's Pot Belly, John's of 12th Street, Lanza, Ye Old Waverly Inn, The Beatrice Inn, Cafe della Artiste, El Faro, The Grand Ticino, Ballato, La MaMa's, Provincetown Playhouse, Judson Church Theater, The Blue Note, The Bitter End, The Bottom Line, and more.

Square west past the house where Revolutionary writer Thomas Paine died (**59 Grove Street**) and the boyhood home of poet Hart Crane (**45 Grove Street**). As lovely as the streets are east of Seventh Avenue, they are even more charming in this area. Continue west on Grove until you reach the intersection of Grove and Bedford Streets. On the northeast corner stands one of the few remaining clapboard houses in the city (**17 Grove Street**). Wood construction was banned as a fire hazard in 1822, but the builders of this house managed to erect this structure just in time. The house has served many functions, including a brothel during the Civil War period. Continue on down Grove to the point where the street curves in front of an iron gate. This is **Grove Court**, an enclave of brick town houses built during the mid-1800s as apartments for workers. Today it is home to much more affluent homeowners; in fact, one of these townhouses recently sold for $3 million.

Continue on Grove Street until you come to Hudson Street. Take a peek into the churchyard of St. Luke's Church and school, located on Hudson Street at the end of Grove Street. You may want to rest your feet in the lovely garden. Then, walk north to the corner of Christopher and Hudson, turn east on Christopher, and walk east until you come to Sixth

Avenue. Jog south one block to 8th Street and continue east until you come to Washington Square Park and your hotel.

Actually, you could spend days—even weeks—exploring Greenwich Village. For additional suggestions, see "Glittering Literati." Also, don't be afraid to lose yourselves among the winding, romantic streets. The Village is so small you can't really get lost, and the natives are so friendly that if you do get lost, somebody will help you.

DAY TWO: EVENING

Dinner

If you want to try something wildly different—and very "downtown"—check out ***Tony N' Tina's Wedding*** (for tickets, call Ticket Central; 212–279–2100), an event that has been entertaining audiences for almost a decade. Part play and part performance art, it is entirely hilarious. The audience participates in the "wedding," or more specifically, is "drawn into the drama." After the wedding ceremony, which takes place at **St. John's Church** (81 Christopher Street), you attend a reception around the corner at **Vinnies** (147 Waverly Place), which includes a not-exactly-gourmet dinner, which is in keeping with the play. It's also not exactly quiet and romantic. As you might expect at a wedding, you'll witness a fair amount of family angst; in fact, you'll be drawn into the action all evening long. If you're in the mood for this sort of silliness, give it a try.

If *Tony N' Tina's Wedding* is not quite what you had in mind, I would suggest you check out a quintessential Village restaurant of the 1990s: **The Gotham Bar & Grill** (12 East 12th Street between Fifth Avenue and University Place; 212–620–4020; expensive; reservations are necessary). Considered one of New York's trendiest restaurants, the Gotham is American cuisine at its tastiest and most beautifully presented, created by chef Alfred Portale. Try the seafood salad or the rack of lamb. The desserts are also incredible.

After dinner, indulge in some classic Village entertainment. See *The Fantasticks* at the Sullivan Street Theater (181 Sullivan Street; 212–674–3838). Running since 1960, *The Fantasticks* is the quintessential Greenwich Village romance. Better yet, it's best known for the song, "Try to Remember." What could be more appropriate?!

DAY THREE: MORNING

Sleep late this morning. You deserve it. You've had a lot to absorb, but by now, you're probably beginning to feel kind of "with it." You've reminisced; you've checked out today's action; you're ready to assimilate.

Brunch

For brunch, either catch a taxi or stroll downtown to TriBeCa, which is an acronym for "Triangle Below Canal Street." Twenty years ago, TriBeCa didn't even have a name, let alone an identity. It was just a hodgepodge of large, old buildings that housed printing factories, garment factories, and other businesses that were known mainly as the gray mass that separated Wall Street from the Village. Today, TriBeCa rivals SoHo as Manhattan's most "in" neighborhood in which to either live or play. I'm still flabbergasted by its growth—and I've watched it develop from its beginnings in the sixties.

Have brunch at **The Tribeca Grill** (375 Greenwich Street at Franklin Street; 212–941–3900; moderate to expensive; reservations recommended). The Tribeca Grill is co-owned by Robert De Niro, Bruce Springsteen, Bill Murray, Sean Penn—and a host of other Hollywood types. The food is American with a hint of Japanese. Much of it is grilled, and it is excellent. (For Sunday brunch, the menu is a bit more traditional, featuring omelettes, hamburgers, waffles and the like.) The decor is also very attractive, with high ceilings, widely spaced tables, and interesting but unintrusive activity—including loads of fashionable young people. This is "downtown" New York as it is today—and at its most pleasant.

When you leave the Tribeca Grill, walk east along Franklin Street to West Broadway, turn north and walk three or four blocks north to Canal Street. These streets may appear a bit ramshackle, but, in fact, they comprise the heart of TriBeCa, the trendiest neighborhood in 1990s Manhattan. Nestled in these old buildings are incredibly gorgeous lofts owned by such beautiful types as John F. Kennedy, Jr. and his wife Carolyn. (Actually rumor has it that John and Carolyn live on N. Moore Street, one block north of Franklin.)

When you get to Canal Street, cross at a safe intersection, turn right or east, and continue for two blocks until you come to **Greene Street**. Stroll up Greene Street and take note of the incredible cast-iron buildings that have become the architectural hallmarks for New York City's SoHo neighborhood. The buildings that make up Numbers 8 through 34 Greene Street form the longest continuous row of cast-iron buildings in the city—or anywhere, for that matter.

From 1860 to 1890, as "skyscrapers" were becoming the architectural rage, many cast-iron buildings were built in this area and became popular because they did not require massive walls to bear the weight of the upper stories. As a result, these buildings were able to have more interior space and larger windows. Also the cast-iron material permitted elements to be produced from molds, and therefore they could mimic any style. Notice particularly 28–30 Greene Street, a building nicknamed "The Queen of Greene Street"; it features dormers, arches, columns, and bay windows. These buildings were originally commercial, often housing textile manufacturers; today, however, many of them house affluent residents.

When you reach Prince Street, turn left or west. If you want to browse through a few art galleries, consider the **Paula Cooper Gallery** (155 Wooster Street; 212–674–0766), one of SoHo's oldest galleries, or continue west on Prince until you come to West Broadway. Here, along the block between Prince and Spring Streets are several of SoHo's most famous galleries, including **420 West Broadway**, which houses two of SoHo's biggest names: **Leo Castelli** (212–431–5160) and the **Sonnabend Gallery** (212–966–6160); and **OK Harris** (383 West Broadway; 212–431–3600).

By now, you must be feeling like a very hip—and perhaps a rather tired—New Yorker. Still, I hope the romance of your youth has not diminished and you feel more alive than ever.

FOR MORE ROMANCE

Make a pilgrimage to Strawberry Fields in Central Park (located just inside the park off the West 72nd Street entrance). Strawberry Fields is a lovely international peace garden, designed by Yoko Ono in tribute to John Lennon. Gifts for the garden have come from all over the world. A mosaic set in the path includes the word "Imagine," the title of one of Lennon's famous songs.

If you come to New York over Halloween, don't miss the Greenwich Village Halloween Parade. I'm afraid it has become quite a scene. It used to be a little neighborhood get-together on Bethune Street, but in spite of its expansion, its intrinsic humor remains. Anyone can be part of the procession, and the more outrageous the costume, the better. You'll still see big, hairy guys dressed as ballerinas or nuns, moms pushing toddlers in strollers, and teenagers with fuchsia hair and rings in their noses defying their parents. The parade begins about 6:00 P.M., usually at Spring Street, and marches up Sixth Avenue to 23rd Street. (Check the papers for the exact route, which nowadays changes almost yearly.)

If listening to avant-garde poetry is of interest, catch deejay Jeannie Hopper's Liquid Sound Lounge at the **Nuyorican Poet's Cafe** (226 East 3rd Street between Avenues B and C; 212–515–8183; $7). Jeannie reads poetry and plays tribal and jazz records as she recites. Or, try **AlterKnit Theater** (Knitting Factory, 74 Leonard Street between Broadway and Church Street; 212–219–3006; $5), an intimate space where young poets perform.

ITINERARY 20
Two days and one night

X-Rated

*T*his itinerary is designed for the couples from that exclusive club known as Generation X. You know who you are: those sophisticated people who range in age from 18 to 35 and look great in whatever you wear, whether it's black and tight fitting or brown and baggy. Conventional wisdom holds that the Baby Boomers, who are all rapidly turning fifty, are the hip generation. However, it seems to me that you X-ers are the really cool ones; the sexy ones, the ones who seem to be having all the fun. This itinerary is for you. If the word *romantic* sounds too old-fashioned, let's just call this a "very sexy" weekend.

Practical notes: Unless you've amassed quite a bit of disposable income, you may find the SoHo Grand Hotel out of your price range right now. If so, you might want to try the **Chelsea Inn** (46 West 17th Street; 212–645–8989; under $100 per night depending upon the room). This charming, renovated nineteenth-century town house in Chelsea offers a choice of suites or single rooms with private or shared baths. I suggest that you ask for a room with a private bath.

This weekend would be fun anytime of year—the hottest summer weekend or the coldest winter weekend.

DAY ONE: LATE AFTERNOON/EVENING

In the late afternoon, check into **The SoHo Grand** (310 West Broadway; 212–965–3000 or 800–965–3000; rooms, $199–$249; penthouse suites, $949 and $1149), the first hotel located in the heart of SoHo in over a century. Don't think for a moment that this is a historic renovation. Opened in the summer of 1996, it is a spanking new building that architecturally alludes not only to the cast-iron buildings that line SoHo's streets (and provide the neighborhood with its historic importance) but to the latest in modern art. The entrance steps are lined with wire fencing and lighted with glass disks in each step, and the high-ceilinged lobby floors are carpetless granite. The furnishings are very modern and very downtown, but the starkness has a certain friendliness to it that is both handsome and appealing.

The rooms are rather small, but they are decorated in attractive neutral grays, beiges, and greens and are fitted out with every convenience. The views are not exactly lush (depending upon where your room faces, you may see the entrance to the Holland Tunnel or the rooftops of SoHo), but they are pure downtown Manhattan. For a SoHo itinerary, the location of the SoHo Grand Hotel is superb. Simply walk out the front door, turn left, and walk one short block to the heart of SoHo.

SoHo (an acronym for "South of Houston") has been "SoHo" for less than thirty years. In the late sixties, artists began moving into the lofts with the hope of finding cheap space. Within less than a decade, both the rich and the commercial interests had discovered the charms of these buildings, and for good or ill, moved in. Today, SoHo is the trendiest neighborhood in town and a "must" for most travelers, especially Europeans. Most of the

Romance at a Glance

♥ *Stay at the very trendy SoHo Grand Hotel (212–965–3000).*

♥ *Explore SoHo, the East Village, Chelsea, and the Upper West Side*

♥ *Dine at Zoë's, Rain, and La Luncheonette—New York's "in" restaurants.*

♥ *Spend time at the American Museum of Natural History and the Hayden Planetarium.*

struggling artists have had to move to less expensive neighborhoods, but their galleries are here by the score.

If contemporary art interests you, you'll have plenty of galleries to visit. Try **The American Fine Arts Company** (22 Wooster Street), **Amos End Gallery** (594 Broadway at Houston, Suite 404) or **Printed Matter** (77 Wooster Street)—or just walk into any of the galleries that line West Broadway. If shopping is your thing, you'll find shops galore (393 of them to be exact): designer clothing stores, home furnishing stores, jewelry stores (usually pieces designed by local artisans), bookstores—the choices are endless. SoHo is a place to browse through, and many shops stay open late into the evening.

Dinner

Many of New York's best restaurants are located in SoHo, and you can pick from Italian, Japanese, Indian, Chinese, and fascinating combinations. To keep pace with the trendy American spirit of the SoHo Grand, I suggest you try **Zoë's** (90 Prince Street between Broadway and Mercer Street; 212–966–6722; moderate to expensive). Zoë's lovely warm decor is superseded by its remarkable American cuisine and a terrific wine list. Open, friendly, and a little bit on the noisy side, Zoë's differs from the typical romantic formula. Still, I think you'll love it.

❧❀☙

After dinner, you may want to go to a local hangout and just enjoy the ambience of the neighborhood. **The Merc Bar** (151 Mercer; 212–966–2727) and **Naked Lunch** (17 Thompson Street; 212–232–0828) are both great. Nearer to the hotel, there's **Cafe Noir** (32 Grand Street; 212–431–7910) or **Cafe Novecento** (343 West Broadway; 212–925–4706), which features tango dancing. These may all be crowded, smoky, and noisy—but that's part of SoHo's charm. Finally, you could head back to your hotel and have a nightcap in the **Grand Bar** or **The Salon.**

DAY TWO: MORNING

This morning's adventure is designed to allow you to explore a bit of one of Manhattan's most popular neighborhoods, and to pay homage to some of American's most famous Generation–X'ers, stand-up comic Jerry Seinfeld, and his friends, George, Elaine, and Kramer, all of whom star on one of America's coolest television shows. To fortify yourselves for the day, have a hearty breakfast in **The Canal House**, the restaurant in the SoHo Grand.

Head out to explore a bit of Upper Manhattan, also known as "Seinfeld country." Get on the subway at Canal Street; take the A or C train to 59th Street, then change to the uptown 1/9 train at 59th Street, and go to the 110th Street and Broadway stop. When you exit the subway, walk two blocks north to **Tom's Restaurant** (112th Street and Broadway). You'll recognize the facade as the place where Jerry and his pals hang out. The interior is not used on the television series, but you may still want to stop for a cup of coffee or tea—just to say you've been there.

For some months, a guy named Kenny Kramer, who was a former neighbor of Seinfeld's chief writer, Larry David, and served as the model for the show's Kramer character, offered tours of famed Seinfeld spots. Calling himself "The Real Kramer," Kenny Kramer showed willing tourists such places as **Roosevelt Hospital** (where Kramer dropped a Junior Mint into a patient during surgery), the **New York Public Library** (where Jerry returned *The Tropic of Cancer*, twenty years overdue), and the **NBC studios** (where Jerry and George pitched a show about nothing). Kenny Kramer may still be offering these tours, but I wouldn't count on it and I'm not suggesting that you actually *go* to these places. Still, sometime during the day, you may want to walk by **129 West 81st Street** where the real Jerry Seinfeld once lived, and where his television character still resides.

But, before you head back downtown, walk just four blocks north to the beautiful **Columbia University campus** (116th and Broadway). Enter through the gates at 116th Street, and check out the famed Low Library and the statue of Alma Mater, made famous by radical students and other young protesters of the 1960s—who may well now be your parents!

The **Upper West Side**, as this part of Manhattan is called, runs from 116th Street south to 59th Street. A mostly residential area, it is populated by a true cross section of New Yorkers, from older people who have lived here for decades to Columbia University students. Stroll south along Broadway, or else catch a bus or subway on Broadway to 79th Street, then walk three blocks east to Central Park West and the **American Museum of Natural History** (82nd and Central Park West, 212–769–5100; open Sunday–Thursday, 10:00 A.M. to 5:45 P.M.; Friday–Saturday 10:00 A.M. to 8:45 P.M.; $6 donation).

DAY TWO: EVENING

Dinner

When you're ready for the evening, hail a taxi, and go to dinner at **La Luncheonette** (130 Tenth Avenue at 18th Street; 212–675–0342; expensive). That may sound like a funny suggestion for dinner, but La Luncheonette is not really a lunch place. It's a romantic bistro located in an out-of-the way part of Chelsea, offering classic—and delicious—French food. Linger over dinner, enjoy each other, and talk over your day. Then, if the mood strikes you, go dancing for a couple of hours.

❧

One of the best places for dancing is **The Tunnel** (220 Twelfth Avenue at 27th Street; 212–695–4682). Open Friday and Saturday from 10:00 P.M. to 10:00 A.M. and Sunday from 9:00 P.M. to 4:00 A.M., The Tunnel is located in a Chelsea warehouse on Twelfth Avenue and is a veritable department store of dance clubs. The main room has a skateboarding ramp at one end. There's also a disco room, an alternative-rock room, a rap and reggae room, and even conversation zones with cozy couches and padded walls so you can even have some quiet time. Admission is $15 to $20; no minimum.

Or you could go to **Tramps** (51 West 21st Street; 212–727–7788), which is part dance hall, part concert hall. Sometimes it books bands—country, reggae, rock, or funk blues—

perfect for whatever sort of dancing you prefer. At other times, it brings in entertainers like George Jones or Little Richard and turns into a sit-down club. It's a friendly place to hang out for an entire evening. Open Monday through Saturday, it charges $10 to $30 for tickets and has a two-drink minimum.

DAY THREE: MORNING

Breakfast

Go for a hearty diner breakfast at the **Lucky Dog** (167 First Avenue, between 10th and 11th Streets; budget), which offers traditional American breakfasts at great prices. Then spend the day in the East Village.

❦❧

The streets of the East Village are lined with amusing stores, many of which are open on Sundays. For X-rated romance, look into **Love Saves the Day** (119 Second Avenue at 7th Street) for vintage clothing and sixties and seventies memorabilia, **Religious Sex** (7 St. Mark's Place between Second and Third Avenues) for young designers' wares, and **Little Rickie** (49 First Avenue at 3rd Street) for fun nonessentials like plastic nuns, Elvis memorabilia, and weird postcards.

Spend the rest of your day exploring the East Village or walk south on First Avenue, cross Houston, and continue south to Prince Street, then walk west back into SoHo. Don't let your weekend end without taking a look in some of the many galleries in SoHo. Look into the **Guggenheim Museum SoHo** (575 Broadway, 212–473–3500; $5 admission fee; Wednesday through Friday and Sunday 11:00 A.M. to 6:00 P.M.; Saturday 11:00 A.M. to 8:00 P.M.), which offers changing exhibitions of contemporary art as well as pieces from the Guggenheim's permanent collection, or the **Museum for African Art** (593 Broadway, 212–966–1313; $4, Tuesday through Friday 10:30 A.M. to 5:30 P.M.; weekends: noon–6:00 P.M.)

A particularly romantic downtown art gallery is the **Clocktower Gallery** (346 Broadway at Leonard Street, 12th Floor; 212–233–1096). This complex of studios features interesting exhibits by up-and-coming young artists. Equally interesting is the building itself, which was designed by McKim, Mead, and White in 1895. Although the outside of the building looks a bit worse for wear, the inside is remarkably intact, especially the elegant double-storied General Office on the second floor. An exquisite hand-wound clock tops the building. Climb the four flights of the very steep, twisting stairs above the gallery to see the clock's inner workings, which can be viewed whenever the gallery is open. You can come on Wednesdays at noon to watch the city's "clockmaster" wind it. The gallery is open from September through June, Wednesday through Saturday from noon to 6:00 P.M., but call first in case the schedule has changed. Admission is free. Browsers and buyers are welcome.

FOR MORE ROMANCE

If you visit New York over the summer, think about taking the **Sunset Cocktail Cruises** (Pier 16, South Street Seaport; 212–980–6434). On this charming cruise, you can dance to pop and rock music as you enjoy New York's fabulous harbor from the best vantage point—a yacht! Tickets are $20 per adult; reservations are required; cruises depart at 7:30 and 10:30 P.M. and return at 10:00 P.M. and 1:00 A.M.

ITINERARY 21
Two days and two nights

THANKSGIVING FOR TWO, HOLD THE GUILT

If you're not American (or if you were reared in a perfectly functional family), you may be confused by the title of this itinerary. I'll explain: Thanksgiving is an American national holiday conceived more than 130 years ago. It was designed as an occasion to allow families to come together and joyfully give thanks. Celebrated on the fourth Thursday in November, we were all supposed to climb into our buggies or sleighs and go to Grandma's house and consume a gigantic meal centered on a beautifully cooked (not dry) turkey. After dinner, we were all supposed to kick our shoes off, take a nap or quietly chat, and feel all warm and cozy. Sounds nice, doesn't it?

If you're an average American, however, the title of this itinerary may well speak volumes—and the story may not be so nice. The reason? Sadly, for many families Thanksgiving is one of those obligatory "celebrations" fraught with all sorts of family angst. Instead of feeling warm and cozy, many of us feel guilty about—well, just about everything. We're not married yet; we married a jerk; our father always gets drunk on holidays; our gravy is lumpy; we're vegetarian; we're dieting, and we know we'll consume calories in the high five digits. You name it.

Romance at a Glance

♥ *Stay at The Lowell (212–838–1400).*

♥ *Dine at Arcadia and the Hudson River Club, two of New York's best American restaurants.*

♥ *See a Broadway show.*

♥ *Watch the Macy's Thanksgiving Day Parade.*

♥ *Take a walking tour of Old New York.*

♥ *Take the Staten Island Ferry at dusk.*

So, here's a suggestion. This year, why don't the two of you inform your parents, your siblings, your kids, or your Aunt Gertrude to prepare the traditional turkey without you? Then, you two sneak off to Manhattan for a warm, cozy, angst-free holiday—and give thanks for each other.

Practical notes: For this itinerary, I've suggested that you stay at the Lowell—to my mind, one of New York's most romantic hotels. It is expensive, however, and if you're watching your pocketbook (we're reducing guilt, remember?) for this Thanksgiving getaway, consider staying at the **Crowne Plaza Manhattan** (1605 Broadway; 212–977–4000; 800–243–NYNY; fax: 212–333–7393; moderate; Thanksgiving and other special packages available).

The Crowne Plaza may lack the intimate luxury of the Lowell, but it makes up the difference in location and practical amenities. Its convenient 49th Street and Broadway location is central and makes travel to other parts of Manhattan incredibly easy. There's no better spot to watch the Thanksgiving festivities than the Crowne Plaza lobby, which is open only to hotel guests during the parade. It also has a fabulous health club with an indoor pool, plenty of exercise machines of every kind, and sauna and steam rooms, all of which are great for working off the effects of Thanksgiving dinner.

DAY ONE: WEDNESDAY EVENING

Although the purpose of this itinerary is to "get away from it all," it is still a family holiday and should be a retreat that allows you to experience the comfort of home. No hotel in New York is more home-like (in the most luxurious sense of the word) and yet more romantic than **The Lowell** (28 East 63rd Street; 212–838–1400; 800–221–4444; standard rooms, $365–$475; suites from $595–$1,500). One of New York's most discreet hotels, it stands on a quiet residential street in the midst of Manhattan's posh Upper East Side close to Central Park. Every room is decorated with deep rugs, cushy sofas and armchairs, book-lined walls, and in several special rooms, you will find a wood-burning fireplace and a terrace overlooking the Park and Upper Manhattan. Not at all "flashy," it is incredibly beautiful and the ultimate in luxury and comfort.

Settle into your room, and then walk around the block to an equally discreet and beautiful restaurant—Arcadia.

Dinner

Arcadia (21 East 62nd Street near Fifth Avenue; 212–223–2900, reservations necessary; very expensive) is a small, beautifully decorated, and very romantic restaurant situated in a town house. Owner Anne Rosenzweig has been called one of the best chefs in America. She serves New American cuisine that is inventive and sophisticated and yet somehow homey. Try the chimney-smoked lobster with potato/chervil cakes and tarragon butter or the dill-crusted salmon. Her desserts are grand, especially the warm chocolate bread pudding with brandy custard sauce.

⋰⋱

After dinner, get into a festive mood of the holiday. See one of those marvelous long-running plays or revivals you've been meaning to catch. You can try to get tickets for *A Funny Thing Happened on the Way to the Forum* (St. James Theater; 246 West 44th Street; Tele-Charge: 212–239–6200), *The Phantom of the Opera* (Majestic Theater; 247 West 44th Street; Tele-Charge: 212–239–6200), *Sunset Boulevard* (Minskoff Theater; 200 West 45th Street; TicketMaster Hotline: 212–307–4007), or *The King and I* (Neil Simon Theatre, 250 West 52nd Street; TicketMaster: 212–307–4100).

After the play, take a taxi uptown, and spend a few minutes watching the preparations for the Macy's Thanksgiving Day Parade. On Central Park West and 79th Street, workers will be inflating the biggest Snoopy, Betty Boop, Rocky and Bullwinkle—and many other amusing characters—that you've ever seen. It's great fun to watch.

By now, you may be feeling absolutely giddy that you've escaped the annual angst. Celebrate a little bit by taking a taxi to **Mark's Bar** (at The Mark; 25 East 77th Street between Fifth and Madison Avenues; 212–722–4300). This is one of the chicest hotel bars in the city and a marvelous place to linger together for an hour or so before you return to the Lowell.

For something more traditional and perhaps even more romantic, go to **The Rotunda at the Hotel Pierre** (Fifth Avenue at 61st Street; 212–838–8000; expensive). During the day, English tea is served in this beautiful space, but in the evening, the lights are dimmed and cocktails or splits of champagne are served. The luxurious surroundings, with murals, cozy couches, and a profusion of flowers, make this a perfect end to a perfect evening.

DAY TWO: THANKSGIVING MORNING

Have a leisurely late breakfast or brunch in your lovely room. (Since you'll be having Thanksgiving dinner in the late afternoon, I'm not suggesting lunch, so depending upon the hour, order whatever you'll require until dinner.)

Around noon, head over to watch a bit of the Thanksgiving Day Parade, a national tradition. (The weather is precarious this time of year, but if it is warm enough, walk through Central Park, entering at 66th Street. If it's too cold, take a taxi.) Although it will be crowded along the parade route (West 79th and Central Park West south to 34th Street), the onlookers are not too rowdy. You'll enjoy yourselves.

DAY TWO: AFTERNOON

Catch a taxi (if you can) or better yet, take the subway (#1, 2, or 3 from Broadway and 59th Street; A or C from Central Park West and 59th Street to City Hall). When you exit the subway, make your way to Broadway. Because this is a holiday, most buildings and restaurants in the neighborhood will be closed, but it's still fun to wander around these caverns created by the downtown skyscrapers and try to imagine Old New York. You'll need a map and perhaps a more conventional guide book than this one.

Note the **Woolworth Building** (233 Broadway), designed in 1913 by Cass Gilbert, one of New York's most prestigious architects. The Woolworth "Cathedral of Commerce," built in honor of Frank W. Woolworth and his empire of dime stores, was the tallest building in New York until the Chrysler Building went up in 1930. It's an exquisite building, still a dignified highlight of lower Broadway.

Be sure to stop at **St. Paul's Chapel** (Broadway between Vesey and Fulton Streets). During the two years that New York served as America's capital, President George Washington worshipped here. You can see his chair and bible here. Built in 1766, this is Manhattan's only pre-Revolutionary church. It is a lovely Georgian chapel, reminiscent of St. Martin-in-the-Fields in London, and it has a poignant, tiny graveyard through which you can wander. It's fascinating to note that before the adjacent land was filled, the Hudson River flowed right outside the graveyard.

Walk south down Broadway to **Trinity Church** (Broadway and Wall Street). Trinity parish is the oldest—and most prestigious—Anglican parish in New York; the original Trinity church on this site was built in 1697 and burned down in 1776 during the Revolution. This building, designed by Richard Upjohn and consecrated in 1846, was one of the most dominant structures in New York for generations. If the church is open, visit the small museum and the graveyard where Alexander Hamilton, Robert Fulton, and other well-known Americans rest.

Walk down Wall Street one block to **Federal Hall National Memorial** (26 Wall Street at Nassau). Say hello to George Washington, who has been standing here since 1883. The **New York Stock Exchange** located across Wall Street will be closed on the holiday, but take a look and return on Friday if you'd like a tour.

In honor of Thanksgiving, go down to the Smithsonian Institution's **National Museum of the American Indian** (1 Bowling Green at the end of Broadway; 212–668–6624; free). This museum contains a superb collection of Native American art, artifacts, and crafts displayed in uniquely moving exhibits. It is open daily except December 25 from 10:00 A.M. to 5:00 P.M.

If you have time before dinner, try to stop by **Fraunces Tavern** (54 Pearl Street; 212–269–0144; moderate). The original structure on this site was a mansion built in 1719; Samuel Fraunces converted it into the Queen's Head Tavern in 1762. During the American Revolution, it became a meeting place for revolutionary patriots. Today it is maintained as a museum of the Revolutionary War and eighteenth-century New York life. Admission is charged. The lower floor of the building still operates as a restaurant.

Thanksgiving Dinner

Plan to have Thanksgiving dinner late in the afternoon (about 4:00 P.M. at **The Hudson River Club** (4 World Financial Center, 250 Vesey Street at West Street; 212–786–1500; reservations required; expensive). The Hudson River Club offers a menu that features seasonal dishes made from Hudson River Valley foods. For Thanksgiving, you can be sure that there will be some magnificent treatment for the traditional turkey. Or you could get crazy—and nontraditional (remember, no guilt!) and order duck, Cornish hen, or filet of salmon instead of turkey. Speaking of salmon, try one of the restaurant's signature appetizers: mint-cured and apple-smoked salmon.

At the Hudson River Club, the food is sublime and the setting is quiet, handsome, and intimate, with incredible views of the harbor, the Statue of Liberty, and the sunsets. Linger over your very special Thanksgiving dinner *à deux*. Be sure to take note as the sun sets and the city's lights bubble on. This is surely the most romantic Thanksgiving you could have imagined.

∽⟨⊙⟩∾

After dinner, take a ride on the **Staten Island Ferry**—just for the fun of it. Enter at the South Ferry terminal near Battery Park, which is just a ten-minute walk from the Hudson River Club. For 50 cents per rider each way, you'll enjoy an hour of romance crossing the world's most romantic harbor. The return trip is the most thrilling of all, as the lights of New York City twinkle in the distance.

FOR MORE ROMANCE

Thanksgiving is generally celebrated over a four-day weekend, from the holiday itself, which is always the fourth Thursday in November, through Sunday. The Friday after Thanksgiving is traditionally the busiest shopping day in the year, as Americans gear up for the holiday gift-giving season. Therefore, for more romance, take this weekend as a four-day pleasure trip and shopping spree—and don't feel guilty about it!

ITINERARY 22
Three days and two nights

ROMANCE? IN BROOKLYN? WHO KNEW?

*F*or most of the twentieth century, Brooklyn has absorbed the brunt of endless jokes. The one-time home of "Dem Bums," the Brooklyn Dodgers, Brooklyn is known to outsiders, and to many Manhattanites, as that place where people "tawk" funny. So, who would have thought that Brooklyn was romantic? The fact is, Brooklyn, with its marvelous Victorian heritage, its array of fine restaurants, its pastoral parks, and its numerous cultural resources, has long been one of the most idyllic haunts around New York City.

This itinerary is for Manhattanites who harbor prejudices about Brooklyn as well as for out-of-towners looking for not only a delicious little getaway but an opportunity to explore a very special part of New York City.

Practical notes: Brooklyn is a joy to visit any time of year. The trees in Prospect Park are especially beautiful in the spring and fall, and the beaches are at their most romantic in fall or late winter. The Botanic Garden is at its most exquisite at the height of spring when the cherry trees are in bloom.

Be sure to reserve your room at the Bed and Breakfast on the Park at least two weeks in advance. Not all the rooms have private baths, so be sure to request a room with both a king-size bed and a private bath. Ask for "The Lady Liberty," "Birds Eye View," "Park Suite," or "Grande Victoria." Also, guests are required to stay a minimum of two nights on weekends and three nights over holidays.

For more information about events in Brooklyn, call the **Fund for the Borough of Brooklyn** at (718) 855–7882. They will take your name and address over the telephone and send you a calendar of current events.

Romance at a Glance

♥ *Stay at The Bed & Breakfast on the Park (718–499–6115).*

♥ *Dine at the River Cafe, Gage & Tollner, Primorksy's, and other fabulous restaurants in Brooklyn.*

♥ *Stroll through Prospect Park and the magical Brooklyn Botanic Garden.*

♥ *Walk on the boardwalk and beach at Coney Island.*

♥ *Tour Brooklyn Heights and trek across the famous Brooklyn Bridge at sundown.*

DAY ONE: EVENING

The very best way to get to Brooklyn is by way of the bridge. You know which bridge: the Brooklyn Bridge. So, if you are going to Brooklyn from Manhattan, splurge on a cab—it will probably cost about $7—and delight in the views as you cross the famous expanse. (If you are coming from either LaGuardia or Kennedy Airports, both of which are in Queens County, take a taxi to Brooklyn. Since both Brooklyn and Queens are on Long Island, you won't be crossing "The Bridge" just yet.)

As you climb the front stoop of the **Bed & Breakfast on the Park** (113 Prospect Park West, Park Slope, Brooklyn, New York 11215; 718–499–6115; $275–$350 per night), you'll feel as if you've stepped back into the nineteenth century. The oak door provides a hint of the exquisite woodwork and original metalwork that highlight this impeccably restored 1892 limestone town house. The decor is spectacular, including fine paintings by the proprietor's relatives, many Victorian antiques, and glorious lace-, chintz-, and velvet-covered furnishings. The service is both friendly and genteel.

Dinner

Catch a cab to the **River Cafe** (1 Water Street, Brooklyn; 718–522–5200), the restaurant that food critic Gael Greene describes as "an ardent hideaway for romance and seduction." About a fifteen-minute cab ride from your bed and breakfast, the River Cafe is located on a barge directly under the Brooklyn Bridge. If the weather is warm, enjoy a cocktail—and maybe dinner, too—on the deck overlooking the East River. From April to October, you may be able to watch the sun set majestically behind Lady Liberty.

The River Cafe is considered to be the greatest dining experience in Brooklyn and one of the best in all New York City. You have a glorious view of one of the most romantic sights in the world: Lower Manhattan, the confluence of the East and Hudson Rivers, and the Statue of Liberty. Try to reserve one of the nine window tables.

The menu is as great as the view. Dinner is $65 prix fixe for three courses, or, you might try the six-course tasting menu for $85, which will give you a taste of more of the chef's specialties. The menu is a melange of delights created by chef Rick Laakkonen, but the focus is on fish. Choose from among such treats as Penobscot Bay Peekytow crab and asparagus salad, fruitwood-smoked salmon, sauteed yellowfin tuna, or crisp black sea bass. The desserts are also fabulous, especially the chocolate confections. Try Crunchy Praline and Bittersweet Chocolate Torte.

Plan to relax and enjoy a very special evening. By the way, the restaurant claims that more proposals of marriage take place here than in any other restaurant in America! So if such thoughts are on your mind, this is the place.

Taxicabs will be waiting outside the door to take you back to your B&B.

DAY TWO: MORNING

Breakfast

Don't miss breakfast at the B&B. It is prepared personally by the owner, Liana Paolella, or her daughter, Jonna. The menu varies, but Liana or Jonna often include fresh fruit, homemade rolls, German pancakes, crepes, country bacon, or gourmet omelettes. The food is delicious, and the ambience of the warm Victorian kitchen together with the delightful company—even if you wanted to be alone!—is marvelous. Eat up, because this is to be a day of strolling and just "being" together.

✦

As you walk out the front door of the B&B, you'll again have the feeling that you are stepping back in time. Directly in front of you lies **Prospect Park**, which is Brooklyn's answer to Manhattan's Central Park. In fact, it, too, was designed by Frederick Law Olmsted and Calvert Vaux, and some experts believe they did an even more beautiful job here. The park contains 562 acres of scenic woodland, broad meadows, picturesque bluffs, several ponds, a lake, a zoo, a Quaker burial ground, and a Dutch Colonial farmhouse.

Turn left as you leave the stoop and walk down the avenue called Prospect Park West. This street is lined with beautiful houses, most of which were designed and built in the late nineteenth and early twentieth century as developers organized the urbanization of Brooklyn and it became clear to wealthy people that Prospect Park West was going to become a fashionable avenue. One house, **Litchfield Villa**, located between Fourth and Fifth Streets, actually stands within the park. This house was built about ten years before the development of Prospect Park and is the oldest mansion in Park Slope.

As you head north on Prospect Park West toward Grand Army Plaza, consider wending your way up and down a few of these marvelous "suburban" side streets that run perpendicular to Prospect Park West. **Montgomery Place**, for example, is considered Park Slope's

"Block Beautiful." The one-block street was developed between 1887 and 1892 as a single real estate venture by famed designer Cass Gilbert. As you walk down the block, notice the intricate scrollwork, gables, and windows on each of the houses. **Carroll Street**, **President Street**, and **Garfield Place** are three more particularly charming blocks.

At the top of Prospect Park West is **Grand Army Plaza** designed by Olmsted and Vaux as the grand entrance to Prospect Park. The oval-shaped plaza itself was designed in 1862, but its statuary came later. You can't miss the triumphal **Soldiers' and Sailors' Memorial**, erected in 1892 and dedicated to the Union forces of the Civil War. It is Brooklyn's most splendid monument.

Turn right and stroll around the Plaza until you get to **Eastern Parkway**. Bear to your right and continue walking along the Parkway until you reach the corner of Empire Boulevard and Eastern Parkway. There you will find the entrance to the **Brooklyn Botanic Garden**, which is located at 1000 Washington Avenue (718–622–4433) between the two larger streets. (Admission is free.)

The Brooklyn Botanic Garden is not only a monument to Brooklyn; it is considered one of the greatest horticultural centers in the world. The **Cherry Esplanade** is most beautiful in April and May, and the **Cranford Rose Garden** blossoms spectacularly from June through September. The lovely **Shakespeare Garden** features eighty different flowers and herbs mentioned in Shakespearean works. The **Japanese Hill and Pond Garden** are also exquisite, and the **Fragrance Garden for the Blind** is an olfactory marvel. The glass **Conservatory** designed by McKim, Mead and White is filled with tropical and temperate plants from all over the world. In any season, the Botanic Garden is a pleasure to just meander through and enjoy its peace and beauty.

If the weather is bad or if you have extra time, take in the **Brooklyn Museum** (200 Eastern Parkway; 718–638–5000), located right next door to the Botanic Garden. Considered by some to be a small—or even second-rate—Metropolitan, the Brooklyn Museum is neither small nor second rate. It boasts outstanding Greek, Roman, Middle Eastern, Moorish, and Egyptian galleries. The American Collection with works from John Singer Sargent and the Hudson River School is marvelous, and the European art from the Renaissance to the Post-Impressionist period is remarkable. Explore their well-stocked gift shop, too. The museum is closed on Mondays and Tuesdays. On Wednesday through Sunday, it is open from 10:00 A.M. to 5:00 P.M.

DAY TWO: AFTERNOON

Lunch

If the day is warm, enjoy a light lunch at the **Patio Restaurant**, an outdoor cafe near the Conservatory in the Botanic Garden. In inclement weather try the Brooklyn Museum's cafe, which serves typical but tasty cafeteria brunch and lunch fare.

※

To my mind, one of life's most romantic adventures is a slow, leisurely walk along a seaside boardwalk. Believe it or not, Brooklyn has just such a walk; it's at, of all places— **Coney Island**. (See "Winter Beach.") A word of warning: If it is a hot summer day, stay in Prospect Park. Coney Island is always unbearably crowded in the summer, and is, therefore, definitely *not* romantic. (On the other hand, if scary rides turn you on—Coney Island has those, too.) In spring, fall, or even the dead of winter, however, the Coney Island boardwalk is a remarkable source of nostalgia and romance.

DAY TWO: EVENING

Dinner

Have dinner at one of Brooklyn's landmarks: **Gage & Tollner** (372 Fulton Street, near Jay Street in downtown Brooklyn, 718–875–5181; moderate). For over a century, Gage & Tollner has been a Brooklyn landmark. It represented the epitome of Victorian dining in this once Victorian city. Closed for several years, Gage & Tollner has recently reopened, offering old-fashioned American fare in utterly beautiful, glittering Victorian surroundings.

After dinner, enjoy a quiet evening in your beautiful Brooklyn bed-and-breakfast.

DAY THREE: MORNING

Again, the elegant breakfast served at the Bed & Breakfast on the Park is not to be missed. Afterwards, take the #2 or 3 subway to the Borough Hall subway stop and Brooklyn Heights.

Brooklyn Heights is one of the most charming towns in the United States. Gothic churches, a beautiful promenade, and architecturally eclectic government buildings give Brooklyn Heights a unique character than is both urban and suburban.

This tour begins when you exit the Borough Hall subway. You'll be standing across the street from the building that was once Brooklyn's City Hall. This glamorous "Borough Hall" was completed in 1849, during Brooklyn's heyday.

The Borough Hall station is large with several exits; therefore when you come out of the subway, ask directions to Joralemon Street, and walk west along Joralemon until you come to the corner of Joralemon and Clinton Streets. Clinton Street is named after De Witt Clinton, a Manhattan politician who served as mayor of New York City and as governor of New York State.

Turn right on Clinton and walk two blocks until you reach Montague Street. (I know the neighborhood doesn't look like much yet, but don't worry—you won't be disappointed.) Turn left on Montague Street, which is the "downtown" of Brooklyn Heights. Montague Street is linked with the name of Brooklyn's famous baseball team—the Dodgers. In the late nineteenth century, electric trolley cars would take residents through the Heights to the ferry terminal. Since residents of Brooklyn became used to dodging the trolleys, Brooklyn's baseball team became known as the Brooklyn "Dodgers."

As you come toward the western end of Montague Street, you'll see that you are heading toward the East river and the Brooklyn Heights Esplanade or "the Promenade," as it is commonly called.

Arguably one of New York City's greatest attractions, **the Promenade** is also one of its most romantic. I hope the weather is sunny and sparkling when you venture onto the Promenade, but don't worry if it's not. The Promenade is as fabulous in the dead of winter as it is at the height of summer; as marvelous in the morning as it is at sundown.

Take some time to sit on the benches. You'll feel as though you have entered a picture postcard. You'll be struck by the marvelous view of downtown Manhattan, and of course, you can't miss the **Statue of Liberty**. **Ellis Island National Monument** sits majestically just to the right of the Statue. Look for the Staten Island ferry steaming regally across the harbor. At the extreme left, you'll catch a glimpse of the Verrazano Narrows Bridge that connects Brooklyn with Staten Island. And, of course, to the right is the **Brooklyn Bridge**.

After you have absorbed all the wonders of New York Harbor, stroll north on the Promenade toward the Brooklyn Bridge. To your right are the brownstones that line Columbia Heights, the residential street that runs parallel to the Promenade. Needless to say, the houses that command this spectacular view are some of the most expensive—not only in Brooklyn Heights, but in all New York.

When you leave the Promenade, you should be at the corner of Clark Street. Walk east up Clark. Stop at the corner of Willow Street and look right to see one of the more magnificent views of a Brooklyn Heights residential street. You may want to check out two of the more famous houses: 155 Willow was owned by playwright Arthur Miller, and 70 Willow is the place where author Truman Capote wrote *Breakfast at Tiffany's*. Now, make your way east one more block to Hicks Street.

Hicks Street is named for the Hicks family who owned a farm in the Heights in the early nineteenth century. The term "hick" (American slang for a provincial or yokel) comes from this family who used to bring its produce into Manhattan to sell.

Turn left on Hicks and continue north. The streets will begin to bear the names of fruits or trees like Orange, Pineapple, Willow, and Cranberry. Turn right at Orange Street. A half-block up on the north side is one of America's most historic churches, the **Plymouth Church of the Pilgrims** (Orange Street between Hicks and Henry). Unlike many of the Victorian houses of worship found in Brooklyn, this church has a decidedly spartan appearance. Built in 1847, it is the church where its founder and first minister Henry Ward Beecher held forth for forty years and where Abraham Lincoln worshipped on several occasions. At the back of the courtyard that connects the church with the parish house is a statue of Beecher sculpted by Guzon Borglum, best known for creating Mount Rushmore. Beecher was a well-known abolitionist, and the church was a stop on the Underground Railroad that helped fleeing slaves escape to Canada.

Double back along Orange Street to Hicks. Take a right on Hicks and walk to Cranberry Street. At the house near the southwest corner of Hicks and Cranberry, Walt Whitman set the type for his famed volume, *Leaves of Grass.* Continue along Cranberry Street toward the Promenade, and you will pass some of the oldest buildings in the Heights.

Turn right on Willow and walk to **24 Middagh Street**, which some refer to as the "Queen of Brooklyn Heights." This house is one of the few surviving homes built in the Dutch Federal style and is thought to be the oldest house in the neighborhood. As you walk west down Middagh Street, you are in the oldest part of the Heights. At the corner of Columbia Heights, turn right. Walk down the hill to Old Fulton Street and the Fulton Ferry District.

Turn right at the corner of Old Fulton Street and walk a few hundred yards until you reach the **Eagle Warehouse and Storage Company**. This was the site of Walt Whitman's newspaper, the ***Brooklyn Eagle***. You'll also have a view of the **Watchtower Buildings**, owned by the Jehovah's Witnesses, an institution whose world headquarters is in the Heights.

Double back down Fulton Street and walk to the end and pause at the ferry slip. This point was once one of Brooklyn's most vital commercial districts, and the original Fulton Ferry sailed from this slip to Peck Slip across the river. Take a moment to feel awed by the magnificence of the Brooklyn Bridge that hovers above.

DAY THREE: AFTERNOON

Lunch

By now, surely you're ready to rest a bit. You might want to stop for a late lunch at the **River Cafe** (1 Water Street; expensive), where you dined on Friday night. Brunch is every bit as fabulous as dinner, featuring such creative entrees as whole wheat waffles and fresh berries, orange crepes, or Hangtown fry omelette with grilled oysters and tomato-leek fondue. The view is still wonderful, too, only now you can see Manhattan in the full light of day.

For a change of pace, try **Pete's Downtown** (1 Old Fulton Street; 718–858–3510). Pete's features a traditional, reasonably-priced Italian fare of appetizers, pastas, and desserts in a charming "Old Brooklyn" atmosphere.

❧❧❧

After lunch, head east up Front Street. In order to get onto the Bridge, you must climb some discreet steps that are located under the bridge at the juncture where Front Street crosses beneath the bridge. (If you have trouble finding the steps, just ask anyone on the street. You'll probably see pedestrians making their way toward the bridge entrance.) As you begin your trek up the ramp of the bridge, bear in mind that you are about to embark on one of the greatest sights—and walks—quite literally in the world.

The Brooklyn Bridge, the first suspension bridge built in New York City, is not only an icon of Brooklyn, beloved by its residents. It is also a structure with a history to match its architectural beauty. When it was built, a bridge had never been erected over a body of water as wide or as deep as the East River.

John Augustus Roebling, a wire maker from Trenton, New Jersey, conceived the idea for the bridge, but he died in 1869 just as work began. His son, Colonel Washington Augustus Roebling, took over. As a result of endless hours working in great dumbbells filled with pressurized air, Roebling (and many other workers) developed "the bends," or caisson disease. When he became crippled and was confined to his bed, his wife, Emily, took over the day-to-day management of the bridge. Today, a plaque on the bridge acknowledges Emily Roebling's work. The bridge was finally completed in 1883.

It is almost exactly one mile from the steps ascending the bridge until you descend from the bridge in Manhattan. When you come off the Bridge, you'll see the Brooklyn Bridge subway stop. Take the subway (#4 or #5) back to Brooklyn.

FOR MORE ROMANCE

If you wish to attend a concert or the ballet while you are visiting Brooklyn, find out what's playing at the **Brooklyn Academy of Music** (30 Lafayette Avenue; 718–636–4100). Located in central Brooklyn, BAM offers outstanding performances, often tending toward the innovative and avant-garde.

WINTER

ITINERARY 23
Three days and two nights

CHRISTMAS IN MANHATTAN

*T*o my mind, there is no more romantic time to visit New York than during the Christmas season. The air is brisk, Santa manages to appear on practically every street corner, Christmas music rings out from every direction, and shoppers bustle in and out of every store and market.

Every neighborhood in the city is decked out in its holiday finest, with wreaths on brownstone doorways and pine boughs wound luxuriously around wrought-iron fences. Sometimes it even snows, spreading a fluffy white coat over tired sidewalks and streets. It's beautiful.

Christmas is one of America's most traditional holidays. From late November through New Year's Eve, New York is eager to party. So come to the City and create a tradition of your own: a romantic getaway in preparation for a merry Christmas season.

Practical notes: New York City is crowded during the Christmas season—which seems to begin earlier every year. To be sure that your weekend has no disappointments, book your hotel and your restaurants very early. I would suggest you call at least six weeks in advance.

Romance at a Glance

♥ *Stay at the St. Regis Hotel (212–753–4500).*

♥ *Dine at Le Bernardin and One If By Land, Two If By Sea.*

♥ *Shop at special New York shops.*

♥ *Go ice-skating at Rockefeller Center beneath the beautiful Christmas tree.*

♥ *View the Christmas trees at the Metropolitan Museum of Art and the American Museum of Natural History.*

♥ *See* The Nutcracker *at Lincoln Center or the Radio City Music Hall Christmas Spectacular.*

♥ *Go to a midnight carol service at one of Manhattan's wonderful churches.*

DAY ONE: EVENING

When celebrating the birth of a king, there's no better place to stay than **The St. Regis** (2 East 55th Street at Fifth Avenue; 212–753–4500 or 800–759–7550; fax: 212–787–3447; double rooms, $425 to $525 per night; suites, $650 to $4,600; weekend rates available on request). Five years ago, the St. Regis reopened after a three-year refurbishing that restored it to its original 1904 elegance. When it was opened in the early twentieth century by its founder John Jacob Astor, it was designed for "a class of people who want absolutely the best quality of hotel accommodation," and the St. Regis still adheres strongly to that standard.

The "new" St. Regis is somewhat different from the old; reconstruction of the interior resulted in fewer but larger rooms (365 down from 557) and larger hallways and more luxurious suites (fifty-two in all). The lobby appears much the same, but the Astor Court tea room (with its *trompe l'oeil* ceiling), the King Cole Bar, and the divine Cognac Room are all new. Still, nothing in the hotel looks new; care has been taken to give the entire hotel a look of distinguished elegance.

Every room is luxurious and elegant, decorated in a French style. But looks are only part of the story; in fact, the St. Regis specializes in service. A unique aspect of the hotel is its provision on each floor for a *maître d'étage,* a personal butler on call twenty-four hours a day to take special note of each guest's needs. Male and female, all of the butlers have been trained in the English tradition by a former butler to the Queen, and all are visions of accommodation and discretion. What more could you ask for!?

When you have settled in your room, head out to Fifth Avenue. Window shop for an hour or so. Near your hotel you'll find **Tiffany** (57th and Fifth Avenue) and **Trump Tower** (725 Fifth Avenue), the glitziest mall in America. Check out **Asprey**, founded in London in 1781 by William Asprey as *the* source for cultivated gift-givers seeking the elegant and the unusual in antique porcelain, silver, and antique jewelry. One of Asprey's most intriguing items is available only between Thanksgiving and Christmas: an incredible selection of festive English Christmas crackers together with little gifts to fill them. Choose from such trinkets as a champagne stopper, a sterling silver key ring, or an 18-carat gold pin.

Walk south on Fifth Avenue until you come to **Rockefeller Center** (Fifth Avenue at 50th Street). Take a close look at the marvelous gigantic Christmas tree, usually a Norway spruce about 80 feet tall. Nothing is more romantic—especially during the Christmas season—than to go ice-skating at the Rockefeller Center rink with the Christmas tree as background. (You can rent skates at the rink.) Go for a couple of turns either before or after dinner; the rink stays open late into the evening.

Dinner

For dinner, you could return to the St. Regis and settle into the ultimate in luxury, the restaurant **Lespinasse** (see page 119). Or you could try **Le Bernardin** (155 West 51st Street between Sixth and Seventh Avenues; 212–489–1515; very expensive). Many describe this contemporary French restaurant as "magical," and it is one of the most astonishing restaurants in New York. Chef Eric Ripert specializes in seafood, but it's seafood beyond your wildest imagination: osetra-topped mackerel tartar roast, baby lobster tail on asparagus risotto, a puff pastry "pizza" of shrimp, foie gras, and lobster pot-au-feu—and so on. It's a remarkable place.

It's a fifteen-minute walk back to your hotel; put your arms around each other on the stroll back. For a nightcap, stop in the **King Cole Bar** (at the St. Regis Hotel), every New

Yorker's favorite spot for a romantic tête-à-tête. Ask the bartender to explain the hidden meaning in the magnificent Maxwell Parrish painting that hangs majestically behind the bar.

DAY TWO: Morning

Have breakfast in the privacy of your room, then tour New York, doing some Christmas shopping as you go. I, for one, would avoid the midtown crush of shoppers and head to another neighborhood. For many years, I lived on the Upper East Side (95th Street to be exact) and used to do all my Christmas shopping between 79th and 96th Streets, Fifth Avenue to Lexington—no problem. These days, this neighborhood (known as Carnegie Hill) has become much swankier and the shops are even better.

Take a taxi to Madison Avenue and 72nd Street (or just hike up Madison). Stop at the **Polo/Ralph Lauren** (72nd and Madison) and then go on to **Tenzig and Pema** (956 Madison Avenue), a must for unusual toys for both adults and children. Head north; you'll be dazzled by the incredible variety of shops. Two bookstores that you must explore: **The Corner Bookstore** (1313 Madison Avenue) for children's books and special grown-up treats, and **Kitchen Arts & Letters** (1435 Lexington Avenue) for cookbooks and related culinary ephemera. Don't miss the exquisite Christmas tree at the **Metropolitan Museum of Art** (Fifth Avenue at 82nd Street)—or their gift shop, for that matter; it's the best.

Lunch

Plan to have a late lunch. Hail a taxi and take it downtown to the **Union Square Cafe** (21 East 16th Street between Fifth Avenue and Union Square West; 212–243–4020; moderate to expensive; reservations required; book weeks in advance). Union Square Cafe is one of New York's most popular restaurants, featuring American seasonal fare. Owner Danny Meyer and chef Michael Romano delight in using fresh, local produce, and they buy much of the restaurant's fish and vegetables from the Greenmarket down the block. The cafe menu features oysters, which are a must. Try the Tuna Club sandwich; you've never seen a tuna sandwich like it.

DAY TWO: AFTERNOON

Spend the afternoon exploring the revitalized "Ladies' Mile," which runs from Union Square north to 23rd Street, then up and down Fifth and Sixth Avenues. Stop in at **ABC Carpet & Home** (881 and 888 Broadway at 19th Street), less a carpet store than a new-fashioned emporium; **Fishes Eddy** (889 Broadway) for a rather remarkable assortment of institutional china; and **Lola Millinery** (2 East 17th Street) for chic hats. Stroll down Fifth Avenue next. Don't miss **B. Shackman** (85 Fifth Avenue) for great stocking-stuffers like dollhouse furniture and reproductions of old wind-up toys. Stop at **Emporio Armani** (110 Fifth) for elegant designer clothing, then go over to Sixth Avenue for a look into its fabulous shops. **Bed, Bath, and Beyond** (620 Sixth Avenue) is great for linens and kitchenware, **Old Navy** (610 Sixth Avenue) for clothes, **Barnes & Noble** superstore (675 Sixth Avenue at 22nd Street) for books. (Actually, I prefer the **Barnes & Noble** located at 33 East 17th Street, for no other reason than that it is located in a beautiful building.) In either case, you can stop at the B&N cafe, rest your feet, and revive yourselves with a cup of tea or an espresso.

DAY TWO: EVENING

Dinner

For a festive pre-Christmas dinner, dine at **One If By Land, Two If By Sea** (17 Barrow Street, Greenwich Village; 212–228–0822; reservations recommended; expensive). This restaurant is perhaps the most beautiful in the Village—and the most venerable. It's located in a beautifully restored eighteenth-century carriage house and stable formerly owned by Aaron Burr. One of the reasons this setting is so perfect is that it is said that the house is haunted by Burr, a true-life "ghost of Christmas past." Fresh flowers, roaring fireplaces, and beautiful luxurious tables would provide romance enough in other places, but here even more is typical: Each evening at dinnertime a pianist quietly plays love songs, show tunes, and classical favorites. More importantly, the food is tasty and as tasteful as the ambience.

⋐⋑⋐⋑

Have an after-dinner drink in the bar. Snuggle up in one of the sofas next to the crackling fire. A pianist is always there, playing Broadway tunes and favorite love songs. This is a wonderful and festive way to end a delightful day.

DAY THREE: MORNING

Have a late breakfast or brunch in your room or in the Astor Court. If the mood strikes you, take a taxi to the **American Museum of Natural History** (Central Park West at 79th Street; 212–769–5100). Stop in the Theodore Roosevelt Memorial Hall on the first floor to see their annual Origami Holiday Tree, a 15-foot Christmas tree decorated with more than 2,000 origami pieces representing animals and objects in the museum's collection, from bears to meteorites. Otherwise, window shop along Fifth Avenue.

DAY THREE: AFTERNOON

Plan to see a matinee of ***The Nutcracker,*** presented every year by the New York City Ballet (State Theater, Lincoln Center, 70 Lincoln Center Plaza, Broadway at 64th Street; 212–875–5400 for events; 212–870–5570 for tickets.) The Balanchine dancers combined with Tchaikovsky's music are sublime—an ideal way to celebrate the Christmas season.

Buy a special present for your loved one at one of the terrific shops you'll be visiting. Make it something that will last forever, and remind you both of your gala holiday weekend together. One suggestion: Buy a silver frame at Tiffany's. Write down your ten favorite things about your honey and put it in the frame. Merry Christmas.

If something campier tickles your fancy, see the **Radio City Music Hall Christmas Spectacular** (call Ticketmaster's Radio City Hotline: 212–307–1000). The extravaganza features the Rockettes and a varied cast that often includes live camels and the like. It's great fun!

After the show, go for afternoon tea at the **Palm Court** in the **Plaza Hotel** (768 Fifth Avenue between 58th and 59th Streets; 212–759–3000; expensive). Opened in 1907 and now a National Historic Landmark, the Plaza Hotel has been attracting New Yorkers and visitors for a full century. Today, tea in the Palm Court is as delightfully festive as always.

Best of all, if you haven't done so already, visit **F. A. O. Schwarz** (767 Fifth Avenue at 59th Street). A friend of mine always told her children that F. A. O. Schwarz was a museum; that none of these wondrous dolls, stuffed toys, and eye-popping playthings were for sale. That's not true, of course, so indulge the kid in both of you and buy each other a toy.

Happy Holidays!

FOR MORE ROMANCE

If you are planning to spend Christmas Eve and Christmas Day in Manhattan, plan carefully; bear in mind that many (if not most) shops, restaurants, and other public places will be closed on Christmas Day.

On Christmas Eve attend a midnight service. Many churches offer marvelous Christmas music festivals during the Christmas season. Churches famed for their Christmas music are **St. Thomas Episcopal Church** (Fifth Avenue at 53rd Street; 212–757–7013; **St. Ignatius Loyola** (980 Park Avenue at 84th Street; 212–288–3588), and the **Cathedral of St. John the Divine** (1047 Amsterdam Avenue; 212–662–2133). Check the newspapers or call the churches for times. These services are usually extremely well attended, so arrive at least an hour ahead of time to find a good seat.

Some very special restaurants offer wonderful Christmas dinners. Among these are **One If By Land, Two If By Sea**; **Tavern on the Green**; and **The Russian Tea Room**. The Russian Tea Room happens to be one of my very favorites. The restaurant is being refurbished at the time of this writing, but if it has reopened by the time you wish to come to New York, I strongly recommend a Christmas celebration there. Reserve well in advance.

Merry Christmas.

A TRADITIONAL NEW YORK NEW YEAR'S EVE

*R*emember the film *When Harry Met Sally* with Billy Crystal and Meg Ryan? After years of friendship, Harry and Sally finally figure out on New Year's Eve that they love each other. Harry runs all the way from the Washington Square Arch to the Waldorf-Astoria hotel (about 2 miles, actually) to inform Sally of his revelation.

The last place I would recommend being at midnight on New Year's Eve is at Times Square in Manhattan. Peopled with pickpockets, crazies, and well-intentioned drunks, it is anything but romantic. But that's my personal opinion. For me, a romantic New Year's Eve is spent in my own house, sharing a warm, home-cooked dinner and a bottle of champagne with the man I love.

However, if you simply must do New Year's Eve on the town New York style, then by all means go, and enjoy it. Here are my suggestions, designed to ensure not only that you will have a true Manhattan New Year's Eve experience, but also that your evening will be a huge romantic success.

Practical notes: As I've said several times, New York is the city of superlatives—and at no time is this more evident than on New Year's Eve. On New Year's Eve, New York City is at its *most crowded, most rowdy,* and *most expensive.* More than any other evening of the year, it requires planning. Don't wait until the last minute to try to secure hotel, dinner, or air travel reservations. While it may not be impossible, I guarantee that you'll have problems. Make your plans at least six weeks ahead of time and reconfirm your reservations one week before you come.

Romance at a Glance

♥ *Stay at the famous Waldorf-Astoria Hotel (800-WALDORF).*

♥ *Dine at La Grenouille (212–752–1495).*

♥ *Attend First Night activities, including dancing at Grand Central Station, and ring in the New Year from the top of the Empire State Building.*

Traffic is heavy on New Year's Eve, so you probably will not be able to find a taxi. Even if you can, you probably won't be able to travel very far in it. Although the weather may be cold, plan to walk on New Year's Eve.

All that being said, you can still have one of the most memorable evenings of your lives. For the past few years a collection of New York City "business improvement districts" have planned "First Night, New York," an extravaganza that features scores of performances at several landmark sites around the city, such as The New York Public Library, Grand Central Station, and the Empire State Building. The festivities start at 11:00 A.M. on New Year's Eve and continue until 1:00 A.M. on January 1. It includes activities for children (if you really can't find a baby sitter), singles (you'll be together, but you can still attend), and, of course, romantic couples. Alcohol is not sold at the First Night events, which means the problems with drunken revelers are kept to a minimum. If you want to imbibe, you'll have to provide your own—on your own time.

The "button" that allows you admission to the various events can be purchased at the New York Public Library gift shop, Grand Central Terminal, Penn Station, the Bryant Park half-price ticket booth, or many D'Agostino supermarkets. Admission buttons are $20 for adults. For more information, call First Night: 212–922–9393.

Finally, make sure you are well stocked with New Year's Eve essentials: champagne and caviar. Order champagne from **Sherry-Lehman Wine & Spirits** (679 Madison Avenue; 212–838–6151). This is arguably the best liquor store in New York City, and they deliver.

For caviar, order from **The Petrossian Delicacies Shop** (182 West 58th Street at Seventh Avenue; 212–245–2217). Petrossian is arguably the best caviar store in the world! (Really!) They also offer gift baskets with names that hint at their purpose: for instance, "Love at First Bite" offers 50 grams each of beluga, ossetra, and sevruga caviars; "Petrossian Tryst" offers 100 grams of salmon roe, ½ pound of smoked salmon, ¼ pound of crème fraîche, and two vacuum-packed packs of blini. Visit the Petrossian shop to make your selection or order over the telephone (early). Petrossian will deliver in Manhattan, with a purchase of $100 or more.

THE EVENING

Who hasn't heard of the **Waldorf-Astoria**? When the first Waldorf-Astoria opened in 1893 (on the land where the Empire State Building now stands), it instantly became a mecca for New York high society. The well-known Peacock Alley was named such because Victorian dandies strutted through the hotel with the hopes of catching the eye of beautiful ladies. In 1931, the Waldorf moved to its present site on Park Avenue, and today the majestic lady commands the entire block between 49th and 50th Streets, Park Avenue to Lexington.

Arriving at the Waldorf is thrilling—even if you've been there a hundred times. Always busy, it will be bustling overtime on New Year's Eve. The lobby is awe-inspiring, a landmark Art Deco treasure. Notice the *Wheel of Life* mosaic by French artist Louis Rigal, the tall columns, and the beautiful paneled walls. At the center of the impressive lobby stands the famed bronze and mahogany clock.

The Waldorf is a very large—and very grand—hotel, but each of the 1,120 guest rooms and ninety-five suites is luxurious and impressive. All the rooms, whether single or suites,

Romantic movies set in New York are numerous. Here are a few suggestions: Breakfast at Tiffany's; An Affair to Remember; When Harry Met Sally; Manhattan; Annie Hall; Manhattan Murder Mystery; Barefoot in the Park; West Side Story; Hannah and Her Sisters—*and, oddly enough,* Sleepless in Seattle.

have marble baths, and many of the suites have fireplaces. Needless to say, every amenity is available. The hotel is located at 301 Park Avenue. For reservations and information, call 212–355–3000, 800–WALDORF; or fax: 212–872–7272. Standard rooms are $295–$330; suites are $350–$1,000; weekend packages are available on request.

Luxuriate in your room or suite, then spend some time dressing for dinner. (For New Year's Eve in New York, you could wear anything from blue jeans to a formal gown or tuxedo—which could be great fun. For this itinerary, I'd suggest a silky dress for her and a suit for him.) Before you head out for dinner, you may want to have a drink in the **Peacock Alley Lounge** or the Park Avenue lobby **Cocktail Terrace**. Hold hands and watch the hustle and bustle of holiday New York go by.

Since getting a taxicab on New Year's Eve is next to impossible, you'll be happy to know that even if it is freezing cold outside, La Grenouille, the restaurant you'll be dining at, is only a ten-minute walk from the Waldorf.

Dinner

La Grenouille (3 East 52nd Street, between Fifth and Madison Avenues;

212–752–1495; very expensive) is one of New York's most glamorous French restaurants. This lush, flower-filled restaurant is the ideal place to end the old year and begin the new. It's a place to luxuriate over a romantic, quiet dinner. Start with champagne and caviar, or perhaps the restaurant's venerable lobster bisque. Since you're dining at "The Frog Pond," you might want sauteed frogs' legs or a classic filet of beef. Whatever you select, it will be impeccably prepared, and you'll feel like pampered royalty.

⚘

When you leave the restaurant, prepare to join in the delightful activities that surround "First Night." Walk south down Fifth Avenue to **Bryant Park** (behind the New York Public Library, 42nd Street and Fifth Avenue) and see if there's a performance or party in progress. Then turn east and go to **Grand Central Terminal** (42nd Street between Vanderbilt and Lexington Avenues).

If you've ever scurried through Grand Central at rush hour, you probably won't recognize the place. On First Night, Grand Central Terminal turns into a dreamland. A marvelous dance band is playing, ladies in gowns and men in tuxedos are dancing, and the place is electric with fun. Other dance bands—featuring line dancing, reggae, disco, and other treats—are located in various parts of the station and the lobby of the connecting Met Life building. Be sure to stroll around and join in the fun.

At about 11:00 P.M., start to make your way to the **Empire State Building** (34th Street and Fifth Avenue). It may take you an hour to walk there and make your way to the top, but it will be worth it. Ringing in the New Year atop the Empire State Building is a once-in-a-lifetime event. So have your own affair to remember, and give each other a kiss as the clock strikes midnight.

You will probably have to walk back to the Waldorf (it's about 15 blocks from the Empire State Building), but you'll hardly feel like you're hiking. The streets will be bustling, and everyone will be happy. It's all part of the party.

When you get back to the Waldorf, you could go for a last dance on the hotel's Starlight Roof. (Big bands still play there on New Year's Eve—and yes, it is televised!) If I were you, I'd go back to your room, break open that marvelous bottle of champagne you carefully bought, open up your caviar, and have your own very private party.

Happy New Year!

ITINERARY 25
Three days and two nights

HARLEM DREAMS

*H*arlem is one of the most romantic neighborhoods in New York City. I mean it. Yes, sadly, the word *Harlem* evokes thoughts of urban blight and crime. But from the earliest days, Harlem in fact was always a beautiful refuge—first for the Indians, then for the colonial rich, and, starting in the early twentieth century, for affluent blacks who thought they had finally found a place where they could buy safe and attractive properties.

By the 1920s, during the Harlem Renaissance, Harlem was home to an astonishing number of America's greatest artists and writers: Zora Neale Hurston, Langston Hughes, Cab Calloway, Scott Joplin, Bill "Bojangles" Robinson, Fats Waller, Ethel Waters, and Richard Wright, to name a few. The numbers of prominent African-Americans who were either born or at some time lived in Harlem are incredible: Alvin Ailey, Thurgood Marshall, Willie Mays, James Baldwin, Eubie Blake, Duke Ellington, Ella Fitzgerald, Billie Holiday, Marcus Garvey, W. E. B. DuBois, Althea Gibson, Billie Dee Williams, Malcolm X, Sammy Davis, Jr., David Dinkins, Jimi Hendrix—the list is endless.

Then came the Depression, which was devastating to the black community. The awesome poverty resulted in the blighted streets now so readily associated with Harlem. In recent years, however, great strides have been made to bring Harlem back to its glory days and to pay tribute to its rich African-American culture.

After you've spent a couple of days exploring this lively and fascinating neighborhood, you'll fall in love. This won't be a candlelight-and-roses romantic getaway, but it will be one of the most exciting weekends you will ever spend in New York.

Practical notes: Black History Month (January), especially over the long Martin Luther King holiday weekend, is an excellent time to visit the city and celebrate black culture. Contact the **Harlem Visitors Convention Association** (212–427–3317) for more information. The summer months, especially when the New York Jazz Festival is in full swing, is also another prime time to incorporate a trip to Harlem. For details, write or call the **JVC Festival New York** (P.O. Box 1169 Ansonia Station, New York, New York 10023; 212–787–2020).

When you visit Harlem, you can follow the guidelines in this itinerary or you can take an organized tour. One of the best tours is **Harlem Spirituals, Inc. Gospel & Jazz Tours** (212–757–0425; call for information, prices, and times). This company offers many lively tours of important Harlem spots, including a special Sunday morning gospel tour and a Saturday night "Harlem by Night/Soul Food and Jazz Tour." **The Discovery Tour** (489 Fifth Avenue, New York, New York 10017; 917–763–8051) also offers jazz and gospel tours.

DAY ONE: EVENING

Check into the **Hotel Wales** (1295 Madison Avenue between 92nd and 93rd Street; 212–876–6000; fax: 212–860–7000; standard rooms, from $155 per night; suites, from $215 per night). The Hotel Wales is a European-style hotel that has been restored to its original 1901 charm. The atmosphere is serene, intimate, and friendly. The rooms are modest but comfortable, with original marble baths and brass fittings. The suites are rather like having your own little Manhattan pied-à-terre for the duration of your stay. Breakfast and tea are served in the Pied Piper Room, a Victorian drawing room.

Dinner

Once you've settled yourselves, start your weekend off with some pizzazz and take a taxi to **Sylvia's** (328 Lenox Avenue between 126th and 127th Streets; 212–996–0660; moderate), the most famous soul-food restaurant in Manhattan. Sylvia Woods, herself a neighborhood icon, is known to those who know as "The Queen of Soul Food." Since 1962 she has been serving classic dishes from her native South Carolina, including chicken and dumplings, salmon cakes, smothered pork chops, chicken and ribs (fried or barbecued), collard greens and candied yams. Be sure to save room for her delectable cinnamon sweet potato pie.

Since you're in the throes of an evening of venerable institutions, catch the evening show at **The Apollo Theater** (254 West 125th Street; 212–749–5838; call ahead of time to see who is performing and to reserve tickets). Built in 1913, the world-famous Apollo was originally a "whites-only" burlesque theater. However, by the 1930s (and for forty years thereafter), the Apollo had become the most famous landmark in the history of black music in America, presenting the best black reviews in the city and featuring everyone from Bessie Smith, Mahalia Jackson, Billie Holiday, Ella Fitzgerald, and Duke Ellington to Sammy Davis, Jr., James Brown, Smokey Robinson, and Gladys Knight and the Pips. In the late 1980s, it was completely renovated and has since enjoyed a resounding renaissance with many stage shows and a popular amateur night (usually Thursday). The Apollo has a marvelous intimacy about it; with no trouble you'll feel like you're a part of the neighborhood.

If you want to end your evening with another Harlem institution, go over to **The Cotton Club** (656 West 125th Street; 212–663–7980; moderate). During the 1920s the Cotton Club was Harlem's most dazzling nightclub catering, like the Apollo, to a whites-only clientele. Duke Ellington, Cab Calloway, Louis Armstrong, and Bill "Bojangles" Robinson all performed here, and the Cotton Club's "high-yaller" chorus girls were famous. The Cotton Club withered during the Depression, but in 1978, this modern version of the legendary club opened. It's a bit on the "touristy" side, but well worth a visit.

For something perhaps a bit more authentic, go also or instead to the **Showman's Cafe** (2321 Frederick Douglass Boulevard near 125th Street; 212–864–8941; moderate). Over the years, Showman's Cafe also featured the great jazz musicians, including Lionel Hampton, Count Basie, Dizzy Gillespie, and Nat King Cole, and it still features wonderful live jazz. Many greats came here to listen to their fellow musicians. It's a pretty straightforward kind of place, but you'll love it.

When you can't keep your eyes open another minute—or you find that you only have eyes for each other—catch a taxi on 125th Street back to the Wales.

DAY TWO: Morning

Breakfast

Have breakfast in the hotel's Pied Piper Room or go right next door and treat yourselves to some of the marvelous muffins, pastries, or granola at **Sarabeth's Kitchen** (1295 Madison Avenue; 212–410–7335; moderate).

The "A" train is the A subway line, made famous by Duke Ellington in the song called, of course, "Take the A Train." In the 1920s, the "A" train was the fastest way to get uptown to where the streets were jumpin'.

⁓⊶⊷⊷⊶⁓

Hail a taxi or take the Madison Avenue bus north (M4) to the neighborhood known as **Sugar Hill** (Edgecombe Avenue north of 145th Street). Between the 1920s and the 1950s, this area represented the "sweet life of Harlem," hence its name. Many famous blacks have lived here, including Cab Calloway, Duke Ellington (935 St. Nicholas Avenue near West 156th Street), W. E. B. DuBois (402 Edgecombe Avenue), Thurgood Marshall, and Roy Wilkins.

Make your way south again to **Striver's Row** (West 138th and 139th Streets between Adam Clayton Powell, Jr. Boulevard and Frederick Douglass Boulevard). You may be surprised at the beauty of many of these streets, and Striver's Row is the quintessential example of Harlem's unheralded architectural finery. This marvelous block is known officially as **St. Nicholas Historic District** or The King Model Houses. They were built in the late nineteenth century by David H. King, Jr., a distinguished developer, and were designed by several architects including McKim, Mead and White. By 1919, when Harlem became a refuge for blacks, many successful professionals and artists came to live here, which resulted in the tongue-in-cheek name, "Striver's Row." W. C. Handy, Noble Sissle, and Eubie Blake are just a few of the artists who have lived here.

Lunch

Stop for lunch at the **Jamaican Hot Pot Restaurant** (2260 Adam Clayton Powell, Jr. Boulevard; 212–491–5270). This little spot offers what some consider to be the best Jamaican cooking in the city. Check out the ackee and fish, jerk chicken, the fried plantains, and especially the homemade fruit punch.

DAY TWO: AFTERNOON

During the afternoon, you can explore some of Harlem's centers for black history and culture. The first stop is the **Schomburg Center for Research in Black Culture** (515 Lenox Avenue; 212–862–4000, Monday–Wednesday, noon to 8:00 P.M.; Thursday–Saturday 10:00 A.M.–6:00 P.M.; Admission is free). The Center was founded by Arthur A. Schomburg, a Puerto Rican of African descent who was told as a child that Negroes had no history. He spent his life proving otherwise. The Schomburg Center is a research library with an extensive collection of cultural and historic papers, art, music, and memorabilia from the United States, Africa, and the Caribbean. It has a permanent display of African-American art by Harlem Renaissance artists. It's well worth a visit.

Your next stop is the **Studio Museum in Harlem** (144 West 125th Street; 212–864–4500; Wednesday–Friday; 10:00 A.M.–5:00 P.M.; Saturday and Sunday, 11:00 A.M.–6:00 P.M.; admission is charged), the centerpiece of New York's contemporary African-American art community. Dedicated to the preservation of the art of black America and the African diaspora, it also offers many exhibits on the history and culture of Harlem. It is impressive with its open space, modern architecture, and dramatic lighting of paintings, sculpture, and photos.

You could take the bus (M2, M3, or M4) down Fifth Avenue and back to the hotel, or catch a taxi. Think about getting off the bus or having the cabbie drop you at the **Conser-**

vatory Garden (in Central Park at Fifth Avenue between East 103rd and East 106th Streets). After the liveliness of Harlem, you'll welcome the serenity, privacy, and romance of the Conservatory Garden. Walk around the lawns, the beautiful English and French gardens, and rest for a few minutes in the pergola. It's less than a mile back to the Wales. Why don't you walk? (Turn right as you leave the park. Walk south for 13 blocks, then turn east one block to Madison and 93rd.)

DAY TWO: EVENING

Dinner

This evening head downtown. For dinner, try **Chez Josephine** (414 West 42nd Street, between Ninth and Tenth Avenues; 212–594–1925; moderate to expensive). Chez Josephine is a French bistro with a tinge of "soul." It is owned and operated by Jean-Claude Baker, one of the many adopted children of famed black singer and dancer, Josephine Baker. Jean-Claude is usually on the scene, giving the restaurant an aura of friendliness and intimacy. The menu is basically French, and the atmosphere is sexy and fun.

You're dining in the heart of the theater district, so if you can get tickets for a show by a black playwright, go for it. Two-time Pulitzer Prize–winner August Wilson, for example, is one of the best-known African-American writers at work today and has written many plays about the African-American experience, keeping audiences riveted. One of his more recent successes was *Seven Guitars*. If dance is more to your taste, see if the Alvin Ailey Dance Company or the Dance Theater of Harlem are performing. Also, Savion Glover's *Bring in 'da Noise, Bring in 'da Funk* is a remarkable vision of tap and jazz.

If you want to end your romantic evening with a bit more jazz, try **Birdland** (2745

There is always something left to love. And if you ain't learned that, you ain't learned nothing.

—Lorraine Hansberry, American playwright

Broadway at 105th Street; 212–749–2228; moderate). Again, this is not the original Birdland, but it is still worth the trip.

DAY THREE: MORNING

You can't celebrate a weekend in Harlem without going to church on Sunday morning. This won't be a quiet Quaker service, but, in most cases, a lively session marked with gospel and choir music. The most famous church with the largest black congregation in the country is the **Abyssinian Baptist Church** (132 West 138th Street between Lenox Avenue and Adam Clayton Powell Jr. Boulevard; 212–862–7474; call for hours). A splendid Gothic and Tudor structure with circular pews and red carpeting, over the years it has boasted several famous pastors, including Adam Clayton Powell, Sr.

For another sort of experience, you might want to go to **Mother A. M. E. Zion Church** (14-146 West 137th Street between Lenox Avenue and Adam Clayton Powell, Jr. Boulevard; 212–234–1545). This was the first church in New York City organized by and for blacks. The church was originally founded in 1796 at 156 Church Street in lower Manhattan through money donated by a former slave. Also known as the "Freedom Church" because of its connections with the Underground Railroad, its roster of former members reads like a volume of African-American history: Harriet Tubman, Paul Robeson, Sojourner Truth, and Frederick Douglass.

St. Philip's Protestant Episcopal Church (214 West 134th Street; 212–862–4940) is the most exclusive church in Harlem. It, too, has great history; the original congregation was founded in 1809 as part of the original Trinity Episcopal parish. It moved, with its black congregation, uptown, finally settling in 1918 in this building designed by two African-American architects, Vertner W. Tandy and George W. Foster.

Brunch

After church, a jazz and gospel brunch is a must. Head for brunch at **Copeland's** (549 West 145th Street; 212–234–2356; inexpensive) or **Copeland's Country Kitchen** (209 West 125th Street and Seventh Avenue; 212–666–8700; inexpensive). With live harp music in the background, Copeland's features down-home Southern and Cajun fare, including peanut soup, oxtail soup, crab cakes, gumbo, and barbecue. Or try **Snooky's** (63 West 117th Street between Fifth and Lenox Avenues; 212–281–3500; moderate) for soul food and jazz. You can wile away the entire day here.

If you've had enough stomping for today, go downtown and try the lovely **Cafe Beulah** (39 East 19th Street; 212–777–9700; moderate). Cafe Beulah calls itself a "Southern Revival Bistro" and favors the "comfort, good taste and elegance that made life gracious and meals joyful." The cafe is decorated with soft butter-yellow walls, quiet ceiling fans, and polished brass fixtures. The food is decidedly Southern, with a unique sense of refinement and style. Here's a place where you can wile away the afternoon quietly, enjoy each other, and allow the marvelous sights and sounds of New York's black experience to take firm hold in your minds, hearts, and dreams.

FOR MORE ROMANCE

For a look at two special history spots in Harlem, travel farther north to the **Jumel**

Terrace Historic District (160th and 162nd Streets between St. Nicholas and Edgecombe Avenues), which is an area featuring a number of preserved row houses. Be sure to go to the **Morris-Jumel Mansion Museum** (Roger Morris Park at West 160th Street; 212–923–8008; Tuesday through Sunday, 10:00 A.M. to 4:00 P.M.; $3 admission). Built in 1765 by Roger Harris, this was one of several country mansions in the area built as retreats for rich New Yorkers whose town homes stood below Wall Street. This house was General George Washington's headquarters during the Revolutionary War and is the only pre-Revolutionary residence still extant in Manhattan. The gardens are lovely as well, featuring a dramatic view of the Harlem River.

WINTER BEACH

To me, few activities are more romantic than a walk along a windswept beach in winter. The only other aspect that would transform such a walk into utter perfection would be to take it with someone I adored. Amazingly, New York City has a breathtaking windswept beach. It's at Coney Island, of all places.

From mid-autumn until early spring, the magnificent boardwalk at Coney Island is one of the most enchanting places in the region to spend a quiet day together. The salt air is brisk, the weather often turns moodily foggy, the shuttered amusement park rides offer a kind of down-at-the-heels nostalgia. If you have just met and want to know each other better or if you have been married for fifty years, take the train to Coney Island, catch each other's hands, and prepare to be transported to a very special sort of paradise.

Practical notes: You could take this walk any time of day. You could go in the morning and then have lunch instead of dinner; you could go, as this itinerary suggests, in the afternoon and end your romantic day with dinner. I would suggest, for the sake of safety, that you take your seaside walk before the late afternoon sun goes down. This part of Brooklyn is actually quite safe, but I would not tempt fate or frustrated teenagers.

AFTERNOON

You could drive or hire a taxi cab to take you to Coney Island, but I strongly recommend that you ride the subway, which will cost each of you $1.50. Catch a B, D, F, or N train to Stillwell Avenue, Coney Island. The ride takes about forty-five minutes from mid-Manhattan and offers a certain romance all its own. For starters, you can sit, hold hands, and watch a fascinating theater of humanity go by. Also, these trains are among the few in New York that emerge aboveground in mid-Brooklyn, which, in itself, is interesting. You'll see New York City neighborhoods that you never imagined existed. The Stillwell Avenue subway station, even in its proud seediness, is also rather fascinating. It's the last of the old stations that evoke a kind of 1940s nostalgia. You can almost hear Frank Sinatra and Gene Kelly tapping by in *On the Town*.

Romance at a Glance

♥ *Take a romantic subway ride to Coney Island.*

♥ *Walk along the boardwalk at Coney Island.*

♥ *Explore Brooklyn's fascinating Russian enclave.*

♥ *Have dinner in one of Brooklyn's most fabulous restaurants.*

Lunch

As you exit the Stillwell subway station, you'll see the original **Nathan's Famous Restaurant** (corner of Surf Avenue and Stillwell Avenue; inexpensive). Although you've seen hundreds of ersatz Nathan's (they are now part of the chain), this is the original. Stop by for a hot dog, which back in Frank and Gene's day was a nickel and is now about $1.50. Or try a shrimp boat, some fried clams, the fabulous french fries, or even some cotton candy.

In its heyday at the turn of the century, Coney Island played host to millions who came from around the world to see its amazing amusements and rides. Some parts of the island, like Luna Park, Steeplechase Park, and Dreamland, are now just memories. But some of the famous rides are still going, particularly **The Cyclone** (1927), long considered one of the world's scariest roller coasters, and the **Wonder Wheel** (1920) a Ferris wheel, which is a marvelous work of art and has been declared a New York City landmark. Both are still as wondrous as ever. If they are operating on the day you are here, take a turn. Both demand that you grab onto each other for dear life.

Coney Island always had one of the world's greatest wide, sandy beaches—and it still does. It also has 4 miles of boardwalk, which is a delight to stroll upon. Or you can sit on the beach or boardwalk and soak up the sunshine (even in winter) and the salt air.

A short way down the boardwalk, you will come to **New York's Aquarium for Wildlife Conservation** (Surf Avenue and West 8th Street; 718–265–FISH. You can enter the Aquarium from the boardwalk.) The Aquarium is home to thousands of fish and marine creatures including beluga whales, sharks, walruses, and dolphins. For 100 years, it has been one of New York's favorite attractions. Let the kid in both of you experience the Discovery Center where electric fish "go zap," walk under a crashing wave (you'll stay dry), listen to the beluga whales click and whistle, or giggle at the penguins and walruses. It's a remarkable place—and a joy to visit. It is open Monday–Friday 10:00 A.M. to 5:00 P.M.; weekends and holidays 10:00 A.M. to 7:00 P.M.; admission is charged.

Continue walking down the boardwalk for about a mile until you come to Brighton Beach, Brooklyn's Russian-Jewish enclave. At the turn of the nineteenth century, Brighton Beach was the Atlantic City of its day, the place to which, in hot summer weather, New Yorkers took their pleasure boats and headed to Brooklyn for a picnic at the beach. Later, racetracks, music halls, and fancy hotels made it a haven for gamblers, including the likes of Diamond Jim Brady, and other high-livers. When the subway extended to Coney Island in 1920, Brighton Beach turned into a year-round suburb, and after World War II, many Jewish refugees from Europe settled here. The neighborhood has had its ups and downs, but for the past two decades, it has been settled by middle-class Soviet Jews, many from Odessa, who were escaping Russian prejudice. Today, a younger Russian population also lives in Brighton

Beach, giving its restaurants, shops, and nightclubs a certain Eastern European pizzazz. Stroll along the boulevard and explore the many dashing stores and markets. They provide a fascinating look at a very special neighborhood.

EVENING

Dinner

As evening approaches, you have to make some decisions. On one hand, you could stay in the Brighton Beach and Coney Island neighborhood. If you are feeling in the mood for a unique treat, consider having dinner at **Primorski's** (282 Brighton Beach Avenue; 718–891–3111; moderate). It serves delicious Russian-Jewish fare—borscht, Circasian chicken in walnut sauce, *soylanka* or lamb stew, outstanding Georgian bread—and vodka by the gallon. Live singing, music, and dancing (both Russian and American) is offered nightly starting at 8:00 P.M. What Primorski's lacks in the glamour of, say, The Russian Tea Room, it makes up for in its uniqueness and fun.

On the other hand, you can get back on the subway, head to Brooklyn's downtown Williamsburg section and go to **Peter Luger's Steak House** (178 Broadway; 718–387–7400, expensive). Together, take the # 2 or 3 subway to Clark Street or the A train to the High Street/Brooklyn Bridge stop. Established in 1887, Peter Luger's is one of New York City's oldest and most revered steak houses, serving what some believe is the best steak in New York. If all that sea air has readied both of you for some hearty red meat (as well as some great fried potatoes and creamed spinach) this is your place. The ambience is more sawdust and beer than rosebuds and wine, but it is the perfect accompaniment to Brooklyn's nineteenth-century flavor.

Kisses and Knishes

As you stroll down the boardwalk, leave time to steal a kiss. If you pause here a while, you may run into Albert, one of Coney Island's certifiable characters. He's the friendly guy pushing the cart with the handwritten sign boasting the "best knishes in the world." It would seem impossible, but guess what? The knishes are, possibly, the best in the world. Be sure to buy one from Albert—and, while you're at it, let him fill you in on all the Coney Island boardwalk gossip. If Albert's fare seems too "iffy" for you, be sure to stop by Mrs. Stahl's Delicious Knishes (1001 Brighton Beach Avenue; 718–648–0210) for her—yes, delicious!—knishes.

FOR MORE ROMANCE

You may find that you'll be seduced by the Russian mood in Brighton Beach. If so, try going to one of the popular Russian discos. In some places, like Primorski's, the music and dancing is on the conservative side with a combination of Russian slow dancing and American disco. Other dance clubs are less staid, to say the least, with Russian rock and rap and an incredible "night club" scene. If you want a taste of Russian chic, try **Odessa** (1113 Brighton Beach Avenue; 718–332–3223; moderate to expensive) or **Paradise** (2814 Emmons Avenue at Nostrand Avenue; 718–934–2283; moderate to expensive). Unlike typical American discos, you can have dinner at these two. That, together with all the iced vodka you can drink is all part of the evening.

ITINERARY 27
Three days and two nights

NOW AND ZEN

*T*he influence of the countries that line the Pacific rim has become very strong in Manhattan in recent years. The contributions of Chinese, Japanese, Korean, Thai, and Indonesian cultures to the flavor of New York life can be experienced all over the city in thousands of ways.

The Chinese have lived in Manhattan for well over a century. In the late nineteenth century, only a few hundred Chinese settled in lower Manhattan. Today, more than 250,000 Chinese, primarily of Cantonese descent, live in Chinatown and have almost overtaken the old Jewish and Italian neighborhoods that border the original Chinatown. Many Vietnamese and Cambodian people have also moved into Chinatown in recent years, adding to the neighborhood an Indonesian influence. Japanese, Thai, and Korean people have also flowed into Manhattan, particularly in the past ten years, settling in various other neighborhoods all over the city. They, too, have brought marvelous aspects of their cultures to the New York scene.

This itinerary does not focus on one nationality in particular; instead it offers a plan to taste, in a rather lavish way, many of the most dazzling—and romantic—ways Asian culture has affected New York life.

Romance at a Glance

♥ *Stay at The Peninsula (212–247–2200; fax: 212–903–3949).*

♥ *Dine in Shun Lee Palace, Vong, Honmura An, and other Asian restaurants, classic and contemporary.*

♥ *Explore the magnificent Asian art at the Metropolitan Museum of Art, the American Museum of Natural History, and The Asia Society.*

♥ *Tour Chinatown and other Asian centers.*

Practical notes: This itinerary is ideal if you will be visiting New York during Chinese New Year, which occurs in late January or early February. Chinese New Year is marked by two weeks of street festivals culminating in a wild and festive parade. (Contact New York's **Chinese Chamber of Commerce**, 33 Bowery, New York, New York 10002; call 212–226–2795 for the exact dates and other details.)

Another marvelous time to celebrate Asian New York is mid-spring. At that time, a visit to the Brooklyn Botanic Garden or the New York Botanical Garden is incredibly delightful—the Japanese cherry trees are in full bloom generally from mid-April to early May.

Yet another fascinating time to visit is during **The Moon Festival**, which occurs in September (specifically, on the fifteenth day of the eighth lunar month). The moon is thought to be at its brightest at this time, and young girls are meant to ask *Yeuh Lauo,* "the man in the moon," for a vision of their future husband. For this occasion moon cakes, actually beautiful cookies, are made from black beans, red beans, lotus seeds, and egg yolk—all symbols of fertility. Ornate boxes of moon cakes can be purchased in pastry and grocery shops all over Chinatown during the Moon Festival.

If The Peninsula is fully booked, consider staying at **The Kitano** (66 Park Avenue at 38th Street; 212–885–7000; fax: 212–885–7100; standard room, $245–$270 per night; suites, $425–$1,200 per night; Japanese suite $1,200 per night). The Kitano is a handsome Japanese hotel decorated with sleek Japanese-style mahogany and cherry fittings. **Nadaman Hakubai**, the hotel's Japanese restaurant, is one of the most authentic Japanese restaurants in the city.

DAY ONE: EVENING

Arrive at the elegant **Peninsula** (700 Fifth Avenue at 55th Street; 212–247–2200; fax: 212–903–3949; standard rooms, $340–$440 per night; suites $700–$3,750 per night; weekend packages are available upon request), the sister hotel of the venerable Peninsula Hong Kong. Its central and chic location marks this hotel as equally important as its Asian counterpart. When you enter, the grand staircase, the elegant chandeliers, and the gorgeous Oriental rugs and tapestries will assure you that you will be cared for with the same classic luxury as you would be at the original. Although this is a large hotel (242 rooms), it has a feeling of romance and intimacy. Your room or suite, decorated in tasteful art nouveau style, will be as luxurious as the lobby rooms. You won't want to check out.

One of the most delicious aspects of the Peninsula is its incredible spa. If you have time before dinner, go for a swim in their rooftop pool or have a massage or facial. Whatever you do, allow yourself to be pampered. You may feel, as I did, that you want to curl up and stay in bed for the next three days. If you're eager to explore New York's Asian delights, however, go out for a special dinner.

Dinner

For a classic Chinese dinner, you could go to **Shun Lee Palace** (155 East 55th Street, between Lexington and Third Avenues; 212–769–3888; expensive) or **Shun Lee West** (63rd Street between Columbus Avenue and Central Park West; 212–595–8895; expensive). Michael Tong, who owns both establishments, is considered New York's premier Chinese restaurateur. Both restaurants offer gourmet Chinese fare at its best.

If you'd prefer something less traditional but equally elegant, try **China Grill** (60 West 53rd Street; 212–333–7788; expensive). It tends to attract a somewhat younger crowd, and its chic decor and remarkable menu are well worth the price.

For something truly unique, you must try **Vong** (200 East 54th Street at Third Avenue,

212–486–9592; expensive), one of the most magical dining experiences in New York. The restaurant itself is decorated in vivid gold leaf with black, salmon, coral, and burnt orange lacquer trimming. A large pagoda dominates the dining room. All of this may sound gaudy, but it's gorgeous.

The French-accented Thai food created by chef Jean-Georges Vongerichten is pure ambrosia. Vongerichten has taken classic Thai spices and flavorings (lemon grass, mangos, lotus root, chestnuts, and ginger) and created dishes that are sublime. All are excellent, from appetizers such as foie gras to the fish, lamb, or other main dishes to the desserts. How does passion fruit with white-pepper ice cream sound? Don't be afraid to try something exotic!

✍️

Before you return to your luxurious room, have a nightcap at the **Pen-Top Bar and Terrace** on top of the Peninsula. This is one of the best bars in New York and, with its fabulous views, is an ideal place to end a very romantic evening.

DAY TWO: MORNING

Breakfast

Luxuriate in your marvelous room until you feel inspired to get out into the real world. Have a light breakfast in your room, then head out to explore.

✍️

Both the **Metropolitan Museum of Art** (Fifth Avenue at 82nd Street) and the **American Museum of Natural History** (Central Park West at 79th Street) have remarkable collections of Asian art and artifacts. You could spend the morning (actually you could spend weeks!) exploring either of these treasure troves.

For something quite special, plan a morning visit to **The Asia Society Galleries** (725 Park Avenue at 70th Street), which also has a very special collection of Far Eastern art and artifacts. Located in a red granite building designed by Edward Larrabee Barnes and opened in 1982, The Asia Society was founded in 1956 by John D. Rockefeller III as a nonprofit institution dedicated to fostering understanding of Asia and communication between Americans and the people of Asia. The Society has a splendid permanent gallery of Asian art from the Rockefeller collection as well as changing exhibitions.

If you have time, also try to visit the **China Institute** (125 East 65th Street; 212–744–8181). It offers many courses in Chinese art, language, and culture, many of which are one-day lectures. Call the Institute to see if they are offering an event you might like to attend.

Lunch

For lunch, catch a taxi and take it to SoHo to **Honmura An** (170 Mercer Street, between Houston and Prince Streets; 212–334–5253; expensive). In recent years, scores of Japanese noodle (*soba*) shops have sprouted around Manhattan, but Honmura An is by far the most elegant. The atmosphere is quiet (rather Zen-like, one might say), and the restaurant is beautifully appointed. You can watch the chefs creating the exquisite noodles, and all the dishes are delectable.

On the other hand, if something decidedly trendy sounds interesting, try **Nobu** (105 Hudson Street at Franklin Street; 212–219–0500). This incredible TriBeCa restaurant, centering on the cuisine created by chef Nobu Matsuhis, and owned by Robert De Niro among others, is an awe-inspiring space with a miraculous menu, the ultimate in designer Japanese food, with a touch of South American flavors. Be sure to try the sushi.

Chinese Wedding Bells

As you explore Chinatown, watch for a Chinese wedding in progress. Perhaps you will catch a glimpse of the bride either as she leaves the temple or as she enters a restaurant for the wedding banquet. Often the bride is married in a white Western-style dress and then changes for the wedding banquet into a beautiful Chinese wedding dress, called a Qua. It is a traditional, tight-fitting gown made of luxurious red silk embroidered with gold and silver thread. Like all brides, a Chinese bride is incredibly beautiful.

DAY TWO: AFTERNOON

Spend the afternoon strolling through SoHo. Buy a map and as you walk and shop head southward toward Chinatown. If you want to rest your feet—and try something incredibly romantic and different—stop in at **Kelley and Ping** (127 Greene Street; 212–228–1212; moderate) for a cup of tea and some atmosphere. Kelley and Ping is primarily a noodle shop, but it also serves marvelous salads and a wide range of Asian teas. A fine selection of packaged teas, as well as pots, cups, and other tea utensils are also for sale. Like many of the restaurant suggestions here, Kelley and Ping is an American invention with a decidedly Asian twist. It is quite special, and you'll love it.

When you reach Chinatown, be sure to explore the **Museum of Chinese in the Americas** (70 Mulberry Street, Second Floor; 212–619–4785). This marvelous little gallery offers changing exhibitions about the life of the Chinese people in the United States. It has become an important Chinese cultural center. Check the bulletin board outside the gallery for announcements of Chinese dance performances, plays, concerts, or other events that might be of interest to you.

DAY TWO: EVENING

If you are visiting over **Chinese New Year**, you'll have no trouble finding Chinatown in the late afternoon. Whether the new lunar year is the year of the ox, dog, rabbit, or pig, Chinatown is a blizzard of movement during this, the year's most important celebration. Chinese men and women (and many non-Chinese!) crowd the markets, stocking up on holiday foods such as oranges, tangerines, lotus seed buns (lotus seeds insure fertility) fresh fish and chicken, and cherry blossoms. You'll hear the words *"Gung Hoy Fat Choy,"* or "Happy New Year" in Cantonese everywhere you go.

Dinner

Go to one of the fancier restaurants for a real Chinese banquet in honor of the Chinese New Year. Try **Triple Eight Palace** (78 East Broadway between Division and Market Streets; 212–941–8886; moderate) or the **Silver Palace** (50 Bowery at Canal Street; 212–964–1204; moderate). The glittery Triple Eight specializes in fish dishes while the Silver Palace offers a complete range of Chinese dishes and has long been a favorite with New York politicos.

The order of a traditional Chinese banquet may seem odd to Westerners. The banquet usually starts off with four cold appetizers and has at least eight main courses, including a steamed fish course and a duck course. The traditional—and delicious—Peking Duck is the best known of these. Soup ends rather than begins the meal. Plan to spend several hours at dinner.

✑✑✑

Late in the evening, pandemonium breaks out on Mott Street. Crowds throng, drums beat, firecrackers pop loudly, and a stunning parade begins. The focal point of the parade is a gigantic dragon created with as many as eight dancers covered in a silky red cloth and tassels. The dragon, a symbol of good luck, power, and strength, winds through the streets as other dancers bait him like a toreador. It is very exciting.

The atmosphere becomes quite intense, and sometimes the popping firecrackers can be a bit scary (and not a little bit dangerous). The only way to escape the partying is to begin walking north and to find a taxi (or a subway) to take you back to your hotel.

To unwind before you settle in your room, stop for a quiet nightcap at the **Gotham Lounge** back at the Peninsula.

DAY THREE: MORNING

The best time to explore Chinatown is not in the evening—especially during Chinese New Year—but in the relative peace of an early Sunday morning. The earlier you can come, the better; but even if you sleep in, the place offers delights all day long. Take a taxi to the **Confucius Statue** at the corner of Mott Street and Chatham Square. This fascinating black and green marble icon represents the focal point of the local Chinese culture.

Stroll north up Mott Street. Explore all the open markets and shop for Chinese pastries, including buns, balls, tarts, or cookies sculpted to look like fish or birds at **Maria's** (174–176 Canal Street) or **Lung Fong Chinese Bakery** (41 Mott Street), which has an excellent moon cake.

For curios and antiques, browse in the scores of shops along Mott. Among them are **Quong Yeuen Shin & Company** (32 Mott Street), which offers tea sets in delicate porcelain, or **Don Enterprises** (36 Mott Street), a tiny store that offers urns and other porcelains. For a special romantic treat, look for a Chinese zodiac chart or book. Just like a western zodiac, you can identify your signs—be they rat, ox, tiger, rabbit, dragon, snake, horse, sheep, monkey, rooster, dog, or pig—then check to see if the pair of you are compatible!

As you are walking up Mott, take a detour down Pell to **Doyers Street** between Pell and the Bowery. This narrow street with a wishbone-shaped curve was once known as

During Chinese New Year Sui Xien roots are sold in earthenware bowls in shops and market stalls. The roots look humble but will soon sprout into lovely, delicate flowers. They are considered a sign of new life and fertility.

Bloody Angle. Opium dealers, who thrived here in the last century, lured their competitors here then ambushed them.

Brunch

First-time or anytime visitors to Chinatown must try the traditional Chinese meal of *dim sum*. Two good choices for dim sum are **Mandarin Court** (61 Mott Street near Canal; 212–608–3838; offers dim sum from 8:00 A.M. to 3:00 P.M.) or **Hee Seun Fung Teahouse**, or HSF (46 Bowery between Canal Street and Chatham Square; 212–374–1319; moderate to expensive; offers dim sum from 10:00 A.M. to 5:00 P.M.). The dim sum at Mandarin Court is more authentic, and the atmosphere is more intimate. At HSF, the dim sum is designed to appeal to the western palate, with lots of delicious shrimp and pork *shiu mai* but no marinated chicken feet or taro root to tantalize those with more adventuresome palates. At HSF, the mood is more bustling.

If you'd like to try some delectable Vietnamese food, check out **Mekong** (44 Prince Street near Mulberry; moderate), a little storefront restaurant that is turning out some of the best Vietnamese food in the city.

It is impossible to view all the magical Asian treasures in New York City, but their influence has provided Manhattan (and the surrounding boroughs) with a unique sort of romance. Whenever you come, you will find it intriguing—especially as you explore together.

FOR MORE ROMANCE

If you cannot visit New York during the Chinese New Year holiday season, have dinner in Chinatown anyway—regardless of when you visit. Then try to attend a performance (or a reading) at the **Pan Asian Repertory Theatre** (St. Clement's Church, 47 Great Jones Street; information, 212–505–5655; reservations, 212–245–2660; moderate). This theater, under the direction of producer Tisa Chang, is considered one of the most exciting theater companies working in New York today. It presents original works by Chinese, Japanese, and other Asian playwrights concerning aspects of Eastern sensibility and the Asian-American experience—all to great acclaim. Formerly part of the La MaMa experimental group, it is now considered part of mainstream New York theater.

ITINERARY 28

One day and one night

VALENTINE'S DAY

DELIGHT FOR THE HEART

*F*or those souls who are madly in love, thinking about stoking the fires, wishing to rekindle cooled embers, or planning to pop the question, Valentine's Day, our national day of love, offers the perfect opportunity. I have an old friend who always takes a vacation day from work on her birthday. I suggest taking a vacation day on Valentine's Day to give our loves— and ourselves—some extra-special TLC. This itinerary is for cheerful lovers willing to give themselves over unconditionally to a few of life's most sybaritic delights.

Practical notes: Although the Box Tree does not advertise, those in the know are well aware of its numerous charms. As a result, both the restaurant and hotel are always booked for Valentine's Day months in advance. Be sure to make your room and dinner reservations several weeks ahead of time and reconfirm a couple of days ahead of time. The Box Tree is pricey, but if you stay at the inn, you receive a $100 credit toward your marvelous dinner in the Tiffany Room. On Valentine's Day, chef Hans Dieker presents a voluptuous seven-course prix-fixe dinner.

By the way, the Box Tree restaurant has three special private rooms: the Music Room,

Romance at a Glance

♥ *Spend the night at The Box Tree (212–308–3899).*

♥ *Have a light, romantic lunch at the Cub Room Cafe, a chic SoHo bistro.*

♥ *Stroll through Greenwich Village catching a glimpse of the sites of great lovers' trysts.*

♥ *Enjoy a voluptuous dinner at The Tiffany Room at The Box Tree.*

the Blue Room, or the Gold Room. These larger rooms are meant for small parties of ten to thirty-five people and are often booked in advance. But if they are available, a couple can dine in awe-inspiring (or love-inspiring) splendor for an additional charge of $250. If this happens to be the night when you are declaring your love for the first time or proposing marriage, one of the more lavish private rooms is the ideal setting.

MORNING

If you are coming from out of town, plan to arrive in the late morning. If you come by air or rail, take a taxi from the airport or train station to **The Box Tree** (250 East 49th Street; 212–758–8320; fax: 212–308–3899; $290–$320), and check your luggage at the front desk. If you are a New Yorker taking a day off work, drop your bags at the inn early in the day so that you are not encumbered with them.

As soon as you view the warm lobby of this incredibly charming *pension,* you may want to just chuck all other plans and hole up in your room all day. Well, I don't blame you! It's the "day of love." Anticipation sometimes makes the final event even more exciting, however, so you may want to go ahead with the other delights of this itinerary. If so, catch a taxi and take it down to SoHo.

Lunch

Enjoy a light lunch at the **Cub Room Cafe** (183 Prince Street at Sullivan; 212–777–0030; moderate), a relatively modestly priced cafe and bar adjoined to the more pricey Cub Room. It's a very "in" place these days, and chef Henry Meer, formerly of Lutéce, creates marvelous salads, sandwiches, and other bar fare. Meer's creations reveal French origins with an Oriental touch. All the choices will be very tempting, but select something light because dinner will be spectacular.

AFTERNOON

After lunch stroll through the streets of SoHo and Greenwich Village. (See "Glittering Literati," page 147, for a detailed walk.) If you are so inclined, take **"A Lover's Stroll Through Greenwich Village,"** a guided walk that is often offered on Valentine's Day. It takes you past sites of famous love affairs and tragic suicides. It meets at 2:00 P.M. on Valentine's Day afternoon under the arch in Washington Square at the bottom of Fifth Avenue (check the *New York Times* for details).

If you'd rather be alone, just wander unescorted through these romantic streets and take in the delights of this magical neighborhood and each other. You must check out the marvelous shop called **The Gifted Ones** at 150 West 10th Street. On Valentine's Day they offer a host of special Valentine treats, ranging in price from $20 to $125. Each has a witty name. "A Kiss on the Lips" is a 2½-foot-tall lipstick filled with five pounds of chocolate kisses together with a manual called "The Art of Kissing." My personal favorite is called "Feeling Blue," although neither of you will be sad when you open it. It's a basket filled with items for a sensual massage. Designed to dazzle all the senses, it includes a scented candle, massage butter balm, ancient Oriental massage tools, and a large box of chocolate truffles. I'll leave it to you to figure out what to do with these items later this evening.

Valentine's Day is never complete without chocolate, so stop by **LiLac Chocolates** (120 Christopher Street; 212–242–7374). LiLac makes the best chocolate I've ever tasted. On any given holiday, LiLac creates chocolate surprises in appropriate holiday shapes and any size you could possibly consume. On Valentine's Day you'll find giant red satin heart-shaped boxes chock-full of chocolates. Don't miss these or any of the many other chocolate surprises.

Catch a taxi when you're ready to head back uptown, but stop a block before you reach the Box Tree to have a glass of wine at **Top of the Tower** (The Beekman Tower, 3 Mitchell Place at 49th Street and First Avenue; 212–355–7300; expensive). This marvelous piano bar is an ideal place to watch the city twinkle on in the late afternoon. You'll have breathtaking views of the Empire State Building, the United Nations, the Chrysler Building, and other icons of architecture to remind you that you are in the greatest city in the world with the one you love.

EVENING

When early evening has settled, head for the Box Tree. It's only a block away from the Beekman Tower. Each room in the Box Tree is unique, starting with the remarkable hand-painted doors. Whether you choose the **Chinese Suite**, the **King Boris Bedroom**, or the **Consulate Suite**, you can be sure that its lush decor will include chandeliers, marble and lapis lazuli baths, a working fireplace, beautiful screens, and many other marvelous appointments.

After you've settled in your room, you may want to enjoy a glass of champagne alone before going downstairs to dinner. Ask the concierge to bring you a bottle from the inn's excellent wine cellar. You may also choose to have a cocktail in the intimate little bar next to the Box Tree's Tiffany Room, which is the main dining room.

Dinner

On Valentine's Day, the Tiffany Room's chef, Hans Dieker, prepares a formal continental-style seven-course feast. On one recent Valentine's Day his menu included lobster salad, fennel soup with pernod, marinated quail, and filet of beef with Armagnac. Among the

desserts was a dish called Vacherin Box Tree, a glorious lemony meringue that is as light as a feather.

After dinner, have a nightcap in the bar. One of the specialties of the Box Tree is a marvelous cellar of port and other after-dinner drinks. Then, return to your room and enjoy each other.

Happy Valentine's Day.

FOR MORE ROMANCE

For a true New York wedding, get married on the 86th-floor observatory of the **Empire State Building**, a scene made famous in the movie *An Affair to Remember*. On Valentine's Day, up to thirty couples can be married between 10:00 A.M. and 7:00 P.M. by one of three available New York State Supreme Court justices. For more information, call (212) 736–3100.

ITINERARY 29
Two days and two nights

CUDDLING IN CONNECTICUT

*A*mazing as it may seem, less than three hours from the teeming streets of Manhattan lies one of the most beautiful parts of New England. Replete with picturesque villages, country inns, classic spired churches, and, in the middle of winter, a blanket of fluffy white snow, it's a perfect scene for a romantic weekend of fun, fine food, and, best of all, a host of warm snuggles.

Northwestern Connecticut—or the Litchfield Hills as the area is called—offers town after town of picture-postcard New England villages—from New Preston to Salisbury. You'll find plenty to keep you busy: skiing (both cross-country and downhill), ice-skating, antiquing, or just cuddling in front of a fireplace.

Practical notes: Unlike many of the itineraries in this book, you are going to need a car for this weekend. If you don't have one of your own, rent one from the usual car rental enterprises. All of the best-known agencies have locations around Manhattan and, of course, at all the metropolitan airports. Be sure to reserve your car ahead of time.

DAY ONE: LATE AFTERNOON/EVENING

For this special winter getaway, you'll be staying at **The Boulders Inn** (Route 45; 203–868–7918; $100–$225 for rooms; cottages start at $225) in New Preston, Connecticut, one of the state's most beautiful towns. The Inn was literally built with boulders in its fieldstone walls. It is located on a lovely, discreet lake called Lake Waramaug, and the antiques-filled living and dining rooms at the Inn offer marvelous lake views. The rooms in the main building are pretty, but better (and more romantic) are the tiny cottages located on the Inn grounds. Each of the cottages has its own working fireplace.

To get to New Preston from Manhattan, take the Henry Hudson Parkway to the Saw Mill River Parkway to Route 684 north to Brewster, then Route 84 east to Danbury. Take exit 7 to Route 7 north to New Milford, then Route 202 east to New Preston.

Romance at a Glance

♥ *Stay at the Boulders Inn on Route 45 in New Preston (203–868–7918).*

♥ *Ski at Mohawk Mountain Ski Area in Cornwall.*

♥ *Take a sleigh ride at Wood Acres in Terryville.*

♥ *Dine at the Boulders Inn (New Preston), The White Hart (Salisbury), The Mayflower Inn (Washington), and Le Bon Coin (New Preston).*

DINNER

Plan your trip so that you arrive at the Inn about 7:00 P.M., and let the innkeeper know that the moment you arrive you want to settle down to a delectable dinner in the cozy dining room—preferably right next to the fireplace. The Boulders specializes in British specialties like Scottish salmon and steak and kidney pie, an ideal feast after a frosty trip from the city. End your dinner with a glass of brandy, and then retire to your room for a warm sleep.

DAY TWO: MORNING

This is an action day, so indulge in a hearty American breakfast at the Inn. You can afford the calories, since you'll work it off on the slopes. Then head off for Mohawk Mountain. Mohawk Mountain is Connecticut's largest ski area (albeit by Vermont and certainly Colorado standards, it is rather small). It is located about 10 miles north of New Preston near Cornwall, Connecticut.

Mohawk is an ideal place to learn to ski or to practice those parallel turns until they are second nature. For novices, Mohawk offers a special day rate, lessons, rentals, and a slower chairlift. Although the slopes are not as steep or long as they are in bigger ski centers, Mohawk's twenty-four trails and relatively quick lift lines make it a perfect "easy" ski getaway for more experienced skiers. Also, if downhill is not to your liking, Mohawk also offers cross-country skiing, including equipment rentals, lessons, and miles of beautiful trails in the nearby Mohawk State Forest.

Lunch

Enjoy lunch at the attractive Mohawk Mountain Lodge. The menu is fairly standard, but somehow the most mundane hamburger or bowl of chili becomes ambrosia after a morning of skiing. After lunch, rest for a few minutes in the Lodge and enjoy the wonderful views out the huge windows or sit out on the deck if the day is sunny.

DAY TWO: AFTERNOON

Catch a few more runs in the afternoon and maybe enjoy a cappuccino or hot chocolate back at the lodge when you think you've spent enough time on the slopes. Then drive back to the Boulders Inn and take a leisurely hot bath or shower to relax those worked-over muscles. If you're truly bushed, a late afternoon nap is often the perfect close to a day of skiing and the best way to get ready for a jolly evening.

DAY TWO: Evening

If you are feeling adventurous, consider driving to Salisbury, Connecticut, one of the state's most typically New England towns. It is about a forty-five-minute drive from New Preston. Take Route 7 to Route 44 West, which leads to Salisbury. Take a quick stroll around Salisbury's quaint village green. If you are a tea lover, Salisbury boasts two well-known centers for tea. One is a delightful tea room called **Chaiwalla**, which serves delightful light lunches and snacks as well as rare teas. And don't miss **Harney and Sons, Ltd.,** which brews its teas in the back of a small house on the Green and sells them in a tiny room in front. Harney and Sons teas are famous throughout the world.

Dinner

After your walk, enjoy dinner at the **White Hart** (on the green in Salisbury; 203–435–0030; moderate). The White Hart is another of Connecticut's classic New England inns and a not-to-be-missed landmark in Salisbury. What's more, it is adored by Connecticut natives as well as visitors, who delight in its wonderful service and its very special menu.

If Salisbury seems just a bit too far to drive for dinner, try the **Mayflower Inn** (Route 47, Washington, Connecticut; 203–868–9466; expensive), one of the most prestigious inns in the state and just 15 minutes away from the Boulders. Recently refurbished, it offers three fine dining rooms, an excellent menu, and a terrific wine list.

୬୭ତ୬

After dinner have a safe and leisurely drive back to your cozy cottage, linger over a brandy next to the fireplace, and get ready to snuggle into bed.

Romantic Massage

Nothing could be more soothing or more romantic after a day of energetic exercise than a deep, sensual massage. Although one can learn to give an expert massage, you need not be an expert to give pleasure to your partner. Just use your common—and your sensual—sense. After your day on the ski slopes and a hot bath or shower, dim the lights, light some scented candles, put on some soft music, and give each other a massage. To add to the pleasure, use one of these blends of essential oils (they are available at many pharmacies and health food stores).

A Blend to Soothe Muscles

2 drops eucalyptus
3 drops rosemary
2 drops lavender
1 ounce carrier oil

An Aphrodisiac Blend

3 drops ylang-ylang
2 drops sandalwood
2 drops jasmine
1 ounce carrier oil

DAY THREE: MORNING

After yesterday's workout, you may want to linger in bed for an extra hour or two. When you're finally up and going, head out to New Preston's single main street and absorb the charm of this beautiful town.

Brunch

Enjoy brunch at **Thé Café** (Route 202, New Preston, Conn.; 203–868–1787; moderate). A feast for the senses, Thé Café abounds with the aroma of brewing teas, freshly baked bread, and huge bouquets of fresh flowers. You can linger over brunch, sitting on a cozy sofa next to a crackling fire.

After brunch, spend an hour or two exploring the fascinating craft and antique shops nestled into the picturesque old buildings along New Preston's main street. For example, **J. Seitz and Company** features Southwestern furniture, clothing, and jewelry in its location in an old garage. Also look for **Black Swan Antiques** with its European influence, the **Grey Squirrel** with its folk art delights, and several other fascinating little stores.

DAY THREE: AFTERNOON

Just a few miles north of New Preston on Route 202 is the town of Litchfield, one of Connecticut's most historic villages and another place well worth exploring both for its fine shops as well as for its photogenic qualities. In fact, Litchfield is considered to be one of the most beautiful historic towns—and certainly one of the most quintessential Main Streets—in America. What's more, Litchfield's gorgeous historic district is easily strollable—even on a wintry Sunday afternoon. (Most of the houses are private residences and are not open to the public.) More than thirty of its choicest houses are concentrated on two long blocks, North and South Streets, just off the village green. The beautiful white Colonial and Federal houses just seem to go on forever.

The names connected with these fabulous houses are equally impressive. Harriet Beecher Stowe's family lived in the 1787 parsonage next to the famous Congregational Church located on the Green. The 1773 home of Tapping Reeve served as America's first law school and boasted Aaron Burr as its first pupil, followed by alumni that included three Supreme Court justices, two vice presidents, fourteen governors, twenty-eight senators, and more than 100 congressmen.

After your stroll you may want to stop in at the **West Street Grill** (43 West Street, Litchfield; 203–567–3885; moderate) for a mid-afternoon coffee or snack.

If you have the time and the inclination, think about going for a sleigh ride at **Wood Acres** (Griffin Road in Terryville; 203–583–8670), a farm a few miles from Litchfield. (If the snow is too light, Wood Acres also offers hayrides or romantic carriage rides.) This is an ideal way to end your snowy, snuggly weekend.

FOR MORE ROMANCE

To find out more about activities in the Litchfield area, call the Litchfield Hills Travel Council, P.O. Box 968, Litchfield, Connecticut 06759; 203–582–5176.

PUTTIN' ON THE RITZ

*T*his itinerary was specially planned for two reasons. First, it's designed to pay homage to those great American musicians who for most of this century have made all of our lives so happy and romantic: Irving Berlin, George and Ira Gershwin, Harold Arlen, and Cole Porter. Second, just as Mr. Berlin's famous song "Puttin' on the Ritz" implies, it's a put-on—a spoof, designed "just for the fun of it." Fun is, after all, an essential part of romance.

Just like Holly Golightly in *Breakfast at Tiffany's,* don your best duds, hide behind a pair of fancy glasses, and go mix with the Rockefellers (with sticks and umbrellas). Go slumming (and nose-thumbing) on Park Avenue and Madison and Fifth. And have a wonderful time!

Practical notes: Many of the weekends suggested in this book are designed for visitors, but this weekend, perhaps more than any other, is ideal for New Yorkers. Most of us natives work too hard, feel guilty when we take a cab instead of a bus or subway, and feel like we're splurging when we pay full price for a theater ticket. Give this weekend to your beloved to show that you'll be loving him or her always.

You could plan this weekend any time of year, but I would suggest you try it in late

January or early February—a time of year that often gets us down. You know, you're worn out by the holidays, the weather, your job. You need some fun.

If you really want to pull out the stops, think about reserving a car and driver for the weekend. (Frankly, except for transport to and from the airports—or perhaps a grand auto tour if you have never been to New York City before—a car can be something of a nuisance in busy New York traffic. Still, this is a weekend for luxury, so let the driver fret over the traffic—you sit back and enjoy. Not too many years ago, town cars and limousines were considered the ultimate in expensive luxury, but now they are more competitive. Try **Carmel** (212–666–6666), **Sabra** (212–777–7777) or **Allstate** (212–741–7440). If you are arriving by plane from out of town, you can call ahead of time and have the car and driver meet you at your airport. Discuss with the company costs for securing the car for the entire weekend. All of them take credit cards.

Romance at a Glance

♥ *Stay at the Ritz-Carlton.*

♥ *Dine at classic "fancy" New York restaurants.*

♥ *Listen to Bobby Short sing greatest hits at the Carlyle Cafe.*

♥ *Go dancing at the Rainbow Room.*

♥ *Have tea at the Plaza.*

♥ *Shop at the fanciest stores: Tiffany, Cartier, and Harry Winston.*

♥ *Rent a limousine.*

♥ *Take a helicopter ride.*

What if you're planning to "put on the Ritz," but truth is, you can't quite *afford* the Ritz-Carlton? Don't feel bad; neither can I. But don't despair, you can stay at the **Wyndham** (42 West 58th Street; 212–753–3500; doubles, $130–$140; one-bedroom suites, $175–$205; two-bedroom suites, $290–$340). And you won't be alone there. Chances are good that Vanessa Redgrave, Maggie Smith, or a few other rather impressive British types may be in residence. Each room and suite is unique and very homey. Mr. John Mados and his wife, Suzanne, are the gracious owners of the Wyndham. They will make sure your weekend is an utter success.

So, don those dark glasses and have a great time.

DAY ONE: EVENING

Check into the **Ritz-Carlton** (112 Central Park South; 212–757–1900; fax: 212–757–9620; special weekend getaway rate, $295 per night in a superior room; $335 per night in a Park view room; special occasion weekends from $395 to $2,000 for suites). When you enter the beautifully appointed lobby of the Ritz, you'll be transported. With its location right across the street from Central Park, you'll know you've come to the right place for a "puttin' on the Ritz" weekend.

The original Ritz-Carlton, New York, was opened in 1910 by the celebrated European hotelier, César Ritz. It was his first property in the United States and was located in midtown Manhattan on Madison Avenue at 46th Street. It became the grand social center of town. The original Ritz closed down after World War II, and in 1982 the present building was purchased by hotelier John Colemen, completely renovated, and reopened as the Ritz-Carlton in October 1982. Mr. Coleman sold the hotel again in 1989. It was purchased and again refurbished, and today is ranked among New York's few five-star hotels.

If you are really "puttin' on the Ritz" (and can afford it), ask for the Ritz-Carlton Suite, the pièce de résistance of the hotel's 214 rooms. Located on the twenty-first floor of the hotel, this newly created suite features a marble foyer, a living room with a working fireplace, fabulous antiques, and art works, a dining room, two glorious bedrooms, and a master bathroom the size of most average hotel rooms. (There's a giant whirlpool and a special Swedish shower equipped with multiple shower heads.) The suite offers spectacular sweeping views of Central Park, which can be viewed from any of its four balconies. Brunch or evening cocktails on the balconies is the epitome of romance.

However, if you're just going coach class (Ritz-style), ask for a "Park view" room (which may well include a balcony and a fireplace). Even if you can't have the Ritz-Carlton Suite, you won't be disappointed. Every room is exquisite.

Dinner

Since you are embarking on what might be described as a delightfully eccentric weekend, you must (at least try) have dinner at **Cafe Nicholson** (323 East 58th Street between First and Second Avenues; 212–355–6769; moderate to expensive). This unique restaurant belongs to John Nicholson, who serves as chef, host, and server. He prepares relatively simple fare: herbed roasted chicken, filet mignon, and marvelous chocolate soufflé. The ambience is sort of "eccentric aristocrat," yet very personal, faintly sultry, and ever-so-slightly odd, but wonderful. John Nicholson likes to travel and is away most of the summer, as well as any other time he feels so moved. So be sure to plan—and reserve—ahead of time. When he's there, the cafe is open Wednesday through Saturday from 6:30 to 9:00 P.M.

If Cafe Nicholson is closed for the evening or fully booked, walk over to **Bouterin** (420 East 59th Street; 212–758–0323; moderate to expensive). Chef-owner Antoine Bouterin, for many years the chef at the prestigious Le Perigord, has created a rather funky Provençal cottage restaurant that reflects his St. Rémy home. For appetizers, try *pâté de campagne maison* with fresh onions and yams or eggplant caviar with parsley blini; for a main course, try the veal chop with truffles or the old-fashioned lamb stew.

❦

Savor your dinner, then catch a taxi to the **Carlyle Cafe** in time for the 10:45 P.M. late show.

No tribute to Irving Berlin and his compatriots would be complete without a late-night visit to the **Cafe Carlyle** (in the Hotel Carlyle, 35 East 76th Street at Madison Avenue; 212–744–1600; $35 cover charge). As you probably know, the Cafe Carlyle is one of the most—perhaps *the* most—sophisticated bar in New York. Like most things "classy," it doesn't scream at you—it's subtle with salmon-colored upholstered banquettes, tiny tables, and a wraparound mural on the wall by French painter Marcel Vertès. Best of all, during many months of the year, Bobby Short sings Gershwin, Porter, and Berlin in his inimitable style.

If the New York City Ballet is performing "Who Cares?", go see it. It's an homage to George Gershwin, and the combination of his elegant music ("The Man I Love," "Embraceable You") with the Balanchine dancers and Jerome Robbins choreography may actually make you weep.

(Seeing Bobby Short perform even just once is a life goal everyone should set, as far as I'm concerned. If he is not performing during your stay in New York, however, don't be too disappointed. The other regulars—Dixie Carter and Eartha Kitt among them—are quite magical in their own right.)

DAY TWO: MORNING

Breakfast

Have breakfast in your room, or, if you prefer something more formal, have a long, leisurely breakfast in the hotel's restaurant, **Fantino**. An excellent place for breakfast or lunch, Fantino is also rated one of the best restaurants in the city for dinner. The intimate Fantino bar is also quite wonderful and is a popular spot for residents and visitors to have cocktails.

⌘

After breakfast, dress up a little bit (shirt and tie for men; nice day dress for women—remember, you're puttin' on the Ritz) and call your car (if you ordered a car, that is; if not, have the doorman hail a taxi). Go up to **Georgette Klinger** (978 Madison Avenue at 76th Street; 212–744–6900) and have a facial ($70), a massage ($70), or a manicure ($19). They frequently offer special packages, for instance, a facial and full massage for $100. Georgette Klinger salon caters to both men and women, and you can be pampered in (almost) any way you choose.

Lunch

Now that you're all beautiful, lunch at **Le Cirque** (58 East 65th Street; 212–792–9292; prix fixe lunch, very expensive). Considered by many the world's most glamorous restaurant, it is frequented by kings, ex-princesses, wives of U.S. presidents, and various society ladies who are so thin you can't imagine that they eat. Le Cirque is also among the best restaurants in New York. For years, the high quality of Le Cirque was maintained by owner Sirio Maccioni. The restaurant has been going through some changes recently. If it is not open when you visit, you'll be very well taken care of (to put it mildly) at **Restaurant Daniel** (20 East 76th Street; 212–288–0033; very expensive). Restaurant Daniel may end up leading New York's French restaurants into the twentifirst century. It's incredible—I'll say no more.

DAY TWO: Afternoon

After lunch, play Holly Golightly and her sweetie and go cruising at all the fancy stores that line the Upper East Side, 57th Street, and Fifth Avenue. (For some ideas, see "French Kiss," page 117.) Particularly, don't miss **Asprey** (725 Fifth Avenue in Trump Tower). Ask to see the unusual gifts, like the antique Russian travel bidet made in 1885 for Princess Xenia Feodorovna, daughter of Alexander II and sister of Czar Nicholas. It's yours for $25,000. Also look into **A La Vieille Russie** (781 Fifth Avenue at 59th Street). Going here will take a little bit of chutzpah—as it should since these little trinkets are true artifacts gleaned from the troves of Russian nobles. Some of their antique jewelry dates back to the 1630s. Going from the sublime to the ridiculous, don't pass up **F. A. O. Schwarz** (58th and Fifth Avenue). This is the store where Tom Hanks had so much fun in the movie, *Big.* When you're finished

playing, pay special attention to the jewelers on Fifth Avenue. **Harry Winston** (718 Fifth Avenue), **Van Cleef & Arpels** (744 Fifth Avenue), and, of course, **Tiffany & Company** (Fifth Avenue and 57th Street) will have much to tempt you.

Sometime during the afternoon, take tea at the elegant **Rotunda** (The Hotel Pierre, Fifth Avenue at 61st Street; expensive). This room is beautiful, and it's an ideal place for a romantic interlude.

DAY TWO: EVENING

Dinner

For this evening, don your best bib and tucker and go for dinner and dancing at **The Rainbow Room** (30 Rockefeller Plaza, 65th Floor; 212–632–5000; expensive; $20 entertainment charge for dancing).

Since 1934, The Rainbow Room has been the classiest supper club in New York. Twenty-four floor-to-ceiling windows allow you to gaze out over Manhattan's skyscrapers. To my mind, there is no better view in New York. On a clear evening you can see 50 miles in all directions.

Several years ago, the Rainbow Room and the adjoining club, **Rainbow and Stars**, were refurbished to their original 1930s Art Deco splendor. With satin walls and drapery, green carpet, jade-green leather chairs, and every detail thought through to perfection, the effect is marvelous. Paul Goldberger, architecture critic of the *New York Times* described the renovation as *"S'Wonderful."* It is so romantic, in fact, that the Rainbow Room management claims that every weekend five or six couples become engaged here; on Valentine's Day, at least twenty couples celebrate their engagement.

The menu is as nostalgic as the decor—and as delicious. For dinner, you can start with oysters Rockefeller (what else?), then choose from lobster Thermidor, rack of lamb, or duck l'orange. For dessert, indulge in baked Alaska. These classic dishes may sound a little old-fashioned for today's sophisticated palates, but the fact is, at the Rainbow Room, these dishes are prepared exquisitely under the direction of Executive Chef Wady Malouf and are central to the mood of the evening. Select a light champagne to accompany your dinner.

Of course, during and after dinner, you can dance on the gently revolving oak dance floors under the colored lights that give the Rainbow Room its name and twinkle across the arched ceiling. Sublime!

❦

Just to remind yourself, this weekend is all about glamour with a sense of humor—go for a nightcap at **The Monkey Bar** (60 East 54th Street; 212–838–2600; expensive). How about a Manhattan? With its 1930s murals and elegant Art Deco appointments, the Monkey Bar is the perfect ending to a perfect day.

DAY THREE: Morning

If you stayed out until the wee hours, sleep late today. When you're ready, complete your "puttin' on the Ritz" weekend with a final salute to Cole Porter.

Brunch

Head down to the **Waldorf-Astoria Hotel** (49th Street and Park Avenue) and have

Create a little time capsule of your "Puttin' On the Ritz" weekend. Save your ticket stubs, flowers from the restaurant, a menu, a matchbook, a photo, and give them in a small frame or beautiful book to your partner on his or her next birthday, anniversary, or holiday. The keepsake will help preserve your romantic and loving memories.

brunch at the historic **Peacock Alley** (expensive). Cole Porter lived in the Waldorf for years, and Peacock Alley features his own piano. Like the Rainbow Room, Peacock Alley is steeped in nostalgia, but the food is carefully prepared and delicious. As in days of old, Sunday brunch is a real scene, with celebrities and other beautiful people parading through the restaurant.

FOR MORE ROMANCE

For a spectacular end to your "Puttin' on the Ritz" weekend, take a helicopter ride over Manhattan island. Liberty Helicopters (West Side Heliport, West 30th Street and Twelfth Avenue, or Wall Street Heliport, Pier 6, near Battery Park; 212–943–5959) offers a variety of tours from 9:00 A.M. to 9:00 P.M. daily. You can fly through the caverns of Manhattan, so close to the Statue of Liberty you can almost touch her, and past the Empire State Building. For $44 to $150 per person, you can have a bird's-eye view of Manhattan that you'll never forget.

If a helicopter ride sounds too scary or too expensive, you can have an equally romantic ride on the Staten Island Ferry, with an equally remarkable view of New York's harbor, all for fifty cents each.

ROMANTIC RESTAURANTS

Restaurant price categories in this index, represented by one to four dollar signs, designate the cost of an appetizer, an entree, dessert, and one cocktail for one person. The approximate price for each category is indicated in the following key:

Inexpensive ($): Less than $15
Moderate ($$): $15 to $30

Expensive ($$$): $30 to $60
Very Expensive ($$$$): More than $60

(Note: Area code is 212 unless otherwise noted.)

American

Alley's End ($$), 311 West 17th Street, 627–8899, 105

Arcadia ($$$), 21 East 62nd Street, 223–2900, 199

Aureole ($$$$), 34 East 61st Street, 319–1660, 42

Boathouse Cafe ($$), On the Lake, East Park Drive at 73rd Street, 517–2233, 60

Bryant Park Grill ($$), 40th and Fifth Avenue, 840–6500, 151

Café des Artistes ($$$), One West 67th Street, 877–3500, 175

Cafe Nicholson ($$$), 323 East 58th Street, 355–6769, 276

Cedar Tavern, ($), 82 University Place, 929–9089, 182

Cub Room Cafe ($$), 183 Prince Street, 777–0030, 260

Danal ($$), 90 East 10th Street, 982–6930, 181

Edwardian Room ($$$), Plaza Hotel, 768 Fifth Avenue, 759–3000, 36

Gage & Tollner ($$), 372 Fulton Street, Downtown Brooklyn, (718) 875–5181, 211

Gotham Bar & Grill ($$$), 12 East 12th Street, 620–4020, 185

Gramercy Tavern ($$$), 42 East 20th Street, 477–0777, 14

Hudson River Club ($$$), 250 Vesey Street, 786–1500, 202

Iridium ($$$), 44 West 63rd Street, 582–2121, 120

Joe Allen's ($), 346 West 46th Street, 581–6464, 6

Patio Restaurant, Brooklyn Botanical Garden ($$), Brooklyn, (718) 622–4433, 210

Peter Luger's Steak House ($$$), 178 Broadway, Brooklyn (718) 387–7400, 246

Rainbow Room ($$$), 30 Rockefeller Plaza, 65th Floor, 632–5000, 101, 279

Rose Room at The Algonquin Hotel ($$$), 59 West 44th Street, 840–6800, 149

Tavern on the Green ($$$), Central Park West at West 67th Street, 873–3200, 43, 61, 226

Tribeca Grill ($$$), 375 Greenwich Street, 941–3900, 186

Verbena ($$$), 54 Irving Place, 260–5454, 17

Windows on the World ($$$$), 107th Floor, World Trade Center, 938–1111, 86

Zoë's ($$$), 90 Prince Street, 966–6722, 191

American Southern/Soul Food

Cafe Beulah ($$), 39 East 19th Street, 777–9700, 241

Chez Josephine ($$$), 414 West 42nd Street, 594–1925, 239

Copeland's ($), 549 West 145th Street, 234–2356, 241

Copeland Country Kitchen ($), 209 West 125th Street and Seventh Avenue, 666–8700, 241

Jamaican Hot Pot Restaurant ($), 2260 Adam Clayton Powell, Jr. Blvd., 491–5270, 238

The 10 Most Romantic Restaurants in New York City

1. *Café Des Artistes*
2. *The Box Tree*
3. *The River Cafe*
4. *The Rainbow Room*
5. *March*
6. *Les Celebrites*
7. *Lespinasse*
8. *Aureole*
9. *Windows on the World*
10. *Chanterelle*

Romantic Hotels, Inns, and B&Bs

(Note: Area code is 212 unless otherwise noted.)

Very Expensive ($350 per night and up)
Carlyle, Madison Avenue at 76th Street, 744–1600, 80
Four Seasons, 57 East 57th Street, 758–5700, 4
Lowell, 28 East 63rd Street, 838–1400, 199
Peninsula, 700 Fifth Avenue at 55th Street, 247–2200,
    251
Plaza Athenée, 37 East 64th Street, 734–9100, 118
Ritz–Carlton, 112 Central Park South, 757–1900, 275
St. Regis, 2 East 55th Street, 753–4500, 220

Expensive ($225 to $350 per night)
Algonquin, 59 West 44th Street, 840–6800, 148
Bed & Breakfast on the Park, 113 Prospect Park West,
    Brooklyn, 718–499–6115, 206
Boulders Inn, Route 45, New Preston, Conn., (203)
    868–7918, 266
Box Tree, 250 East 49th Street, 758–8320, 260
Essex House, 160 Central Park South, 247–0300, 34
Hotel Elysée, 60 East 54th Street, 753–1066, 119
Inn at Irving Place, 56 Irving Place, 533–4600, 12
Kitano, 66 Park Avenue, 885–7000, 250
Mayfair, 610 Park Avenue, 288–0800, 132
Millennium, 55 Church Street, 693–2001, 160
Mill Garth, Windmill Lane, Amagansett, Long Island,
    (516) 267–3757, 92
Plaza, 768 Fifth Avenue at 59th Street, 759–3000, 36, 225

Soho Grand, 310 West Broadway, 965–3000, 190
Stanhope, 995 Fifth Avenue, 288–5800, 68
Waldorf–Astoria, 301 Park Avenue, 355–3000, 229, 280

Moderate ($100 to $225 per night)
Beekman Arms, 4 Mill Street, Rhinebeck, N.Y.,
    914–876–7077, 49
Best Western Seaport Inn, 33 Peck Slip, 766–6600, 110
Crowne Plaza Manhattan, 1605 Broadway, 977–4000,
    198
Delamater House Inn, 49
FitzPatrick Manhattan Hotel, 687 Lexington Avenue,
    (800) 357–7701, 24
Holiday Inn Downtown, 138 Lafayette Street, 966–8898,
    132
Hotel Wales, 1295 Madison Avenue, 876–6000, 235
Paramount, 235 West 46th Street, 764–5500, 100
Wyndham, 42 West 58th Street, 753–3500, 274

Budget (Under $100 per night)
Chelsea Inn, 46 West 17th Street, 645–8989, 189
Manhattan Seaport Suites, 129 Front Street, 742–0003,
    109
Off SoHo Suites, 11 Rivington Street, 979–9808, 160
Washington Square Hotel, 103 Waverly Place, 777–9515,
    178

NIGHTLIFE

(Note: Area code is 212 unless otherwise noted.)

Dancing

Rainbow Room, 65th Floor, 30 Rockefeller Plaza, 101, 279

Tramps, 51 West 21st Street, 727–7788, 193

Tunnel, 220 Twelfth Avenue, 695–4682, 193

Bars

Blue Bar, Algonquin Hotel, 59 West 44th Street, 840–6800, 149

Cafe Noir, 32 Grand Street, 431–7910, 191

Cafe Novecento, 343 West Broadway, 925–4706, 191

Gotham Lounge, Peninsula Hotel, Fifth Avenue at 55th Street, 256

Grand Bar, Soho Grand Hotel, 310 West Broadway, 965–3000, 247–2200, 256

Greatest Bar on Earth, 1 World Trade Center, 107th Floor, 938–1111, 114

King Cole Bar at the St. Regis Hotel, 2 East 55th Street, 339–6797, 221

Mark's Bar, Mark Hotel, 25 East 77th Street, 722–4300, 200

Merc Bar, 151 Mercer, 966–2727, 191

Monkey Bar, 60 East 54th Street, 838–2600, 280

Naked Lunch, 17 Thompson Street, 232–0828, 191

Pen–Top Bar & Terrace, Peninsula Hotel, 700 Fifth Avenue at 55th Street, 247–2200, 252

Rotunda, Hotel Pierre, Fifth Avenue at 61st Street, 838–8000, 279

Salon, Soho Grand Hotel, 310 West Broadway, 965–3000, 191

Temple Bar, 332 Lafayette Street, 130

Top of the Tower, Beekman Tower, 3 Mitchell Place, 355–7300, 262

The 10 Most Romantic Bars in New York City

1. Promenade Bar at the Rainbow Room
2. The Temple Bar
3. Cafe Carlyle or Bemelman's Bar at the Carlyle Hotel
4. Fifty Seven Fifty Seven at the Four Seasons Hotel
5. Merc Bar
6. Top of the Tower at Beekman Tower
7. Monkey Bar at the Hotel Elysée
8. King Cole Bar at the St. Regis Hotel
9. Terrace Bar at the Stanhope
10. The Greatest Bar on Earth at the World Trade Center

"21" Club, 21 West 52nd Street, 582–7200, 102

View, on top of the New York Marriott Marquis, 1535 Broadway, 398–1900, 84

Pubs and Taverns

Cedar Tavern, 82 University Place, 929–9089, 182

Chumley's, 86 Bedford Street, 675–4449, 158

Fraunces Tavern, 54 Pearl Street, 269–0144, 202

Landmark Tavern, 626 Eleventh Avenue, 757–8595, 31

Mare Chiaro, 176$\frac{1}{2}$ Mulberry, 226–9345, 137

GENERAL INDEX

Note: For Restaurant, Hotel, and Nightlife listings, see the special indexes, which begin on page 282.

ABOUT THE AUTHOR

Pamela Thomas is an editor and writer who has worked in New York City for more than 25 years. In addition to a number of cookbooks and gardening books, she is the author of *Reflections of New York* (Smithmark), and is currently at work on a book about New York's Greenmarket. She lives in Greewich Village, the neighborhood that she swears is New York's most romantic.